Decoding Homes and Houses

Houses are not just assemblages of individual rooms but intricate patterns of organised space, governed by rules and conventions about the size and configuration of rooms, which domestic activities go together, how the interior should be decorated and furnished and what kinds of household object are appropriate in each setting, how family members relate to one another in different spaces, and how and where guests should be received and entertained in the home. *Decoding Homes and Houses* introduces new, computer-based techniques designed to retrieve and interpret this wealth of social and symbolic information. The various representations and measures show how domestic space provides a shared framework for everyday life, how social meanings are constructed in the home and how different sub-groups within society differentiate themselves through their patterns of domestic space and lifestyles.

Julienne Hanson is a Reader in Architectural and Urban Morphology at University College London. Her previous publications include *The Social Logic of Space*, co-authored by Bill Hillier, with whom Dr Hanson founded the 'space syntax' group.

Decoding Homes and Houses

Julienne Hanson
with contributions by Bill Hillier, Hillaire Graham and David Rosenberg

CAMBRIDGE
UNIVERSITY PRESS

PUBLISHED BY THE PRESS SYNDICATE OF THE UNIVERSITY OF CAMBRIDGE
The Pitt Building, Trumpington Street, Cambridge, United Kingdom

CAMBRIDGE UNIVERSITY PRESS
The Edinburgh Building, Cambridge CB2 2RU, UK
40 West 20th Street, New York NY 10011–4211, USA
477 Williamstown Road, Port Melbourne, VIC 3207, Australia
Ruiz de Alarcón 13, 28014 Madrid, Spain
Dock House, The Waterfront, Cape Town 8001, South Africa

http://www.cambridge.org

First published 1998
First paperback edition 2003

Typeset in Trump Medieval 9.25/14pt, in QuarkXPress™ [SE]

A catalogue record for this book is available from the British Library

Library of Congress cataloguing in publication data

Hanson, Julienne.
Decoding homes and houses / Julienne Hanson: with contributions
by Bill Hillier, Hillaire Graham, and David Rosenberg.
p.   cm.
Includes index.
ISBN 0 521 57284 3 (hardback)
I. Architecture, Domestic – England.   2. Space (Architecture) –
– England – Psychological aspects.   3. Personal space – England –
– Psychological aspects.   4. Architecture and society – England.
I. Title.
NA 7328.H26   1998
728′.37′0942–dc21   98–43344 CIP

ISBN 0521 57284 3 hardback
ISBN 0521 54351 7 paperback

Contents

Acknowledgements

Like so many academic endeavours, this book is the product of many minds. The debt I owe to Professor Bill Hillier, my colleague, mentor and co-inventor of 'space syntax' is inestimable. He has always been, and remains my inspiration. My thanks are also due to Professor Patrick O'Sullivan for granting me sabbatical leave to complete the text and for his unflagging patience and encouragement during the inevitable teething-troubles on the way to publication. I am indebted to my close colleagues Alan Penn and John Peponis for their generosity in sharing ideas and constructive criticism, and to Nick 'Sheep' Dalton for the elegant and stylish computer software which has turned configurational analysis from a dream to a reality. Many people have contributed directly to the production of this book, notably Hillaire Graham and David Rosenberg whose case studies of houses form the basis of two of the chapters. I am grateful to Luiz Amorim, Wendy Bustard, Laurel Cooper, Justin De Syllas, Circe Monteiro, Abdulrazzaq Muhammad-Oumar, Deniz Orhun, Freida Peatross, Edja Trigueiro, Jason Shapiro and Jian fei Zhu all of whose work was influential in identifying future directions for research, to Luiz Amorim, Kayvan Karimi, Mark David Major, Tim Stonor and Reem Zako who helped with the daunting task of compiling the illustrations and to Eva Culleton-Oltay, Joanna Saxon and Reem Zako who so generously proof-read the typescript. My thanks are due to all of these. I greatly appreciate the assistance and advocacy of Professors Mike Batty, Lionel March, Tom Markus, John Musgrove, Philip Steadman and the late Barry Wilson over a period of many years. This book would not have been possible without the constant challenge and example of my Master of Science and Doctoral students at the Bartlett, the stimulating and supportive atmosphere which exists within University College London and the strength and determination of the production team at Cambridge University Press. I apologise in advance if I have inadvertently failed to acknowledge an intellectual debt. The final credits are due to my long-suffering family, David, Jessica and Rebecca Thom who have given me the conceptual space and practical support to enable me finally to bring this work to fruition.

Chapter one

An introduction to the study of houses

Summary

Vernacular and cross-cultural examples of dwellings are explored in order to illustrate the complexity of human habitation and to suggest ways in which houses can carry cultural information in their material form and space configuration, and in the disposition of household artefacts within the domestic interior. It is proposed that the analysis of domestic space configuration provides the link between the design of dwellings and their social consequences, and an outline is given of the methodological approach which will be adopted in succeeding chapters. The major themes of the book are introduced.

The most complex building

The publication of *The Social Logic of Space* in 1984[1] was the culmination of a decade of research into the lawfulness of space created for human social purposes. At that stage, the aim was to expound a general theory of what was inherent in the nature of space that might render it significant for human societies and how space might, in principle, be shaped to carry cultural information in its form and organisation. The book was deliberately wide-ranging in content, reflecting the variety of spatial behaviours which human societies exhibit, practices which any powerful theory of space organisation would need to account for.

In the ensuing decade, our understanding of the significance of space in structuring social relations has been greatly increased by empirical research. Much more is now known about the effects which the physical form and structure of the urban grid have on observed patterns of human co-presence and movement, and about how large building complexes accommodate the programmed and unprogrammed activities of organisations. Our research has now confirmed that the spatial measure of how integrated or segregated a particular space is within a building or a settlement is a powerful predictor of how busy or quiet it is likely to be. Integration is the key by which we can understand the social content of architecture and show how buildings and places function at a collective level. This is not a naive 'architectural determinism' which says that buildings and places compel people to behave in particular ways. The effects which we have identified are from spatial patterns to patterns of movement among collections of people, which arise from everyone going about their business in a very ordinary way.

In parallel to the more public programme of research at the urban scale and into the buildings for work, welfare and leisure which shape most people's experience of architecture, systematic investigation has continued over the past two decades into the ways in which people's dwellings embody and express cultural and lifestyle preferences. The dwelling is the original building historically, and a universal building type today. Nearly everyone has some kind of a place to live, so everyone feels entitled to a view on what counts as good design in housing and what as bad. Nowhere is the relationship between architecture and life so passionately debated as in the association between house form and culture.

Houses everywhere serve the same basic needs of living, cooking and eating, entertaining, bathing, sleeping, storage and the like, but a glance at the architectural record reveals an astonishing variety in the ways in which these activities are accommodated in the houses of different histori- cal periods and cultures. The important thing about a house is not that it is a list of activities or rooms but that it is a pattern of space, governed by intricate conventions about what spaces there are, how they are connected together and sequenced, which activities go together and which are separ- ated out, how the interior is decorated, and even what kinds of household objects should be displayed in the different parts of the home. If there are principles to be learned from studying the design of dwellings, they do not yield easily to a superficial analysis of 'basic human needs'.

It is, moreover, in the history and evolution of houses that the distinc- tion between 'architecture' and 'building' is almost impossible to side-step and, for some authors, 'architecture' – superior, elitist, high-style – as opposed to 'building' – inferior, popularist, vernacular – is a sub-text to the views that are voiced.[2] In looking at houses we are frequently invited to make formal and aesthetic judgements, as well as judgements about fitness for purpose. In non-residential buildings of a public nature it is normal to speak of good and bad architecture, taking for granted that the nature of architecture is well-understood. In discussing the design of houses, what is meant by 'architecture' is called into question by almost every statement uttered.

The house is therefore an ideal vehicle for exploring the formal and experiential dimensions of architecture, hence the attraction of houses for the great twentieth century architects whose continued interest in gener- ating housing prototypes demonstrates that the intellectual challenge of the archetype is limitless. At the same time, the everyday familiarity of the house renders it apparently so innocuous that architecture teachers tend to locate a proposition for the design of a house early in the sequence of student projects. The same brief for a house may generate solutions of breathtaking sophistication and mind-numbing banality. Domestic char- acter and small physical scale apparently are deceptive, and a little reflec- tion suggests that the house is perhaps the most complex building of all.

The deceptive and inherent complexity of the dwelling may go some way to account for its central place in the evolution of 'space syntax' theory. The first studies of domestic space organisation pre-dated our excursions into configurational analysis and, at just about every stage, developments in theory and research methodology have been spearheaded by pilot studies on samples of houses, several of which are published here for the first time. Research into the ethnographic record has been complemented by a study of the evolution of domestic space organisation and family structure in Britain, and by accounts of historic houses and examples of innovative, contemporary domestic architecture. An extensive database of housing from all over the world has been accumulated over the years, in the work of our graduate and research students. *Decoding Homes and Houses* now makes this material public, by bringing together for the first time in one volume historical, contemporary and cross-cultural studies of dwellings with interpretations of modern, architect-designed homes.

Primitive huts and elementary buildings

In its elementary form, human habitation embodies fundamental spatial gestures such as those which pertain among the !Kung bushmen of the Kalahari Desert[3] described by Marshall:

> The fire is the clearest visible symbol of the place of residence. One can see who lives at each. Always, summer and winter, every nuclear family has its fire, which is kept burning all night. . . . The fire is the nuclear family's home, its place to be. In a way, a fire is a more unchanging home than a house on a spot of ground from which the family might depart. A fire-home is always where the family is. Fires are constant, shelters are whims. . . . It takes the women only three-quarters of an hour to an hour to build their shelters, but half of the time at least the women's whim is not to build shelters at all. In this case they sometimes put up two sticks to symbolise the entrance to the shelter, so that the family may orientate itself as to which side is the man's side and which is the women's side of the fire. Sometimes they do not bother with the sticks.[4]

Simple as this fire-home is, it embodies a set of spatial concepts which gives the lie to the architectural notion of the 'primitive hut' as a sort of 'portable cave' which expressed only the bare essentials of human existence – shelter, cooking, warmth. Although the boundary of the fire-home is unclear, space is nonetheless differentiated into an inside zone for the family members and a surrounding region outside where people may pass by. The fire-home forms a semicircle, orientated by sticks and sometimes

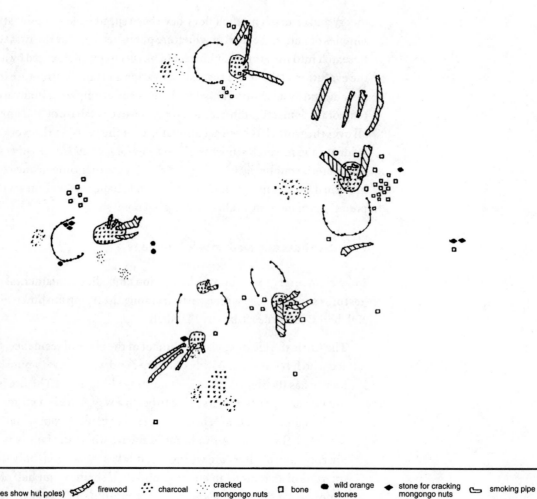

| | hut (circles show hut poles) | | firewood | | charcoal | | cracked mongongo nuts | | bone | | wild orange stones | | stone for cracking mongongo nuts | | smoking pipe |

Figure 1.1
!Kung bushman's encampment

defined by a rough framework of woven, grass-covered branches along a front–back axis. The sticks also mark the threshold, and entrance to the dwelling. The space within is laterally delineated into the woman's space to the left and the man's, to the right. Belongings hang in an adjacent tree (see figure 1.1).

!Kung dwellings may be analysed and understood according to several binary oppositions acting in concert to categorise space: inside–outside, front–back, left–right, up–down. By contrast, no exogenous concept like shape or orientation to the compass governs the layout of the encampment. Shelters take up any direction, facing each other, back to back or side by side, touching or non-contiguous, seemingly as the fancy dictates.[5] The only detectable principles are those of proximity and centrality. Within the encampment, fire-homes huddle closely in an arrangement which has been likened to a 'swarm of bees', as close as two arms' length apart so that neighbours can hand things to each other. Family dwellings tend to hug the periphery of the campsite, leaving an empty space between them which belongs to no one in particular, but where collective activities such as dancing or the distribution of meat take place.

In !Kung living arrangements, a simplicity of material culture and architectural expression are used to convey complex social information which goes well beyond the bare necessities to support human existence. Wherever we look in the ethnographic record, the evidence suggests that, even at its most simple, human shelter is already complex and imbued with a sense of purpose which the French prehistorian Leroi-Gourhan has referred to as the 'domestication' of space and time.[6]

It has even been suggested that this is why the idea of the 'primitive hut' has been central to architectural history. It is the attempt by succeeding generations of theorists to articulate the primary ideas in which architectural forms have their origin, and therein to give substance to the elementary building blocks out of which the most elaborate architectural statements may be assembled. As Rykwert[7] has observed, 'The primitive hut will . . . retain its validity as a reminder of the original and therefore essential meaning of all building for people: that is, of architecture. It remains the underlying statement, the irreducible, intentional core.' This definition is similar to the morphological concept of an 'elementary building' as we tried to define it in *The Social Logic of Space*. In common with those architects who have been preoccupied with the idea of the first house, the specification for an elementary building is an attempt to build a model of the irreducible structure from which all buildings spring. Unlike most previous attempts to speculate on the origins of architecture, the elementary building is not a form drawn from the archaeological record or from ethnography, but a logical construct in space and time.

The elementary building as it was defined in *The Social Logic of Space* is a closed or bounded cell related by a permeability to a contiguous open cell or space outside. The open segment of space may be traversed, while the closed cell is a dead end. The closed and open cells were seen as made

Figure 1.2
The representation of the elementary building

a   b

up of two kinds of raw material: continuous space and the stuff of which boundaries are made, which has the effect of creating spatial discontinuities. In arriving at an ideographic language for architecture, space organised for social purposes was viewed as neither purely continuous nor purely bounded, but some conversion of the spatial continuum by a system of boundaries and permeabilities, to effective space organised for human social purposes (see figure 1.2).

Sociologically speaking, the elementary building was identified with at least one 'inhabitant', in the sense of a person with privileged rights of access and control of the category of enclosed space created by the boundary. An inhabitant was defined as, if not a permanent occupant of the closed cell, at least an individual whose social existence is mapped into the category of space within the cell and thus, strictly speaking, more of an inhabitant of the social knowledge defined by the cell than of the cell itself.

All buildings were then seen as selecting from the set of possible 'strangers' in the external universe, a sub-set of 'visitors' who were defined as persons who may enter the building temporarily, but who do not control it. If the closed cell is the domain of an inhabitant, the open space is the locus of the 'interface' between inhabitant and visitor. Every building is therefore at least a domain of knowledge, in the sense that it is a spatial ordering of categories and at the same time a domain of control, in the sense that it is a certain ordering of boundaries, which together constitute a social interface between inhabitants and visitors.

A building may therefore be defined abstractly as a certain ordering of categories, to which is added a certain system of controls, the two conjointly constructing an interface between the inhabitants of the social knowledge embedded in the categories and the visitors whose relations with them are controlled by the building. All buildings, of whatever kind, have this abstract structure in common: a building type typically takes these fundamental relations and, by varying the syntactic parameters and the interface between them, bends the fundamental model in one direction or another, depending on the nature of the categories and relations to be constructed by the ordering of space.[8]

Finally, it was suggested that all buildings, of which dwellings are a type, are elaborations on this most basic, irreducible spatial structure, which is already redolent with sociological meaning.

The elementary building can be represented graphically, in order to clarify its relational structure (see figure 1.2). The interior may be conceptualised as a point and represented by a circle, with its relations of permeability represented by lines linking it to others. Thus, a cell with one entrance can be thought of as an unipermeable point (see figure 1.2a) while a cell with more than one entrance can be conceptualised as a bipermeable point (see 1.2b). The unbounded open space, immediately outside the cell in the vicinity of the threshold can also be considered as a point, and represented by a circle with a cross to distinguish it from the bounded interior space of the cell.

Elementary buildings in this pure, logical state are found rarely, if they have ever existed, though one rather obvious and instructive candidate is the hermit's cell. Those who wished to live an eremitic life often sought to inhabit a simple closed cell, located in an inhospitable environment at the margins of human habitation. The intention was to lead a solitary life of religious contemplation. In this sense, the hermit's cell is the purest realisation of the domain of an inhabitant. Paradoxically, to the extent that the hermitage succeeded in becoming a place of veneration, a steady stream of pilgrims would recreate the inhabitant–visitor interface, in the vicinity of the entrance to the cell. A holy man's power was seen as emanating from a particular place to such an extent that people often felt a compulsion to visit or a fear of passing by. Pilgrims would not be visitors in the socially accepted sense, for they were seeking counsel, prophecy, intercession or bodily healing from the hermit within. Occasionally the relationship would be directed from the hermit to his visitors in the form of 'action at a distance' activated by cursing, a rather extreme illustration of the general notion that the hermit was 'set apart' from the everyday world of social interaction and encounter. As a manifestation of the logical categories of inhabitant and visitor, the spatial set-up is suggestive.

A hermit's cell is a pure illustration of the theoretical type, but it is a far from typical example of human habitation. However, the ethnographic record provides us with a rich source of portable dwellings from nomadic cultures which, whilst not the earliest forms of habitation, often require considerable technical sophistication and provide a living link with the dwellings of our pre-settled ancestors. Tents are deceptively simple. The space is not large and a nomad's possessions are necessarily few, since they must be transported, but the economy of their material form may be supported by an elaborate system of social practices, which builds upon the concepts inherent in the elementary building and which finds its expression in forms of spatial categorisation and control.

Figure 1.3 illustrates three simple, cell-like tent structures of nomadic tribesmen, reproduced from *The Social Logic of Space* and as described by Torvald Faegre in his study of nomadic architecture.[9] The Bedouin black tent (see figure 1.3a) shows a basic structure, to which key details must be added if the logic of the interior is to be fully understood.

A stranger must approach the tent from the front, which is usually orientated to the south or east. The tent is divided into two by a curtain. The smaller and more opulent men's side is covered with carpets and mattresses. The larger, more functional women's area is used for living and working. The host's camel saddle is set on the mattress in the deepest part of the men's side, and the host and guest of honour sit either side and talk across it, whilst less important guests sit in a semicircle facing them. The space outside is a place for prayer, an activity which ensures that, according to Bedouin cultural conventions, it is a male-dominated space. Although the rules governing hospitality are extremely strong – a Bedouin must entertain even his sworn enemies for three days – there is a strong prohibition on guests seeing into the women's side of the tent.

The abstract rule system which this system encapsulates is extremely clear. Inhabitant–visitor status is manifested on the dimension of depth into the domestic interior, in that the principal host–guest pair occupy the deepest space within the tent. Not only this, access to the open space at the front of the tent is denied to women and reinforced through religious restrictions on its use, so that the inhabitant–visitor interface is controlled by men. The inhabitant–inhabitant relation – that between men and women – is realised in segregation, effected through the strength of the boundary between their respective domains.

If we compare this with a typical Teda mat tent (see figure 1.3b) from the Berber tribes of the southern Sahara, again taken from Faegre[10] and

Figure 1.3
A comparison of the plans of three tents

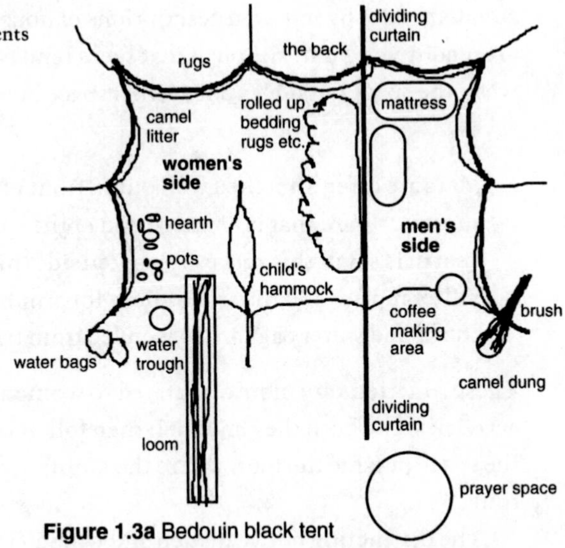

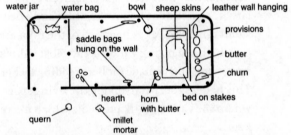

Figure 1.3a Bedouin black tent

Figure 1.3b Teda mat tent

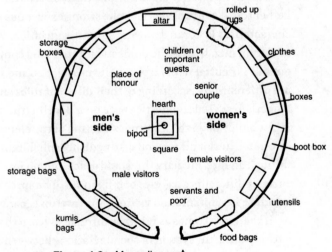

Figure 1.3c Mongolian yurt

supplemented by reported descriptions of household practices, we find a great contrast. First, although mat tents tend to be orientated towards the west, the space outside is not a ritual space but a practical one. As Faegre says:

> Mats are often stretched well out in front of the tent, making an enclosure courtyard that is an extension of the space inside the tent. The hearth is set in this space . . . just outside the tent are placed the wooden millet mortar and the stone quern for grinding grain, while the goatskin churn and water bags are suspended from tripods nearby.[11]

These functions are more orientated to women's work than to masculine activities, and both they and their men folk receive their guests in the space outside the tent, where the family spends the greater part of its time.

The distinction between men and women is not made inside the family home, rather the interior is organised to follow culinary practices. Water jars are stored at one end of the tent and a bed is set up at the other end. In small tents this takes up much of the floor area. Behind the bed is an elaborate leather hanging which is the most valuable item of the bride's trousseau, and is made for her wedding by her mother and female relatives. This hanging serves to divide the living space from an adjacent storage area where the various milk products which make up the subsistence diet are kept.

In both its interior organisation and in its relation to settlement space, Berber social conventions lack the strong exogenous model which characterises Bedouin domestic space organisation. Women are not separated from men within the domestic interior, and control of the space outside is neutral with respect to its use by men and women. Visitors are not differentiated according to their different roles and statuses. Nonetheless, Teda domestic space is still well-structured. Properly speaking, it builds upon the minimal structure of the elementary building. The interior–exterior dimension distinguishes inhabitants from visitors through an intermediary threshold space, but no internal structure differentiates different categories of inhabitant. The space outside serves to interface inhabitants and visitors, the interior separates people from things.

It therefore comes as no great surprise to learn that the Teda have an entirely different system of social relations between men and women. Teda women own their tents and all the interior furnishings. Not only are they a matriarchal society, but the women have a highly developed craft industry – the leather work that dominates the interior decoration of the tent. They are famous as warriors, may divorce their husbands at will and it is even said that they take the initiative in sexual matters. As Faegre observes, the status of Teda women is a constant source of irritation to their Arab neighbours. Berber liberation is amply demonstrated in their virtual reversal of the spatial model of the Bedouin tent.

Moving half way round the world, the Mongolian yurt[12] is comparable to the Berber mat tent in its lack of interior subdivisions, but comparable to the Bedouin black tent in the development of its internal organisation. Within the yurt, everyone and everything 'has its place' (see figure 1.3c). The entrance always faces south or south-east. Entering, it is considered impolite to step on the threshold. Opposite the entrance, against the north wall in the deepest space from the door, is the household shrine. To the west lies the men's side, whilst to the east is the women's side. The centre of the yurt is marked by the hearth, while around the perimeter household objects are stored. The tent is further divided into named sections, within which status and gender dictate the correct situation of people and storage of things. Household implements are physically associated with their users. Men's objects – saddles, guns and ropes – lie in their accustomed places within the men's domain, whilst women's possessions – churns, cooking implements and cradles – are placed in an invariant order around the women's side of the yurt. Guests are seated in the 'place of honour' on the men's side and to the rear of the central hearth, out of the cold. Children and animals sit close to the door. Traditional nomad hospitality requires that anyone who stops outside the entrance to the yurt is invited inside to eat. When strangers enter the dwelling, they will find that the relative position of people and things is identical to all other yurts, right across the steppes.

Mongols persistently categorise objects and people in terms of their position in space. People and things 'out of place' constitute 'pollution', so much so that it is often necessary to conduct a special ceremony to restore the purity of the home. Family life is organised in an exceptionally rigid and formal manner so that, although people may move about within the yurt, all forms of social interaction are ritualised and people have to sit, eat and sleep in their appointed place. The spatial structure guarantees a powerful model for the categories of spatial being, and organises the daily life of its occupants.

So strong is the symbolic structure of the yurt that through the centuries it has come to represent the cosmology of its inhabitants. To the Mongols, the roof is the sky, and the hole in the roof the sun – the Eye of Heaven. The central hearth is regarded as an embodiment of the five elements from which all life springs: earth on the floor, wood in the framework enclosing the hearth, metal in the grate, water in the kettle on the grate, and fire in the hearth itself. Each morning, as a libation is poured over the hearth, the vapours mingle with the smoke and rise to heaven. The interior of the dwelling is synonymous with a microcosm of the universe, held in common with all other yurt dwellers. The model includes the relationship between people and their gods, and is confirmed by the existence of an 'altar' in the deepest, most sacred space of the yurt.

The organisation of the yurt has key elements in common with the !Kung encampment. The elaboration of the 'elementary building' is based on its sectioning according to the spatial dimensions of front–back, left–right, high–low, centre–periphery. But in contrast to the !Kung, among the Mongols every aspect of position is developed in terms of social difference, within these broad dimensions. Depth from the yurt's entrance indicates differences in rank for both inhabitants and visitors, culminating in the 'altar' at the rear of the yurt, in the deepest space of all. At the same time, differentiated regions within the interior record every possible difference in status among household members and guests, whether by gender, age or degree of wealth. The centre marks the focus of the dwelling, the hearth, and the perimeter regulates the disposition of household objects. Yet all this is done without boundaries of any kind.

The yurt is an extreme development of a structured interior which is brought into being, not by the multiplication of boundaries, but by their elimination.

> Here everything is synchronised: but above all the relationships of inhabitants to each other are synchronised and made parallel to the relations between inhabitants and visitors, and both are realised in a powerful and complex model which depends on the non-existence of boundaries. The yurt is a structural interior that is maximally orientated towards the global structure of society: it builds its local relationships in the image of society as a whole.[13]

The effect of all this is to make the rank of each member of society absolutely explicit by manipulating their relative positions in space, whilst at the same time stressing an identity among all yurt dwellers which is embodied in shared practices and values.

Compounds and townships

Houses articulate relations between social groupings, not individuals, and so most dwellings, however simple, are already elaborations of the elementary building. The forms of habitation which we have considered so far have been relatively stable in their internal layout over time, but in many cultures dwellings take on a dynamic aspect, growing, partitioning and eventually fissioning and re-forming, in a cyclical pattern dictated by the evolving composition of the domestic group. Under these conditions, the 'fit' between the internal organisation of the space of the dwelling presents a fairly precise map of the social relations of the members of the household. As the composition of the dwelling group changes, the use of rooms may change, or rooms are added or demolished accordingly.

This has led to an important distinction within the archaeological and ethnographic record between circular hut compounds and villages of rectangular houses. Compounds or homesteads are locally organised collections of circular, single-cell huts linked together by a wall: houses are globally organised and planned arrangements of rectangular rooms within a rectilinear boundary. In some cases, the house may consist of rooms grouped around three or four sides of a courtyard in what amounts to a modular layout. Flannery has even suggested that these two forms of habitation are the outward manifestation of different systems of social and political organisation.[14]

A typical compound consists of a male elder – the compound head – together with his wives and their young children, unmarried adult daughters, adult sons and their wives and children, and occasionally the elder's widowed mother. The concept of the 'family' is not spatialised in a single dwelling. Rather, each of the constituent huts of the compound is designed to house one, or at the most two individuals. The same space may also serve to house children or livestock. Additional huts may be used for storage, cooking, animals, or for the reception of guests. Thus, the number of people in a compound is likely to be somewhat less than the number of its constituent cells.

The cells are frequently arranged in a rough circle or oval surrounding a cleared space where most of the work of the inhabitants is carried out.

Often, walls are raised between the huts so that the boundary of the compound is secured. Some cultures group huts together systematically within the compound. In many cases, food storage is shared by all the members of a compound, though food may still be prepared and consumed separately.

Rectangular houses, by contrast, are designed from the outset to accommodate a family rather than individuals, though the precise definition as to who counts as 'family' may vary widely between cultures. A common though by no means invariant family grouping is a man, his wife or wives and their unmarried children, and their more distant single or widowed relations. Occasionally, siblings and their families may share a house – an expanded family or horizontal lineage – or a married child and his family may share with parents – an extended family or vertical lineage. Each house has its own food storage, and some have walled courtyards so that work space is not shared between households.

Both compounds and houses may accommodate change within the domestic group, but compounds are particularly responsive to processes of growth and fission within the domestic group. A striking example of this spatial dynamic which, in common with many of the dwellings in this introductory chapter was referred to in *The Social Logic of Space*[15] and which has had a significant part to play in building our theoretical spatial models, is to be found in the domestic compounds of the Tallensi of Northern Ghana, as their way of life was depicted by Fortes in the 1940s and 1950s[16] and by Prussin in the 1960s.[17] Tallensi compounds differ considerably in size and complexity, but they are always based on a strong underlying model which can be seen in figure 1.4.

The basic, irreducible unit of Tallensi society is the homestead, a compound made up of simple, circular, mud-built huts with thatched roofs joined together by a perimeter wall. The space in the vicinity of the entrance is marked by a boabab or 'shade' tree, and ancestor shrines. The entrance, in spite of being the only way in for the entire household, is usually dirty and untidy. It gives into a small cattle yard, which has only one room facing onto it. This is the headman's personal space, though he rarely uses it for any purpose other than to keep his belongings in. More important, it is also said to be the abode of his ancestors' spirits. Both the space outside the compound and the cattle yard are strongly identified with males, and this identification is reinforced by prescriptions which derive their authority from religious observances. Transactions between

Figure 1.4
Tallensi compounds

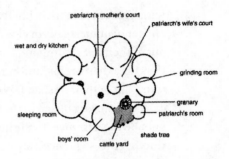

Young man

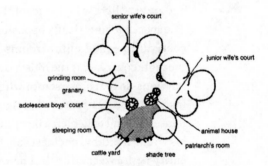

Middle aged man

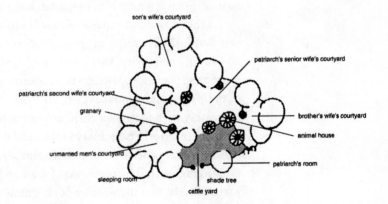

Elderly man

homesteads take place under the shade tree, and are likewise under the
control of men.

The words for homestead and the people who live there are the same in
the Tallensi language. The Tallensi are a patrilineal and patrilocal society,

which means that male kin live together in the same compound, or in a cluster of homesteads in close proximity to one another. Women marry out of their natal compound, and go to their husband's homestead where they take their status, and hence their relative position in the compound, from that of their husband. Within the homestead, domestic space is conceived of and organised in the form of a sequence of spaces from the space outside the entrance, to the heart of the compound. Only by passing through this sequence may visitors arrive at the much larger women's domain.

The women's quarters are separated from the cattle yard by a low wall, and are at a slightly higher level. They are usually well-furnished and tidy. The spaces geometrically opposite the entrance are invariably the outdoor courtyard area and suite of rooms of the senior wife of the patriarch. Just as the male courtyard is the most powerful space governing inside-to-outside relations, so that of the senior wife is the most powerful in organising the inside-inside relations. To her right, looking out, is the second woman of the household and to her left a more junior wife of the patriarch, or the wife of his younger brother or eldest son. Each sub-compound is a self sufficient entity with a wet and dry kitchen, sleeping room and exterior space where the woman and her children may live independently. Far from there being a sense of co-operation in household affairs, there is a strong sense of conflict, so strong that it is a source of segmentation as the compound grows.

As the compound expands towards a more complex form, the domains of individual wives adopt a specific location within the living compound according to seniority. Various hierarchical social practices – a visitor must greet the senior wife first on entering the living area – are associated with this rigid internal space organisation. Others – wives cook and eat separately with their own children – are associated with the segregative, tree-like interior. The granary is the focal point of the entire Tallensi compound, standing between the men's and the women's domains. Powerful sanctions govern the dispensing of grain, which may only be done by the patriarch. Neither the women nor his male relatives may take produce from the granary in the headman's absence.

The way in which a boy becomes a man in Tallensi society is recognised within the layout of the homestead. At puberty, adolescent boys leave their mother's sleeping hut and live together in a separate subcompound for unmarried sons. Proscriptions against a patriarch's meeting his male kin in the doorway of his homestead mean that he can exercise a subtle spatial control over the entry and egress of all the male kin under his jurisdiction. It is not uncommon for married Tallensi men still to be subject to restrictions on their movement in this way. The first stage to full independence is, therefore, for a son to 'cut his own doorway'. This marks a formal separation from his father, and at this point the young man begins to elaborate his own sub-compound. However, this is only the first step in achieving full adult status. To become economically independent, a man must have his own shade tree and ancestor fetishes, in other words, his own compound.

Socially speaking, Tallensi society is a hierarchical lineage system. Every minimal lineage of a compound head is a segment of a more inclusive lineage defined by reference to a common ancestor, and this pattern is repeated until everyone in the whole society can trace their affiliation to each other by reference to the collective ancestors. This elaborate lineage system is erected on a strongly territorial basis. House sites are continuously occupied over many generations. Elaborate purification rituals govern the location of new homesteads in relation to the ancestral home of the patriarch. However, in spite of the strong spatial investment in the location and layout of homesteads, there is no apparent spatial organisation above the level of the compound. On the contrary, compounds appear to be spread across the landscape in a completely random manner.

In addition to living in close proximity to each other, each level in the invisible spatial hierarchy is identified with shrines within the landscape, though to the stranger these may have little significance since they may take the form of a sacred grove, pool, a pile of boulders or a bare patch of earth in the fields or on the hillside. The principles for Tallensi social organisation are enacted well away from places of human habitation, in ancestor rituals where sacrifice to the shrine of a common ancestor requires representation from the senior male in every segment of all the lower orders. Women are banned from taking part. This rule applies to all corporate activity among the Tallensi.

Despite their dispersed settlement form, Tallensi men achieve a degree of social solidarity for which there is no equivalent counterpart among women. Men derive a distinct social advantage through the ritual organisation of the landscape and the local control of the entrance to the compound. Women, on the other hand, remain isolated within their suites of rooms in the women's compound, subject to innumerable rules and restrictions in their daily lives.

In a Tallensi compound, the norms of wifely behaviour within the deterministic spatial order of the compound will in effect be a primary means by which the inequality of men and women is realised. Perhaps in a way we have uttered no more than a truism: the strategy of domination is to isolate and separate the dominated, and to establish local behavioural forms through which the system reproduces itself effortlessly.[18]

To drive the point home, the wives of a patriarch do not even form a cohesive group within the compound, even in the day-to-day performance of household tasks. Unlike the men of the household, who are united by kinship and who have lived together all their lives, wives are permanently institutionalised visitors in their husbands' homesteads, and their daughters are guests who will grow up only to leave home.

The Tallensi are a segmental society. Although there are considerable differences in wealth and status among individual patriarchs, these are not institutionalised in forms of social inequality such as ranks or classes. Each homestead is a more or less self-sufficient entity, and its members are able to supply all the labour necessary to economic subsistence and the roles and statuses required in order to participate in ritual and ceremonial life. At the other end of the spectrum, habitation includes the homes of the aristocracy, governors and rulers who are accustomed to exercise considerable authority within a more stratified society, such as the 'palaces' of the Ashanti chiefs in West Africa, mapped by Rattray[19] in the 1920s. This chiefly residence has become almost urban in its morphology, in that it is made up of a large number of discrete buildings defining a series of courtyards, set within an overall boundary and joined together by open courtyards and narrower passages (see figure 1.5a). Ordinary people's houses are more simple arrangements of rooms grouped around an open court (see figure 1.5b). However, whilst it is the case that the form of the paramount chief's palace is considerably more complex than is that of a typical village home, many of its morphological features can be traced back to these simple origins.

Over and above the fact that the layout of the Ashanti palace is rectilinear and its internal organisation is more geometrically ordered than a typical Tallensi compound, a number of visual differences is immediately obvious. First, the Ashanti palace has several entrances, six to be precise, and these are linked together by the courts and 'streets' so that the whole

Figure 1.5
Comparison of an Ashanti palace and house

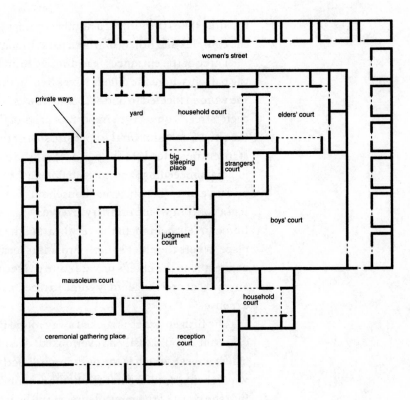

Figure 1.5a Ashanti palace

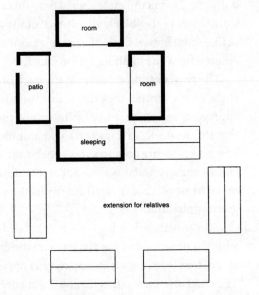

Figure 1.5b Ashanti house

building takes the form of a number of rings, some of which are internal to the complex and others of which pass through the space outside.

Three of the entrances lead directly to an L-shaped area to the rear of the palace, where the chief's wives live. In the Ashanti case, not only are the women located in one of the shallowest spaces in the complex, but also their 'street' connects to important parts of the interior which form part of the chief's domain. On the opposite side of the building, a fourth – main – state entrance leads to the place where the chief presides over important judicial proceedings and hosts major receptions. To the side is a more private court where internal household disputes are dealt with and beyond it is a court in which ordinary, everyday cases are heard in public. Immediately behind, in the very heart of the building, is 'the big sleeping place' where the chief's suite of rooms is located. Next door and directly connected to the chief's private suite is a second small courtyard where any subject or stranger may come to receive hospitality at the chief's expense.

The fifth entrance is tucked away round the back, and is so insignificant that it could easily be overlooked. Guarding it is the room of the 'ghost wives', which is the only space directly connected to the outside whilst being quite separate from the remainder of the complex. It leads into the court of the mausoleum, at the heart of which is a small detached building. This is the most sacred domain of the palace, the 'house of the spirits' where the 'blackened stools' of the ancestors are kept. To the side of the 'stool house' is a gathering place for religious ceremonies which is entered from the main reception court.

The final entrance, is also at the back of the building by the room of the ghost wives. Unlike the others, this leads into a covered building not a courtyard, and is described by Rattray as the 'private ways'. This suggests that this route at least is open to inhabitants of the palace and not to visitors, and possibly only to some inhabitants and not to others. Unfortunately, Rattray does not elaborate, but spatially the effect is to make some parts of the building much less accessible to visitors than it does to inhabitants.

The 'private ways' lead to a yard behind the chief's sleeping quarters which is described as the place where the chief goes when he wishes to be alone, that is in his private capacity as opposed to in his public function. The chief also eats here when he is not entertaining guests. There is a direct access from this more domestic area to the 'big sleeping place', and those parts of the building beyond where the chief enacts his ceremonial role as leader. It is also connected directly to those parts of the building where bodily functions are catered for, and where household goods are stored, food is prepared, rations are issued and sheep are slaughtered. This in turn leads to a small court where the chief and his elders meet to discuss affairs in private. Beyond this is one of the largest of the exterior courts, which has no buildings opening onto it. This is described as a place where the small boys who serve the chief's wives may play. It has direct access to the women's street, and to the main reception space at the front of the building.

The Ashanti palace has a great deal of spatial differentiation according to function. Special spaces are set aside in the building for the chief to entertain his subjects or strangers. The religious function of chiefdom is celebrated in other parts of the palace. A series of spaces is dedicated to the judicial functions of government, where major and less important cases are heard. Other spaces are provided where the chief and his elders may confer in private, realising the political function of government in open-ended negotiations rather than closed and pre-determined ritual. Finally, it is a place of production, not just for the household economy but also for more specialised goods like weapons and gold-work.

Rooms are one step deep from the open courts and, for the most part they are simple, rectangular or L-shaped, open-sided or screened cells with no elaboration of the interior space. The layout seems in one way or another to be dedicated to maintaining relations with the outside world in general, and more specifically to maintaining interfaces between the Ashanti chief and his subjects. Much of the ritual which takes place in the palace is dedicated to expressing this relation between chief and people – judgements, enthronements, and so on. The Ashanti palace is an elaboration of the inhabitant–visitor interface where the Tallensi compound enshrines distinctions among inhabitants – both between men and women – and in respect of women among themselves. At the same time, the chief occupies an especially privileged position, in that the doorways, rooms and courtyards within his personal control relate the discrete parts of the building together internally. Women seem to relate more to the space outside.

The Ashanti live in dense semi-urbanised settlements. Their social structure is one in which descent passes through women. A typical Ashanti house consists of a grandmother, her sons and daughters and their children. The legal head of the house is one of the old lady's sons. He will have inherited the title from his maternal uncle and he will eventually pass on his role to one of his sister's sons. Often this means that husbands and wives do not co-habit, but remain with their natal households, with husbands visiting wives and wives sending food across to their husbands. Typically, children participate in two households, that of their father and that of their mother's brother, and frequently they play one off against the other. This type of social organisation clearly demands a looser control on the building boundaries than that which obtains among the Tallensi, and a more flexible definition of the family house as a place which 'provides shelter for a group of people of varying ages, from very young children to elderly people, who provide mutual assistance . . . and . . . are connected by a complex web of relationships to people in adjoining compounds, creating the need for a flexible system of communications between houses and an entrance that is informal in location'.[20] The use of the space outside and between houses is a common feature of Ashanti village life. It is also a pronounced feature of this elaborate building of the embryonic state.

Elements and relations

The flexible, evolving compounds of the Tallensi are at the opposite end of the domestic spectrum from the palaces of the Ashanti chiefs, which seem spatially to have more in common with a township than with the residences implied by the western concept of a 'palace' which, however large and ramifying, remains essentially a large dwelling planned under one roof. Yet both can be interpreted as elaborations on the inhabitant–inhabitant and inhabitant–visitor interfaces which are the fundamental social generators of buildings.

These contrasting examples also serve to highlight the problem that, in order to compare dwellings with one another and to interpret their sociological significance, we have to solve a prior problem, that of identifying the elements and relations which make up the space pattern. To compare spatial patterns we have to know what a pattern is, and how to tell one configuration from another. Configuration, in this instance, means something quite precise. Spatial relations exist where there is any type of link between two spaces. Configuration exists when the relations which exist between two spaces are changed according to how we relate

Figure 1.6
Basic configurational relationships

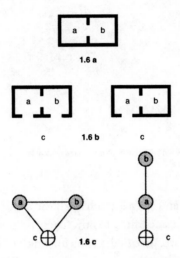

each to a third, or indeed to any number of spaces. Configurational descriptions therefore deal with the way in which a system of spaces is related together to form a pattern, rather than with the more localised properties of any particular space.

A simple graphic illustration may serve to explain. Figure 1.6a shows a simple, rectangular building divided by a partition into two, cell A and cell B, with a doorway creating a relation of permeability between them. It is clear that the relation is symmetrical in the algebraic sense, since A is to B as B is to A.

Now consider figure 1.6b, in which we have added relations to a third space, C (which is in fact the space outside) but in two different ways so that, on the left, both A and B are directly permeable to C whereas, on the right, only A is directly connected to C. This means that in the latter case we must pass through A to get from B to C, whereas in the former we can go either way. In the second example, A and B are different with respect to C. The relation has become asymmetrical. There is a configurational difference between the two examples, and also between the two constituent cells which make up the second illustration.

We have found it useful to show configurational differences in a simple, graphic way, which we call a 'justified' access graph (see figure 1.6c), in which we imagine ourselves to be in one space – in this case the outside

Figure 1.7
Justified access graphs of simple
dwellings

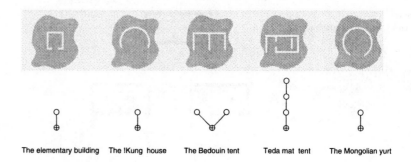

The elementary building   The !Kung house   The Bedouin tent   Teda mat tent   The Mongolian yurt

space, C – and align a graph of all the other spaces in the configuration up the page, according to how 'deep' or how far away each space is from where we are. Justified graphs for small numbers of spaces tend to show configurational differences rather clearly. They capture significant properties of spatial configurations in an immediate, visual way.

If we now represent the elementary building as a configuration, and then compare it with the four very simple structures of the !Kung shelter, the Bedouin and Berber tents, and the Mongolian yurt, then we can begin to identify some configurational similarities and differences among them (see figure 1.7). The !Kung fire-home and the yurt are spatially identical to the elementary building, which maps the relational structure 'interior–exterior' but which is not yet a space configuration. The Bedouin and the Berber tents are more complex domestic space configurations. The former is, configurationally speaking, two contiguous, separate and spatially identical cells, representing the male and female domains, which are linked, or perhaps more accurately separated, by the differentiated space in front of the entrance. The latter is made up of a simple interior sequence of three cells.

The illustrative power of the justified graph can be shown by studying some examples which are a little more complex, and which have been deliberately designed to show the relative independence of building geometry and emergent configurational principles (see figure 1.8). All four 'houses' are based on a three by three square grid, with identical room adjacency. However, from the point of view of permeability, the four examples could not be more different from each other. Room adjacency is a pre-condition for permeability but, within this constraint, the same simple 'courtyard' form can be radically differently configured to make a shallow bush, a deep tree-like sequence, a shallow ringy complex, or a deep ringy room

Figure 1.8
Plans and open spaces of four 'houses'

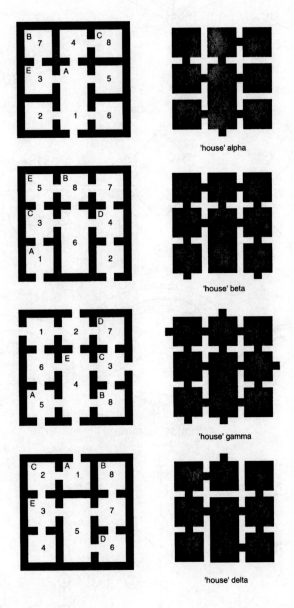

'house' alpha

'house' beta

'house' gamma

'house' delta

arrangement when this is justified in each case from the space outside (see figure 1.9).

However, the invention of the justified graph is more than a simple illustrative tool to clarify space configuration in buildings and settlements. So far as 'space syntax theory' is concerned, the configurational

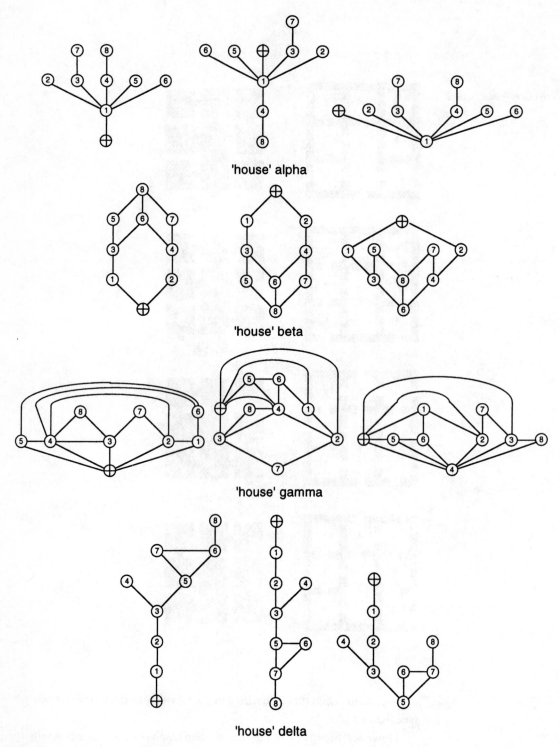

'house' alpha

'house' beta

'house' gamma

'house' delta

Figure 1.9
Justified graphs from the exterior, the
deepest space and the courtyard

variables 'depth' and 'rings' turn out to be fundamental properties of architectural space configurations, and also the means by which architecture can carry culture. There can be no more depth from a point in a configuration than a sequence, nor less than a bush. A tree has the minimum number of connections to join the configuration up into a continuous space pattern. Rings add extra permeability, up to a theoretical maximum where every space is connected to every other. This enables us to begin to measure the degree of depth and relative ringiness of a complex, to capture in numbers the kinds of difference we find in architectural objects.

Justified graphs of house plans unwittingly provided the breakthrough which led to quantitative analysis, for it was by re-drawing the permeability graphs of a simple house from different points within the interior, that we were able to see that the configuration did not just seem different from different rooms, but that it actually was different. As the house was re-drawn from different rooms, the pattern of depth in the graph changed. Some rooms seemed to draw the entire configuration towards the root: other rooms seemed to push most of the rest of the house deep. The depth or shallowness of the whole layout varied, often quite dramatically, depending on where you were positioned within it, as we can immediately see if we compare the respective views of each of the four theoretical 'courtyard houses' in figure 1.8 with the graphs of the same configurations re-drawn from the outside, the deepest room and from the courtyard which are shown in figure 1.9.

We can express this variability mathematically, as the depth from each point compared with that for a bush and a sequence of the same number of spaces, in a measure we call 'integration', because it seems to capture the extent to which each spatial element contributes to drawing the whole configuration together into a more or less direct relationship. The mathematics of the measure are explained in figure 1.10. Shallow graphs will tend to be configurationally more integrated: deep graphs more segregated. The integration values of the four building complexes illustrated in figure 1.8 are tabulated in figure 1.11.

The first thing to look at is the mean integration values for the four 'houses'. Mean integration expresses how shallow or deep on average spaces in the complex are from one another. Unsurprisingly, the shallow, ringy complex has the lowest mean integration and the deep tree-like form is the most segregative configuration, over twice as deep overall. What is perhaps less obvious is that, despite their differences on the ringy

Figure 1.10
The calculation of integration values

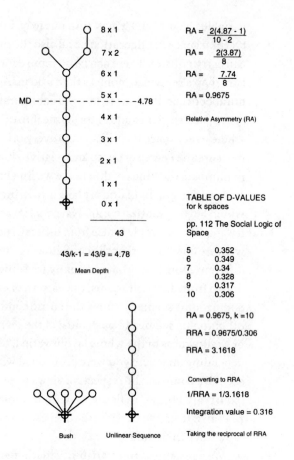

RA = $\dfrac{2(4.87 - 1)}{10 - 2}$

RA = $\dfrac{2(3.87)}{8}$

RA = $\dfrac{7.74}{8}$

RA = 0.9675

Relative Asymmetry (RA)

8 x 1
7 x 2
6 x 1
5 x 1 ———— 4.78
4 x 1
3 x 1
2 x 1
1 x 1
0 x 1

MD ——————— 4.78

43

43/k-1 = 43/9 = 4.78

Mean Depth

TABLE OF D-VALUES
for k spaces

pp. 112 The Social Logic of Space

5	0.352
6	0.349
7	0.34
8	0.328
9	0.317
10	0.306

RA = 0.9675, k =10

RRA = 0.9675/0.306

RRA = 3.1618

Converting to RRA

1/RRA = 1/3.1618

Integration value = 0.316

Taking the reciprocal of RRA

Bush   Unilinear Sequence

dimension, the shallow bush and the deeper ringy complex have the same mean or overall integration. The difference between them lies in how integration is distributed.

Figure 1.11 shows integration values calculated with and without the space outside. This allows us to investigate the interior–exterior relation which, in some cases, has a profound effect on the overall space configuration whilst in others it makes very little difference whether the relation to the exterior is included or omitted from the calculations. The effect of omitting the exterior from the bushy complex, House alpha, is marginal. Considered as a configuration of internal rooms, all the cells become marginally more segregated if the exterior is disregarded, but the rank order of their values from the most integrated space to most segregated is unchanged. In the case of the deep tree, House delta, disregarding the

Figure 1.11
Integration values of the theoretical 'houses'

House alpha			House beta			House gamma			House delta		
space	.	.	space	.	.	space	.	.	space	.	.
⊕		1.015	⊕		1.240	⊕		0.338	⊕		2.480
1A	0.290	0.226	1 A	1.740	1.127	1	1.015	0.676	1 A	2.175	1.691
2	1.160	1.015	2	1.740	1.127	2	0.725	0.451	2 C	1.305	1.127
3 E	0.870	0.789	3 C	0.870	0.789	3 C	1.305	0.676	3 E	0.725	0.789
4	0.870	0.789	4 D	0.870	0.789	4 E	0..580	0.451	4	1.595	1.578
5	1.160	1.015	5 E	1.160	1.127	5 A	1.740	0.902	5	0.725	0.902
6	1.160	1.015	6	0.580	0.676	6	0.870	0.789	6 D	1.305	1.466
7 B	1.740	1.578	7	1.160	1.127	7 D	1.160	0.902	7	1.160	1.353
8 C	1.740	1.578	8 B	0.870	1.015	8 B	1.015	0.902	8 B	2.030	2.142
Mean	1.124	1.002	Mean	1.124	1.002	Mean	1.051	0.676	Mean	1.378	1.503
DF	0.548	0.496	DF	0.782	0.928	DF	0.775	0.827	DF	0.781	0.761

exterior also has very little effect on the overall integration of the complex, which is marginally more integrated if the exterior is disregarded. The effect on the rank order of integration of the constituent cells is slight. We can deduce that, in these complexes, configuration is principally organised so as to structure interior relations, and hence the inhabitant–inhabitant interface.

In both ringy cases illustrated in figure 1.8, the exterior is an important means of forming large rings through the complex, but in the deep ringy example, House beta, unlinking the ring which passes through the exterior does not produce a radical effect on the distribution of integration. The effect of disregarding the connection to the outside upon the mean integration value of the shallow ringy complex, House gamma, however, is to make it much more segregative overall, particularly affecting those cells which do not feature on the two remaining internal rings. The integration values of its constituent interior spaces also become more differentiated. Because the way in which each cell features within the configuration is strongly affected by the way the complex relates to the exterior, the inhabitant–visitor interface is implicated in the sociogram of this building at least as much as the relations among its inhabitants.

Looking at houses with and without the links to the exterior is an important dimension of configurational analysis which helps us to understand the relative importance of inhabitant–inhabitant and inhabitant– visitor relationships for the planning and organisation of the home. Where there are several entrances to a dwelling from the exterior, it may also be helpful to look at how the building unfolds as a justified permeability graph for each way in considered separately, particularly where these are functionally differentiated. In some homes men and

women enter through a different sequence of spaces. In other cases, front
and back doors differentiate formal and informal visiting patterns, or the
way the householder enters the home from the tradesmen's and servants'
entrances. Where entrances are used to separate functions or categories of
people in this way, they often encapsulate entirely different spatial viewpoints of the internal workings of the home.

Variations in the integration values of different spaces in a single
complex can be quite as striking as the justified graphs from different
rooms which we looked at earlier. One way of quantifying the extent of
variability is to compare the values of the most integrated and most segregated spaces with the mean integration value for the complex, this time
taking account of links to the exterior. For example, in the shallow bushy
complex of figure 1.8, the most integrated space, A, is over four times more
integrated than the mean for the complex, and about seven times more
integrated than the most segregated rooms in the complex, which are
labelled B and C. In the shallow ringy complex, the most integrated space
is the outside, which is almost exactly half the mean and about one third of
the maximum value, which is shared by three spaces, D, B and A. A similar
distribution of values is found in the deep tree, but here E in the middle of
the graph is the most integrated space, while the most segregated space of
all is the outside. In the deep ringy complex, the maximum value is only
about twice the minimum. Here too, the most integrated space, numbered
6 in the middle of the graph, links three large rings of circulation through
the complex including the exterior, which again is the most segregated
space of all.

In this case we are looking at single complexes which have been
designed to illustrate syntactic features. However, where the degree of
difference between the integration values of any three (or more) spaces or
functions is consistent for a sample of house plans, so that the most integrated space is shallow and pivotal and most segregated space is very
secluded and private, we can infer that this has not occurred by accident.
To measure this we have developed an entropy based measure called the
'difference factor', which quantifies the spread or degree of configurational
differentiation among integration values. Figure 1.12 gives details of how
the measure is calculated but it is sufficient to know that the closer to 0
the difference factor, the more differentiated and structured the spaces or
labels; the closer to 1, the more homogenised the spaces or labels, to a
point where all have equal integration values and hence no configurational

Figure 1.12
Calculating the difference factor

$$H = - \left[\frac{a}{t} \ln\left(\frac{a}{t}\right) \right] + \left[\frac{b}{t} \ln\left(\frac{b}{t}\right) \right] + \left[\frac{c}{t} \ln\left(\frac{c}{t}\right) \right]$$

$$H^* = \frac{H - \ln 2}{\ln 3 - \ln 2}$$

Max RRA	= 2.348
Mean RRA	= 1.238
Min RRA	= 0.968

$$H = - \left[\frac{a}{t} \ln\left(\frac{a}{t}\right) \right] + \left[\frac{b}{t} \ln\left(\frac{b}{t}\right) \right] + \left[\frac{c}{t} \ln\left(\frac{c}{t}\right) \right]$$

$$H = - \left[\frac{2.348}{4.554} \ln\left(\frac{2.348}{4.554}\right) \right] + \left[\frac{1.238}{4.554} \ln\left(\frac{1.238}{4.554}\right) \right] + \left[\frac{0.968}{4.554} \ln\left(\frac{0.968}{4.554}\right) \right]$$

$$H = - \left[0.5156 \ln\left(0.5156\right) \right] + \left[0.2718 \ln\left(0.2718\right) \right] + \left[0.2126 \ln\left(0.2126\right) \right]$$

$$H = - \left[-0.3415 \right] + \left[-0.3541 \right] + \left[-0.3292 \right] \qquad H = 1.0248$$

$$H^* = \frac{H - \ln 2}{\ln 3 - \ln 2} \qquad H^* = \frac{1.0248 - \ln 2}{\ln 3 - \ln 2} \qquad H^* = \frac{0.3317}{0.4055} \qquad H^* = 0.82$$

differences exist between them. The difference factors for maximum, minimum and mean integration for the four courtyard buildings with and without exterior connections are given in figure 1.11. Of the four theoretical courtyard complexes, House alpha turns out to be most spatially differentiated, both with and without the exterior. The remaining houses invest rather less in spatial differentiation.

If we now consider the labels, or more precisely the relation of the various labels within the space configurations in figure 1.8, we can begin to detect certain regularities in terms of the relations between syntactic positions within the complex and way in which labels are assigned to spaces. For example, the space labelled A is always as shallow as any other in the complex, whereas space B is always as deep as it is possible to go from the outside. Space D is always on a ring, except where there are no rings in which case there is no space D. Space E is always on the shortest path from A to B. Finally the position of C is randomised. Since this is the only space which is so, this may well be considered significant. These consistencies in the visual patterning of the complexes do not, however, extend to a standardisation of the rank order of integration values for the labelled spaces. On the contrary, all permutations occur, as figure 1.11 shows.

These theoretical 'courtyard' examples show us that it is unwise to believe the evidence of our eyes. Not all plans that look alike are configured alike. In dealing with space configuration as opposed to the more recognisable features of buildings such as shape, geometry or room adjacency, we are frequently dealing with a degree of subtlety which cannot simply be left to intuition. Incidentally, these 'theoretical forms' can be found in the ethnographic record of real 'courtyard' houses from different parts of the world, making the point that an apparent typological identity can mask great configurational diversity across space and through time (see figure 1.13).

Integration has emerged in empirical studies as one of the fundamental ways in which houses convey culture through their configurations. Unlike our four theoretical buildings, we began to find that in cases where we were able to work with a statistically reliable sample of real houses from the traditional and vernacular record, different functions or activities were systematically assigned to spaces which integrated the dwellings to differing degrees. Function thus acquired a spatial expression which could also be assigned a numerical value. Where these numerical differences were in a consistent order across a sample of plans from a region, society or ethnic grouping, then we could say that a cultural pattern existed, one which could be detected in the configuration itself rather than in the way in which it was interpreted by minds. We called this particular type of numerical consistency in spatial patterning a housing 'genotype'.

What we were finding in these early housing studies was a relation between the way space is configured and the way it is used. Functional patterning was imprinted into the physical and spatial form of the house. We might best think of this not as a background to behaviour but as a record of behaviour transmitted through the building, perhaps through several generations. Configurational analysis of plans can be conceived of as an 'archaeology of space'. If houses display configurational regularities then the buildings speak directly to us of culturally significant household practices which have been crystallised in the dwelling in the form of an integration inequality genotype.

This insight allows us to return to the irregular, ramifying Tallensi

Figure 1.13
Four courtyard houses from the
historical record

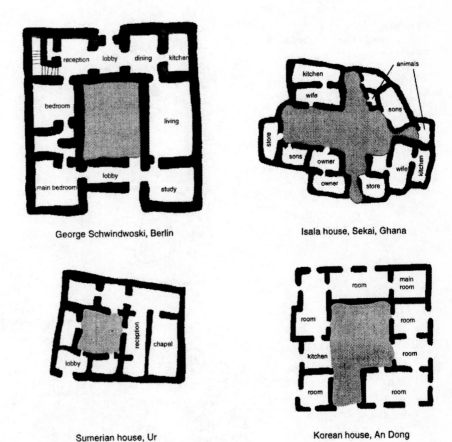

George Schwindwoski, Berlin

Isala house, Sekai, Ghana

Sumerian house, Ur

Korean house, An Dong

compounds which were described earlier, to see if it is possible to capture
the pattern of invariance in inhabitant–inhabitant and inhabitant–visitor
relations which was described earlier, in a more precise, numerical form.
Figure 1.14 gives the justified graphs from the exterior for the three
Tallensi homesteads first shown in figure 1.4. The first example is a
minimal lineage comprising a patriarch, his elderly mother and his wife,
together with their children. In the second example, a more mature man
has two wives who share a compound, whilst in the final and most extensive compound, a patriarch's younger brother and eldest son are both resident, together with their families. We may therefore compare homesteads
at different stages in the domestic cycle.

Justified access graphs immediately clarify the principles for growth.
The homesteads are all organised in the form of a deep, tree-like graph. If

Figure 1.14
Plans and justified graphs of the Tallensi
compounds

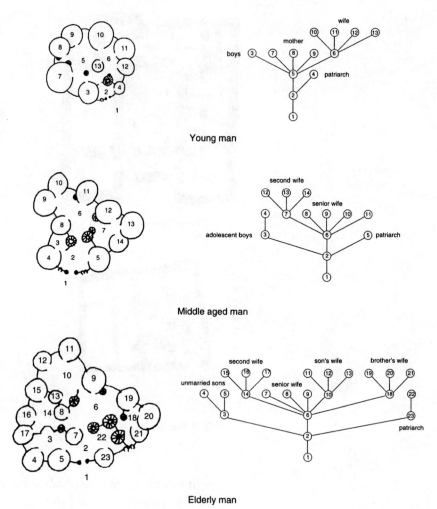

Young man

Middle aged man

Elderly man

the space outside the entrance, where the shade tree and ancestor shrines
are located, is taken as the 'root' of this tree then, by analogy, the room of
the patriarch and the courtyard of the adolescent boys are the lower
branches. The senior wife's courtyard and her suite of rooms are strategically located at the branching point of the trunk. She controls access to the
courtyards of more junior wives, and to the grinding rooms where millet,
which is the staple diet, is prepared for cooking each afternoon. In the
small compound the women share a grinding room, but where one woman
habitually monopolises the room, the patriarch is obliged to provide

House	Order								DF
A	mother's court	wife's court	cattle yard	mother's rooms	wife's room	patriarch's room exterior			
	0.3299	0.4949	0.7194	0.9348	1.0998	1.3197			0.750
B	senior wife's court	cattle yard	second wife's court	senior wife's room	adolescent boys' court	patriarch's room exterior	second wife's rooms	boys' sleeping room	
	0.3844	0.5766	0.6727	0.9610	1.0571	1.1532	1.2493	1.6333	0.762
C	senior wife's court	cattle yard	second wife son's wife brother's wife's courts	senior wife's rooms	unmarried men's court	patriarch's room exterior	second wife son's wife brother's wife's rooms	unmarried men's sleeping room	
	0.3836	0.5994	0.6952	0.8391	0.9590	1.0549	1.1508	1.4145	0.720

Figure 1.15
Space genotype of Tallensi compounds

several to pacify his womenfolk. This seems to have occurred in the largest homestead, but it is also striking that here, where the senior wife has an enhanced supervisory role over food preparation, she seems no longer obliged to cook and her kitchens have been demolished to make way for the courtyard of her son's wife. The canopy of the tree is formed by the sleeping rooms and wet and dry season kitchens of the junior women. Buried deep within the configuration of these irregular, wandering and organic compound forms are principles for social organisation which could not be more clear.

Figure 1.15 then tabulates integration values for the three examples. The integration inequality genotype is clear and invariant. Though relatively deep, the senior wife's courtyard invariably integrates the living complex. The male-orientated cattle yard tends to be the next most integrating courtyard, followed by the courtyards of the junior wives. All the senior woman's rooms, including the grinding room, are more integrated than the mean. Where it exists, the adolescent boys' courtyard is more segregated than the mean integration value for the compound. The space outside the entrance and the room of the patriarch, though very shallow from the outside are segregated with respect to the compound as a whole. The rooms of junior wives and adolescent boys are the most segregated spaces of all. The strength of this genotype, as measured in the difference factor among labels, is suggestive of a rather strong spatial model for Tallensi domestic space.

Wherever we have looked at samples of traditional and vernacular houses, we have come across genotypical stabilities of the sort we have identified here. We have therefore come to believe that this is one of the most general means by which culture is built into housing layout. Housing genotypes, unlike housing layouts which are often quite different from each other, depend on fewer and more general spatial characteristics. Every home configures a 'lifestyle' by constructing social interfaces among family members and between the household and visitors to the home, often extending to the way in which rooms are decorated and household objects placed within the domestic interior, and the genotype, if it exists, will stabilise these generic cultural relations. Everything else can be allowed to vary as circumstances dictate, which is why houses may bear rather little resemblance to one another at superficial level.

In the case of the Ashanti palace, we are dealing with a single building so it is not possible to identify its building genotype. Nonetheless, configurational analysis is able to clarify aspects of spatial organisation which are not immediately open to visual inspection. Figure 1.16a is a justified permeability graph of the palace, and figures 1.16b and 1.16c show separately the structure of the ringy courtyards and the distribution of rooms.

This immediately clarifies the relationship between the shallow, ringy and distributed structure of courts and streets which are open to the air, in relation to the various groups of buildings which make up the palace. The most shallow places in the Ashanti palace are the reception and audience courtyards and the court of the mausoleum, where the public and ceremonial functions associated with chiefly rule are acted out. The street of the women and the boys' play areas are all relatively shallow. The deepest courtyards are those for hygiene, animal slaughter and the dispensing of food, where the chief sleeps, and where he entertains his guests privately and meets his elders in secret. If the 'private ways' are closed, these public and private functions become even deeper with respect to the outside.

Differentiations among the rooms are no less informative. The main reception rooms surrounding the front courtyard, the chief's bathing and robing rooms, the places where his attendants sleep, and the women's houses are clustered together in sets, relatively shallow in the palace complex. The ceremonial and religious functions associated with the 'house of the spirits' form small, non-distributed sub-complexes of deeper spaces accessed through courts which are not part of the general, ringy circulation. The rooms where ritual celebrants gather and where internal disputes are resolved are among the deeper clusters, but so also are the rooms where household goods are stored, where people sit to pass the time

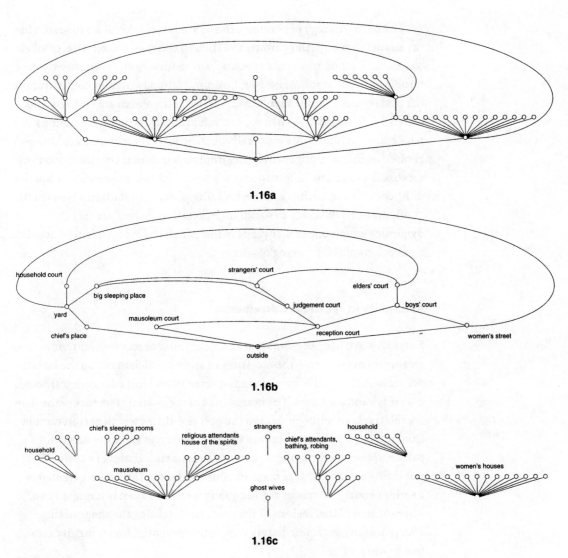

1.16a

1.16b

1.16c

Figure 1.16
Justified graphs of an Ashanti palace

of day and where polluting activities associated with bodily functions and slaughter are carried out. There are only two isolated rooms in the palace, the room of the 'ghost wives', which is outside the rear entrance, and the place where strangers may come for hospitality at the chief's expense. Looked at this way, the Ashanti palace seems not so much a 'machine for living in' as a sophisticated 'ruling machine' which constitutes a microcosm of the society in a single building complex.

The basic strategy of configurational analysis is therefore to search for invariants in the spatial pattern and then to consider the relation of labels to spaces. To the extent that space is systematically and consistently patterned across a sample of houses, buildings embody in their configuration the social intentions of their makers. When differences are strongly and consistently replicated, then we can infer that the structural relations which are articulated are culturally significant. Where rooms are homogenised within a configuration, the implication is that the functions they serve do not need to be so strongly supported by marked configurational differences. Even within a single building, sharp differentiations in spatial configuration give clues to social interpretation and may reveal the dynamics which underpin everyday life which are independent of people's perceptions of the meaning of space.

Ambiguity in spatial arrangements

So far we have been dealing with simple cellular or rectangular room arrangements in which the constituent spaces which make up the layout are separated by walls, partitions and screens, and linked together through doorways and openings. The boundaries of the spatial elements of the plan are relatively unambiguous, and the permeabilities which permit circulation to take place amongst them clear. However, even in the Ashanti palace, space began to take on some of the characteristics of a town. The ramifying arrangement of open air courtyard areas which were treated as a series of bounded spaces could equally well have been interpreted as a series of articulated regions of the plan. Highlighting the shape of the courtyards in grey immediately makes this potential for ambiguity clear (see figure 1.17).

The ambiguity inherent in buildings like these poses problems for arriving at an 'objective' decomposition of a house into its constituent parts – 'objective' not in the sense of being 'true', but in the more limited sense that different people using the same methodology would arrive at an identical spatial description. It serves to highlight a methodological problem that whole classes of buildings seem to behave spatially more like settlements in the very precise sense that the layout of space is essentially continuous.

For some time we believed that, in order to invent an 'objective' representational language for space organisation, we needed to find one,

Figure 1.17
Open space of the Ashanti palace

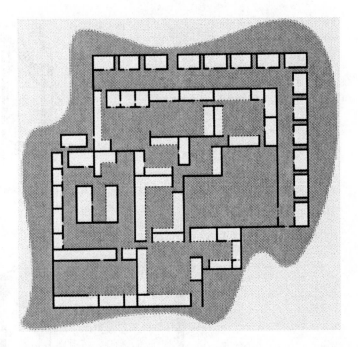

unambiguous method for breaking a pattern of space up into elements. The breakthrough to solving the problem of representing spatial articulation and ambiguity came when we realised that we required not one way of characterising the spatial properties of any building layout or settlement pattern but three. The syntax of space can be considered in its 'axial' or one-dimensional organisation, its 'convex' or two-dimensional organisation, and in terms of its 'isovists'[21] or visual fields (see figure 1.18). Each is related to an aspect of how people experience and use space. Figure 1.19 then breaks up the streets and courts of figure 1.17 into its constituent convex and axial elements. The convex representation shows the set of fewest and fattest two-dimensional spaces, and the axial representation shows the set of fewest and longest lines, which cover the grey shape of figure 1.17, with four lines added to represent the spaces outside the perimeter walls.

The convex break-up of the palace courtyards shown in figure 1.19b turns out to be over four times as elaborate as the structure of its boundaries. In the majority of cases, courts are separated from each other by smaller transition spaces which both link and discreetly separate the activities which take place there. The axial map, figure 1.19a, also suggests

Figure 1.18
Axial and convex spatial dimensions
and convex isovist

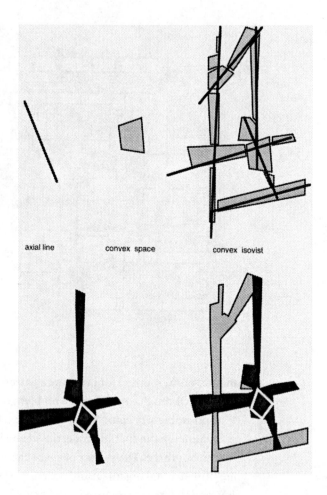

an unobtrusive but persistent manipulation of boundaries and openings. Aside from the entrances on the long sides of the women's streets, all entrances to the palace are chicaned so that visitors cannot see directly into the interior. This effect is reproduced within the complex so that, even though more public and more private activities are accommodated in adjacent parts of the complex, they are screened from each other by placing and shaping of walls and rooms. The articulation is at its greatest in the transitional zone where the chief mutates from enacting his public position to living as a private individual, at the entrance to the big sleeping place. It appears that the manner in which these two ways of seeing a configuration, and how they are related together, tells us even

Figure 1.19
Axial and convex maps of
the Ashanti palace

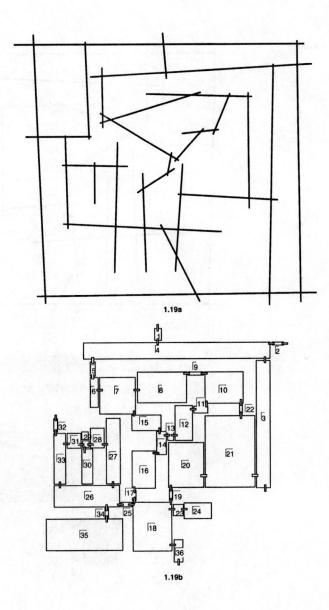

more about the ways in which buildings modulate patterns of encounter
and avoidance.

The spatial property of integration may be computed just as readily for
these axial and convex representations of space as it was for the justified
graphs shown earlier. Figures 1.20a and 1.20b show the integration structure of the open space of the Ashanti palace considered both axially and

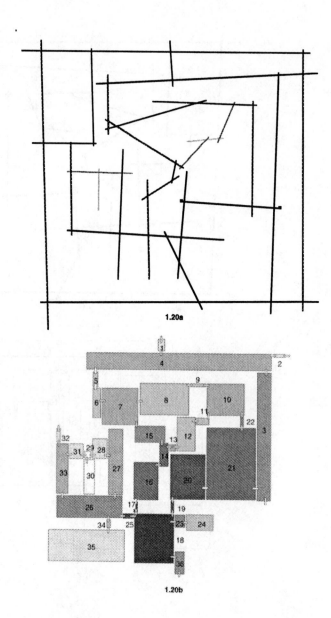

1.20a

1.20b

convexly. The most integrated parts of the complex are picked out in black, and the degree of relative integration is represented by the density of tone from dark to light grey, with the palest grey indicating the most segregated areas of all. In both axial and convex versions of the plan, the main reception court turns out to be the most integrated place in the palace, suggesting that the public interface between chief and subjects is a significant

Figure 1.21
Visual fields of the Ashanti palace

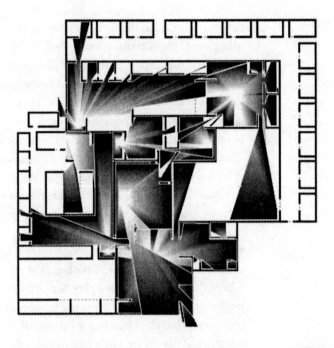

generator of the plan. However, although it is shallow from the outside, the ritual and ceremonial areas associated with the mausoleum and the spirit house, turn out to be the most segregated parts of the building.

In effect, the distribution of integration gives a rather good account of the relative degree of community and privacy which is entailed in the functional organisation of the plan. The combination of strong local enclosure with direct accessibility means that highly ceremonial and intensely intimate activities are able to co-exist in a natural and unforced way. The co-existence of open, roofed shelters and fully-enclosed rooms in each courtyard suggests that manifesting or hiding people and things is an important dimension of Ashanti culture. The exception is the women's street, where domestic privacy is preserved for each of the chief's many wives.

Axial and convex representations map the global configuration of the building. One further representation which looks at each space individually is the representation of its 'isovists' or visual fields (see figure 1.21). Visual fields based on convex or axial representations, show the maximum axial extension of a space, and hence its strategic value in accessing or concealing the remainder of the building. Visual fields may be panoramic, rendering much of the interior transparent, or penetrating, so that narrow glimpses of the interior are revealed, often in several directions. Barriers which end-stop visual fields may be significant architectural or cultural features, or blank walls. The area covered by a visual field may highlight important object arrays, gatherings of people, or movement patterns. The convex visual fields from the set of spaces in the Ashanti palace which are reserved for the chief are superimposed upon one another in figure 1.21. This shows the extent to which the chief acquires a generalised awareness of what is taking place within his palace, simply by going about his every-day business. The only areas which are not subject to his pervasive scrutiny are the streets of his wives, the 'backstage' area of the mausoleum complex where the celebrants gather for religious ceremonies, the rooms where his predecessors' skeletons are housed and the blackened stools of his ancestors are preserved as objects of ritual veneration, and the place where the adolescent boys play. Since these are likely to include his many nephews, among whom is his eventual successor, the conclusion seems inevitable that the visibility structure of the palace presents the chief with a picture of his present role and status, whilst shielding him from visual contact with his ancestral past and his putative successors.

Semantically rich dwellings from the ethnographic record are not the only cases which exploit spatial ambiguity within the domestic setting. It is a particular feature of modern, architect-designed homes, but here ambiguity is created by articulating spatial boundaries within a 'plan libre' or 'promenade architecturale' rather than by differentiating zones within a simple shape. A great deal of the architectural 'buzz' is generated by the plastic manipulation of volume, but here in the interests of the aesthetic experience of a building experienced in movement, rather than the communication of culturally-significant information. For these cases, configurational analysis can be a useful adjunct to the more conventional compositional techniques for architectural criticism, such as an analysis of building proportion or a representation of the 'parti'.

The notations and measures which make up configurational analysis can be applied to any system of elements and relations, provided we specify in advance what these are. Since adjacency is the pre-condition for permeability, it may be of interest to represent and quantify the extent to which the latter is a sub-set of the former in a building or sample of build-ings. Many buildings exploit architecturally the possibility of construct-ing views from one part of the interior to another, or out into the

Figure 1.22
The arrangement of people in the
Mongolian yurt

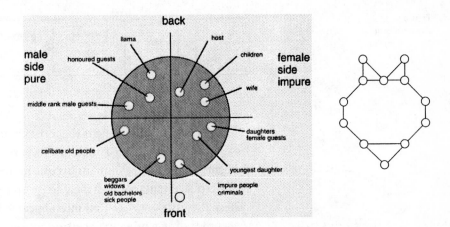

surrounding environment. Under these conditions, relations of visibility –
the transparency or opacity of boundaries – may be compared with
relations of permeability. Whatever the elements and relations under
consideration are, they can still be shown diagramatically as before, where
elements are represented by circles and relations as lines linking circles.

This can even be attempted where the domestic interior is far more
elaborate than its simple boundary conditions might suggest. People, activities and even object arrays can be considered as arrangements whose inter-
relationships can be represented and quantified in order to shed light on the
configuration. The Mongolian yurt will again serve as an illustration.

As we have already seen, this appears to be a simple, domed structure
on a circular plan, yet it constitutes an elaborate and rigid system of invisible rules governing the location of people and things within the domestic
interior and dictating how they may relate to each other. However, despite
the absence of boundaries, different categories of people can equally well
be considered as elements in the layout, which can be located within the
yurt as circles occupying different regions of the plan. In fact, important
differentiations among the places of low and high status individuals are
actually marked on the ground by skins and felt mats, but not all positions are so clearly delineated. Some people find their place by reference
to household objects, which may imply or construct a barrier between
people. The relations of permitted proximity and avoidance which obtain
amongst inhabitants and visitors can then be plotted as lines joining
circles together (see figure 1.22). By this means, the nature of the symbolic
and the practical worlds of the Mongolian yurt can be further clarified.

guest of honour, host, wife		middle rank males, daughters		celibate old people, youngest daughter		sick, impure		llama children		outside
1.0211	>	1.0849	>	1.1488	>	1.2126	>	1.3402	>	1.5317

The symbolic dimension is the most obvious. The 'deeper' into the yurt a person is positioned, the more important is his status: the closer to the centre, the more prominent his role in the proceedings. Within the symmetrical circular plan of the yurt, people's physical positions are systematically skewed so that men appear to be deeper in the house than the women of an equivalent position, and guests are accorded more prominence than family members.

The fine-tuning is quite complex. 'Profane' old people sit closer to the door than 'pure' old people who have refrained from sexual relations, but the latter are more retiring and sit closer to the wall. Unmarried sons and male guests are generally seated deeper and closer to the hearth than female guests and daughters. The host defers slightly to the 'honoured guests' in prominence, but sits slightly deeper in the yurt and closer to the altar. His wife is accorded more status than male guests, but is more peripheral to the proceedings. The youngest daughter is much closer to the door, but is prominently seated opposite the honoured guests. Holy men are in the deepest space of all, but withdraw slightly from socialisation, as do children.

When the physical relationships between them are added and the integration values of the 'people arrangement' calculated (see figure 1.23), we can see that this complex hierarchy is more symmetrical than it appears at first sight. The household head is the linchpin, most integrated and controlling relations between his – largely male – guests and the female members of his family, particularly to his unmarried daughters. Around him, categories are relationally paired and take up balanced positions within the graph from more integrated to segregated: honoured guest and esteemed wife, middle-ranking male guests with daughters, venerable and celibate old people and cherished, chaste youngest daughter, the sick and the outcast, holy men and children, with the outside being the most segregated place. This abstract relational structure is simpler, and suggestive of a more complementary model for social roles in everyday life within the Mongolian home than the relations implied within the superficial distribution of people and things.

Single-cell dwellings with highly elaborated domestic interiors form a class of buildings from the ethnographic record which illustrate the capacity of space to absorb 'fuzzy function'. For these cases, what is not built into space configuration may be stipulated in rules governing behaviour which take the place of rooms, boundaries and openings in generating and controlling social encounters within the home. This is an equally valid observation in the case of more complex houses, for the analysis of space configuration will inevitably portray a partial account of the 'deceptive complexity' of people's homes. In interpreting the social meaning of configuration, it may be necessary to consider such features as orientation, decorative styles, and regularities in the disposition of furniture and domestic artefacts within the home. Interpretation may depend on an understanding of the rules of kinship, marriage, descent and residence within the household, the influence of cosmology or religious belief in the domestic milieu, the daily pattern of household practices, the norms of domestic etiquette and personal behaviour, even people's descriptions and perceptions of home.

This more complex view of the house as a reflection, not just of how individuals and families choose to live their everyday lives, but of the constitution of society at large, has begun to focus scholarly attention in recent years upon a more detailed, cross-cultural examination of domestic architecture. There is now an evolving body of research which suggests that the size and spatial sub-division of people's houses, the development of more complex and differentiated space configurations – whether this is accomplished conceptually by allocating activities to different zones within a space, or physically by partitioning the interior into separate rooms, or by a mixture of both – and the degree of sophistication in the pattern of connectivity, access and spatial integration which obtains among them, may be a direct indication of a society's level of socio-political complexity. This is normally measured through such non-spatial factors as the extent of social stratification, the disparity which exists in material wealth, the amount of occupational specialisation within the division of labour, and the complexity of the household economy.

One of the most detailed studies of this kind by Susan Kent,[22] directly addresses the issue of why it is that some societies segment or partition their homes more than others. Kent describes the use of domestic space and compares qualitatively the extent of spatial sub-division of the dwelling in thirty-eight societies drawn from five socio-political categories. These are ranked according to their level of socio-cultural evolution from nomadic, subsistence hunter-gatherer bands, through segmental societies based on lineages or clans, to more vertically stratified tribal societies which have a degree of social ranking and economic specialisation, class-based chiefdoms in which rank, wealth and social status are inherited not achieved, and finally to societies with a highly structured, specialised and differentiated labour force which is characteristic of the embryonic state. Kent concludes that the segmented use of space and the existence of a segmented architecture correlates directly with the level of social and political complexity of the society in question. In essence, increased social complexity produces increased segmentation and partitioning within the home.

This generalisation raises as many questions for the future of homes and housing, as it suggests novel interpretations of the past. In extending Kent's ideas to modern societies, there clearly is a need to interpret her findings in the light of the complexity of today's built environment, with its tendency to partition and segment the entire city in its urban region into functionally delineated zones, in which the house is an atom and the residential district but a part. Despite a generation of experimental, innovative housing design the essential architecture of past and present homes and housing remains obscure. The studies which follow represent a small piece in the puzzle of understanding what is perhaps the most fundamental and yet most challenging building of all.

The order of the argument

The remainder of the book will use the approach and framework which have been set out above, to explore in more detail the relation between domestic space organisation and the forms of social interface which are constructed by people's homes in different parts of the world and at different historical periods. By taking the physical form and space configuration of the house as a focus, the more complex and interpretative sociological dimensions such as what is meant by 'family' and 'household' in any particular situation become an emergent aspect of the study. The analytic strategy is to examine databases of house plans to identify first any regularities in the way in which the space is configured, and then to see if any configurational invariances which hold across the sample are systematically related to the labels put on particular spaces to describe, or even to circumscribe their use. From this simple starting point, inferences can be made about the way domestic space supports family life and household organisation, even though this may vary in its composition and membership every bit as widely as the range of house types which are to be found in any real situation.

The opening chapters seek to show how configurational analysis can shed light on questions of historical interpretation, contemporary lifestyles and popular tastes as these are manifested in the design of English homes; the later chapters look at houses more as works of architecture which seek to express material and spatial effects over and above the more obvious demands of function or lifestyle. The final chapter reviews current applications in the field and suggests future avenues for research, in a series of methodological sketches which use configurational analysis in entirely new ways, to look this time not at relations of permeability, but at the interpretation and meaning of people's home lives, at the significance of distributions of activities within the home and even at the proportioning of facades and at the massing of the house considered in volume.

The studies presented here span a period of twenty years' research into the relation between house form and culture. They represent the 'tip of the iceberg' in an extensive, multi-cultural corpus of case studies which have been conducted over the years. Whilst they share a theoretical standpoint and draw on the common space syntax research methodology, each has an unique contribution to make to the battery of analytic techniques or interpretative frameworks. If this produces a certain redundancy in the description of research methodology, the gain is that each chapter may be read as a self-contained essay in configurational analysis.

Chapters two and three, 'Tradition and change in the English house' and 'Ideas are in things' come closest to the concept of an 'archaeology of space' in that they use samples of house plans to investigate key questions in the social history of two comparable farming traditions from England and France. The approach shares with more conventional archaeology the difficulty of having to draw on essentially inanimate resources and to breathe life into them by scrupulous analysis and interpretation. Wherever possible, interpretation is supported by contemporary written accounts and historical explanation.

One of our earliest excursions into the study of domestic space organisation was an historical account of a sample of simple, seventeenth-century, three-bay house plans belonging to yeomen farmers from the Banbury region of Oxfordshire which were recorded by Wood-Jones in the 1950s and 60s.[23] *Tradition and change in the English house* presents this previously unpublished work, which turns out to be something of a detective story in which justified permeability graphs hold the key to both housing typology and sociological interpretation. The seventeenth century holds a particular fascination for students of English family structure, since it is at about this period that the family began to emerge in its modern form. It was also a time of political and religious turmoil. The influence of these profound social changes is suggestively linked to the evolution of Banbury farmhouses over time.

Ideas are in things[24] reports one of the first studies to use a sophisticated combination of representational and numerical syntactic techniques to investigate a sample of traditional farmhouses from the Normandy region of France. Conventional interpretations of French rural architecture laid great stress on the orientation of the dwelling, and specifically on the association of particular household functions with front-back and left-right relations. The configurational relationship between visibility and permeability which is reported here also turns out to have important social consequences, suggesting a new interpretation of gender relations within rural French society of the period.

The following pair of chapters explores some of the key features of contemporary English homes. Although most people no longer build their own houses, the houses they buy embody popular values. The difference between speculative and architect-designed houses may therefore help us to gain an insight into ordinary people's desires and aspirations. The original material for chapter four, 'Two domestic "space codes" compared',[25] was gathered during the 1970s, before the greater part of the space syntax research methodology had been developed. It therefore reminds us that detailed observation of the qualitative aspects of people's everyday lives at home can help to identify key binary oppositions which form the dimensions of a space-code underpinning observed cultural behaviours. The chapter looks at everyday life as it was recorded in traditional

London terraced houses during the 1950s by Willmot and Young in their seminal study *Family and Kinship in East London*,[26] and draws a series of spatial and behavioural contrasts with the space culture of the young professionals who began to 'gentrify' these small houses during the 1960s and 1970s.

The research on which chapter five is based, coincided with the twenty-fifth anniversary in 1992 of the foundation of the latest and perhaps the last example of the British new town movement, Milton Keynes. *Shaping the taste of middle England*[27] investigates contemporary lifestyle variables in a much larger sample of speculative houses, built for sale in this thriving new town in the early 1990s. It argues that, despite the reputation which the city enjoys for innovation and futuristic living, the houses which people choose to live in show a continuity of design and purpose with Victorian homes. This seems to relate more to a deep-rooted and very English concern for privacy within the domestic setting than to a superficial affectation for the detailing, decoration and ephemera of the period.

Chapter six, 'Configuration and society in the English country house', looks at four seminal country houses built for members of the English aristocracy between 1590 and 1870. The houses span architectural and social trends which range from late Elizabethan English Renaissance court classicism, through a minimalist and economical style which became popular during the Puritan interregnum, to the celebration of the Palladian villa in the aftermath of the Restoration and the historicist and moralising architecture of the Victorian era. The houses could scarcely appear more different from one another, yet they provide a vehicle through which to explore key themes in the organisation of the domestic interior, including the association between room-centred and corridor-centred plans with what appear at first sight to be fundamentally opposed sensual and spartan lifestyles. Analysis of the space configurations of these houses, however, suggests that they have more factors in common than features which divide them. The houses share a deep, ringy and highly differentiated morphology which supports and regulates both the public and private exercise of power.

The next three chapters share a common theme in the proposition that, when architects are commissioned to design innovative one-off houses, they invariably theorise about how the fundamental features of dwellings should be spatially conceived, whether or not these are

consciously articulated as a part of the brief. Architects' houses can be
rich improvisations of their cultural base, but they can equally-well be
mundane or downright dysfunctional. Dysfunction here acquires a precise
meaning, which is that the house does not modulate generally accepted
social interfaces among household members and/or the conventional
practices for receiving guests into the home, in a natural, unforced way.
Architects may choose not to consider this dimension of housing layout,
but because they configure space, they cannot avoid its consequences.
Turning configurational properties of spatial layouts into phenomena
which can be seen, but which at the same time can also be measured is
one way of moving between analysis and design. The three papers in this
section are united by their concern with the significance of the house as
an ideal type within modern architecture.

The seventh chapter, 'Visibility and permeability in the Rietveld
Schröder house' is a detailed investigation, originally begun by
Rosenberg[28] and completed by Hanson, that looked at one of the best-
known icons of modernity, the blueprint for open-plan living as conceived
in the plan and furniture of the Rietveld-Schröder house in the suburb of
Prins Hendriklaan, Utrecht. Differences are detected in the extent to
which the open-plan living arrangements enhance relations of visibility, as
opposed to permeability, and how this relates to how the house looks as
opposed to how it feels to move about in. As a result, the argument is
advanced for a fresh interpretation of concepts like 'openness' and 'flexibility' as these are customarily applied to the domestic interior.

In sharp contrast, 'The anatomy of privacy in architects' London
houses', draws on a sample of eighteen houses from the 1950s to the 1990s,
originally compiled by Miranda Newton[29] to illustrate a range of architectural solutions to the design of the contemporary home. By focusing on the
domestic architecture of London, the author hoped to minimise differences in land values, construction costs, planning restrictions, development density and thus to turn the spotlight on the value systems, ideals
and design choices which are expressed by a generation of contemporary
architects living and working in one of Europe's most vibrant capital
cities. Chapter eight argues that each home is indeed very much an individual but, even though the sample as a whole does not exhibit the strong
genotypical structure which is typical of traditional and vernacular
houses, underlying consistencies can be detected in the way in which
social relationships are explored and expressed in the built form and space

organisation of these architect-designed dwellings, which relates to a specifically 'architectural' interpretation of the concepts of community and privacy within the family home.

Chapter nine, '"Deconstructing" architects' houses',[30] compares houses by four architectural 'giants' – Botta, Meier, Hejduk and Loos. Visually, the houses share a common preoccupation with the formal dissection of a cube. Spatially, they could not be more different from one another, in that they permutate the morphological properties of depth and rings. The four houses are evaluated in terms of the extent to which, spatially speaking, they can be considered as truly innovative or to which they conceal cultural conformity beneath their rather obvious concern for an uniqueness of architectural expression.

Finally, 'Decoding dwellings: the way ahead' reviews recent research from within the international community of housing scholars which has used space syntax to investigate something of the variety of human habitation in different parts of the world. Cross-cultural comparisons help us to see afresh the fundamental organising principles of houses within our own culture, and students of domestic architecture never fail to wonder at the rich inventiveness in the forms and layouts of dwellings. Yet at the same time, many of the spatial gestures which lie beneath the surface appearance of things, seem to draw on familiar themes which find their genesis in the interfaces which shape the space of human habitation. Despite the heterogeneity of their countries of origin, these studies from Europe, the United States of America, West Africa, Latin America and the Middle and Far East focus in one way or another on the extent to which indigenous cultural traditions can be detected in the form and organisation of the dwelling and the extent to which they exhibit the imprint of modernisation, which may or may not be synonymous with 'westernisation'. The common theme in all these studies is that a configurational approach is linked to more conventional sociological or psychological methods to answer questions about the qualitative and experiential nature of people's domestic space arrangements.

The chapter also sketches some more speculative ways of modelling space which point the way forward to the next generation of morphological techniques by addressing questions of architectural composition, form and aesthetics. It has often been objected that a fundamental limitation of space syntax is that it provides a two-dimensional account of architectural phenomena which are experienced as a three-dimensional reality.

When we use the method to look at building layout in relation to social use this is indeed the case, and for the very real constraint on how people use and experience buildings, which is that people cannot fly. In moving around in buildings, people orientate themselves by reference to what they can see and where they can go. Admittedly, stairs and ramps introduce the potential for movement in the third dimension, but only by reducing it – for practical purposes – to two.

However, in looking at the visual and volumetric qualities of architecture, we need not be constrained by the pragmatics of everyday space use and movement. Indeed we should not be, since architectural speculation almost invariably brings into play the relationship between visibility (what you can see) and permeability (where you can go) through spatial layering, transparency, the inter-penetration of volumes and the dissolving of boundaries. These effects are leading the way to a new generation of space syntax tools which layer three-dimensional axial, convex and isovist representations to capture in the 'solid modelling' of space, the immanence of architectural reality.

Configurational analysis has come a long way since the publication of *The Social Logic of Space*. A recent international symposium to celebrate twenty years of space syntax research attracted seventy-eight abstracts and thirty-five papers, and was attended by one hundred and seventy delegates from nearly thirty countries world-wide. The afternoon devoted to the study of domestic space presented work which ranged from an exploration of how configurational analysis could be coupled to psychological techniques in order to investigate people's perceptions of how and where domestic activities are located within the home environments of different socio-economic groupings in Recife, Brazil, to a series of intriguing archaeological accounts of the morphology of the houses of Chaco Canyon in the American south-west. One feature that all the papers had in common was the attempt to build bridges between the configurational analysis of houses and those methods and approaches which relate more directly to people's social and cultural experience of houses and to individual perceptions of the qualities which are associated with home. After many years of relative neglect, the material culture of homes and houses is emerging as an unified field of study for disciplines as diverse as anthropology, archaeology, architecture, cultural studies, geography, medicine, public health, psychology and sociology. The sharing of information and experiences which has already begun to flow from inter-disciplinary collaboration promises to be both fertile and rewarding for those who seek to understand this most ubiquitous yet most puzzling of human spatial phenomena.

Notes

1 Bill Hillier and Julienne Hanson, *The Social Logic of Space* (Cambridge University Press, 1984), p. 281.

2 Amos Rapoport, *House Form and Culture* (New Jersey: Prentice-Hall, 1969), p. 12 and pp. 126-8.

3 L. Marshall, 'Marriage among the !Kung Bushmen', *Africa* 29 (1959), 354 and L. Marshall, '!Kung Bushman Bands', *Africa* 30 (1960), 342-3.

4 Mary Douglas (ed.), *Rules and Meanings* (Harmondsworth: Penguin, 1973), pp. 95-7.

5 Richard Lee and Victor DeVore, *Kalahari Hunter-Gatherers* (Harvard University Press, 1976), p. 68.

6 André Leroi-Gourhan, *Le Geste et La Parole: La Mémoire et Les Rythmes* (Paris: Albin Michel, 1964), vol.II, pp. 139-40.

7 Joseph Rykwert, *On Adam's House in Paradise* (Cambridge, Massachusetts: MIT Press, 1984), p. 192.

8 Hillier and Hanson, *The Social Logic of Space*, p. 147.

9 Torvald Faegre, *Tents: Architecture of the Nomads* (London: John Murray, 1979), pp. 15-24.

10 Ibid., pp. 61-77.

11 Ibid., p. 73.

12 Caroline Humphrey, 'Inside a Mongolian Tent', *New Society* (31 Oct.1974), 273-5.

13 Hillier and Hanson, *The Social Logic of Space*, p. 180.

14 Peter Ucko, Ruth Tringham and G. W. Dimbleby (eds.), *Man, Settlement and Urbanism* (London: Duckworth, 1972), pp. 23-53.

15 Hillier and Hanson, *The Social Logic of Space*, pp. 242-5.

16 Meyer Fortes, *The Dynamics of Clanship among the Tallensi* (Oxford University Press, 1945) and *The Web of Kinship among the Tallensi* (Oxford University Press, 1959).

17 Labelle Prussin, *Architecture in Northern Ghana* (Berkeley and Los Angeles: University of California Press, 1969), pp. 51-65.

18 Hillier and Hanson, *The Social Logic of Space*, p. 257.

19 R. S. Rattray, *Ashanti Law and Constitution* (Oxford University Press,1929), pp. 56-61.

20 Paul Oliver (ed.) *Shelter in Africa* (London: Barrie and Jenkins, 1971), p.160.

21 M. B. Benedikt, 'To Take Hold of Space', *Environment and Planning B: Planning and Design* 6 (1979), 47-65.

22 Susan Kent (ed.), New Directions in Archeology, *Domestic Architecture and the Use of Space: an interdisciplinary study* (Cambridge University Press, 1990), pp.127-52.

23 Raymond Wood-Jones, *Traditional Domestic Architecture in the Banbury Region* (Manchester University Press, 1963).

24 Bill Hillier, Julienne Hanson and Hillaire Graham, 'Ideas Are in Things: an Application of the Space Syntax Method to Discovering Housing Genotypes', *Environment and Planning B: Planning and Design* 14 (1987), 363-85.

25 Julienne Hanson and Bill Hillier, 'Domestic Space Organisation: Two Contemporary Space Codes Compared', *Architecture and Behaviour* 2 (1982), 5-25.

26 Peter Willmott and Michael Young, *Family and Kinship in East London* (Harmondsworth: Penguin, 1962).

27 Julienne Hanson, 'Selling the dream', *Architects' Journal* (15 April 1992), 36-7.

28 David Rosenberg, 'The Rietveld-Schröder House: Walls and Furniture in the Elaboration of Open-Plan and Conventional Space', (unpublished M.Sc. thesis of the University of London, 1992).

29 Miranda Newton, *Architects' London Houses* (Oxford: Butterworth,1992).

30 Julienne Hanson, '"Deconstructing" Architects' Houses', *Environment and Planning B: Planning and Design*, 21 (1994) 675-704.

Chapter two

Tradition and change in the English house

Summary

A heterogeneous collection of forty-seven seventeenth-century yeoman farmhouses from the Banbury region of Oxfordshire is analysed, to see if any consistencies can be detected in the room arrangements, or in the way in which uses are assigned to different parts of the domestic interior. Configurational analysis of the plans uncovers three distinct forms of domestic space arrangement, the 'through-passage plan', the 'single-entry plan' and the 'multiple-entry plan', which predominate sequentially up to around 1640, between about 1640 and 1660, and from about 1660 onwards. These seem to be related to the types of family structure which were prevalent during the period, the 'open lineage family', the 'restricted patriarchal nuclear family' and the 'closed domesticated nuclear family'. A fourth type, based on a sequence, which occurred mainly during the closing decades of the seventeenth century and throughout the eighteenth century, seems to have been associated with impoverished households in a region where the differences between rich and poor were becoming increasingly differentiated with the passage of time. The evidence is suggestive, not merely because of a coincidence in dating between the recorded house types and the hypothetical family structures, but also because the configurations naturally lend themselves to the forms of family authority and kinds of household activity which are known to have taken place.

Vernacular farmhouses of the Banbury region

The countryside around Banbury in Oxfordshire contains some of the most delightful and picturesque scenery in the landscape of Britain. The region is centred on the Oxfordshire town of Banbury, in the very heart of England, but it also straddles eastwards towards Buckinghamshire and Northamptonshire and westwards in the direction of Warwickshire. It has always been of considerable strategic importance. Throughout the period of British history between the departure of the Romans in AD 410 and the arrival of the Normans in 1066 known as the Dark Ages, it was at the frontier of succeeding waves of invasion and settlement, first by the Anglo-Saxons and then by the Vikings. Many historians argue that this has left an indelible impression on Banbury's cultural heritage, including its regional architecture. The area also saw action during the English Civil War, 1643–5. London and the south-east were for Cromwell, Parliament and the Commonwealth, but Charles I set up his standard at Oxford and he drew his supporters mainly from the north and west of the country. The region had both its Royalist and its Puritan adherents. A number of skirmishes and battles were fought there, including the great Parliamentary victory at the Battle of Naseby in 1645. These facts are not without significance, for it meant that the Banbury region was riven by political and religious dispute throughout the seventeenth century, precisely at the time at which this study is situated.

The houses which are the subject of this study were built mainly between 1600 and 1750. This is the period of the 'great rebuilding', when there was a florescence in house building throughout the country. Forms of construction had evolved to a point where houses had become more durable products, and substantial numbers have survived to the present day. The seventeenth century therefore gives architectural historians the first reliable evidence of how the majority of the population lived. However, most sources show only one or two examples from each region of Britain, and these yeoman houses from the Banbury area are amongst the earliest large samples of regional farmhouses to be recorded systematically. The data are significant in a second sense, in that social historians believe that the concept of the modern family as we know it today first began to emerge at about this time. If how people build provides any clues as to how they think and feel about their social world, then this sample provides a rare opportunity to explore how the early modern family might have patterned and used the domestic interiors of these old houses.

'Through-passage' and 'porch' plans

The data on which this investigation is based were originally assembled by Raymond Wood-Jones[1] in the late 1950s and early 1960s, in an attempt to identify a regional house type for seventeenth-century Banbury farmhouses, which seemed to the author to display a unity of purpose which would justify the research endeavour. Typically, house sites in the Banbury region tended to be long and narrow, with a road at the front and a cart track at the back. Most houses of the period were free-standing properties on large plots, either directly facing or standing gable end on to the road but sometimes one, or more rarely two of the external walls, would be built on the plot boundary. The precise siting of each house seemed to have been determined by the size and qualities of the plot, without reference to neighbouring dwellings or even to the position of roads and open spaces in the village.

The form of construction was a simple timber frame, two or three structural bays in line, running the full width of the house which was only one room deep. Additional structural stability was provided by massive brick chimney stacks. A small number of the later houses were stone-built. In assembling his database, Wood-Jones shows only the layout of the ground-floor rooms. This is because, in the majority of cases, upper floors were used primarily for storage. The original features and uses of rooms were reconstructed and recorded, to show the layout of the house at the time of building.

Wood-Jones distinguishes his examples into two major house types which he describes as the 'through-passage' plan and the 'porch' plan respectively. The defining characteristic of a through-passage plan is that the hall, which in those days was the principal living room of the house, is separated from the kitchen by an entrance passage running from the front door to the back door, to give two-way access from the house plot. The hall fireplace is normally placed on the end wall against the passage. Adjacent to the hall is the parlour, which is often an unheated room. Figure 2.1a shows the archetypal through-passage plan. Real cases may show variations on this pattern, whilst retaining the defining features of the plan.

Figure 2.1
Wood-Jones' plan typology for the
Banbury region, H = hall, P = parlour,
K = kitchen

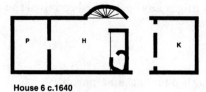

House 6 c.1640

2.1a Typical through-passage plan

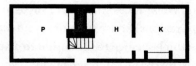

House 28 c.1660

2.1b Typical porch plan

By contrast, the technologically superior porch plan is described
as having a large chimney stack immediately opposite a single front
entrance, which has the distinct advantage of forming a draught lobby to
the principal living rooms on either side. The stack contains back-to-back
fireplaces warming a parlour to one side and a hall to the other. The service
areas are situated beyond the hall. Figure 2.1b illustrates the archetypal
porch-plan, by reference to which real cases are classified.

The through-passage plan is alternatively referred to as the 'upland'
plan, whereas the porch plan is also described as the 'lowland' plan. This
nomenclature gives clues to the suggested origin of the two house types.
The through-passage plan is believed to be characteristic of the upland
areas of Britain, that is, the more mountainous north and west of the
country which were therefore the last regions to be penetrated and settled
by succeeding waves of invaders. The houses, and indeed the culture of the
north and west of England are therefore held by many historians to preserve a more traditional way of life than the south and east, which is seen
to have been subject historically to a succession of foreign influences.
These areas of lowland Britain are more fertile and undulating, and are
therefore more prosperous. Thus, Barley claims that innovations in house
form and lifestyle tend to be adopted first in the south and east of England,
and only gradually diffuse throughout the rest of the country.[2]

Since the Banbury region is located at the border of these upland and
lowland regions of Britain, Wood-Jones assumes the distinction, and seeks

to explain differences within his sample by reference to a gradual process of modernisation in which developments in the plan, often following upon technical innovation, are initiated by the rich and 'ultimately descend to the lower levels of minor domestic architecture'.[3] He classifies the majority of his examples as variations upon the upland, or through-passage plan (see figure 2.2). A further ten examples from the Banbury region are presented as lowland, or porch plans for comparative purposes (see figure 2.3). The earliest examples of porch plans are from the 1630s and the latest from the 1680s, but the implication is that they are all technologically superior to the norm for the Banbury region at this time. Wood-Jones further divides his upland or through-passage sample by size and date of building into small, early examples built between 1603 and 1640, and more substantial, later houses built between 1640 and 1699. He does not elaborate on the significance of these dates, but they clearly have to do with the political and religious climate of the day. A third category of small, mid-century houses completes this part of the typology.

Sixteen more houses from the region are illustrated from the late seventeenth and eighteenth century (see figure 2.4). Having assumed modernisation as the motive power of evolution, Wood-Jones types late seventeenth-century houses which appear to retain characteristics of a previous era as 'archaic' and examples which seem to have adopted some of the features of high architecture, such as well-proportioned facades or decorative detailing, as 'formal'. Again, he distinguishes between smaller and larger examples in locating houses within this classificatory scheme, but he does not comment on whether any of these examples bear any resemblance to through-passage or porch plans.

Wood-Jones concludes that the majority of seventeenth-century yeoman houses of the Banbury region are variants on a through-passage plan, but that a variety of influences may explain the many exceptions to the rule. These influences include structural, constructional and technological features of the houses, their materials, detailing and degree of architectural elaboration, geographical influences and the date of building. Even if this is the case, it still remains to be shown how the through-passage plans in the Banbury sample differ from those in other regions where the upland house is found, to suggest what the dimensions of variability within the Banbury region might be, or to show in what sense the houses might be considered to have evolved during the period in question.

But more importantly, there are a number of anomalies in Wood-Jones'

Figure 2.2
Through-passage plans

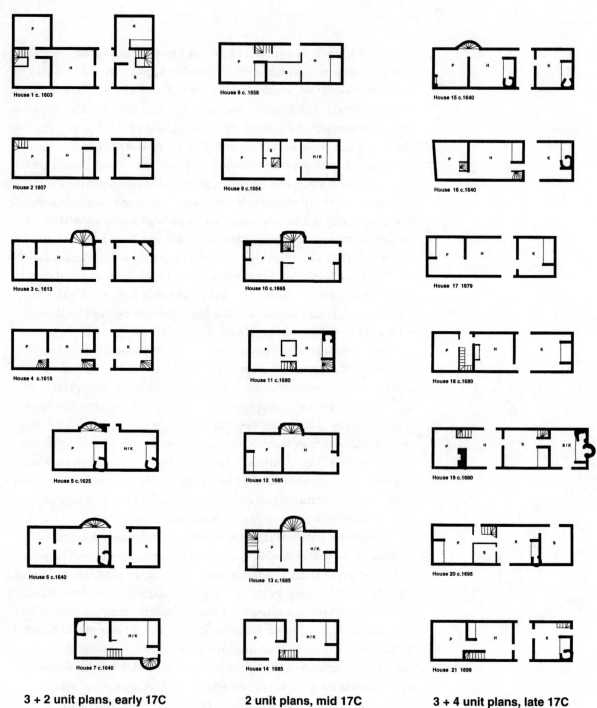

House 1 c. 1603

House 2 1607

House 3 c. 1613

House 4 c.1615

House 5 c.1625

House 6 c.1640

House 7 c.1640

House 8 c. 1658

House 9 c.1664

House 10 c.1665

House 11 c.1680

House 12 1685

House 13 c.1685

House 14 1685

House 15 c.1640

House 16 c.1640

House 17 1679

House 18 c.1680

House 19 c.1680

House 20 c.1695

House 21 1699

3 + 2 unit plans, early 17C   **2 unit plans, mid 17C**   **3 + 4 unit plans, late 17C**

Figure 2.3
Porch plans

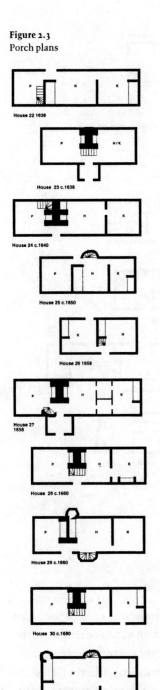

Comparative 17C lowland plans

typology which beg further investigation. Among the twenty-one through-passage plans, only five (numbers 2, 3, 4, 6 and 15) are clear cases with both a through-passage and a fireplace separating the passage from the hall. Seven examples (numbers 5, 7, 8, 10, 11, 12 and 20) do not have any form of through-passage and a further four cases (numbers 16, 17, 18 and 19) have front and back doors giving into a room. Two cases (numbers 13 and 14) have passages leading to the stairs. In house 21 the fireplace is on the far wall which separates the hall from the parlour, whilst in house 9 the through-passage separating off the kitchen is also a non-structural screen. House 1 is clearly a formal plan in the sense that it is the large, well-proportioned and elaborately detailed dwelling of a more affluent social stratum yet, because of its early date, this example is placed with the small house layouts, 1603–40.

In the lowland sub-set, four of the ten examples (numbers 24, 28, 29 and 30) conform to the archetype in all respects. Two cases (numbers 23 and 27) have a projecting porch and two more (numbers 22 and 25) have a lobby formed by the hall fireplace only. One lowland plan, house 26, has an arrangement of front and back doors which is very similar to house 14 in the upland sample and, when handed, house 7 in the upland section is identical to house 31 in the lowland sample in all respects other than the position of the stairs.

None of the later houses conforms to the through-passage or the porch archetypes, but several have features which are similar or identical to the real cases. House 32 is a porch plan with the hall and kitchen to either side of the main chimney stack. House 33 has a chicaned arrangement of front and back doors rather like house 20 of the upland sample. The third formal layout, house 34, associates the main entrance with the stairs. Several of the archaic houses (numbers 35, 36, 37, 39 and 43) have a small porch formed by one fireplace, an arrangement found among both the upland and the lowland examples, whilst in a further six cases (numbers 38, 41, 44, 45, 46 and 47) entry is effected directly into principal living rooms. House 42 has a porch formed by just one fireplace, an arrangement also found in technologically superior lowland cases. Two identical houses (31 and 43) from the same village but dated 1680 and 1800 are shown in the lowland – that is, advanced – sub-set, and in the archaic – that is, retrogressive – sub-set of the typology. Looked at carefully, the data seem to lack an organising model. The question for analysis is whether configurational analysis can shed any light on this puzzle.

Figure 2.4
Comparative eighteenth century
examples

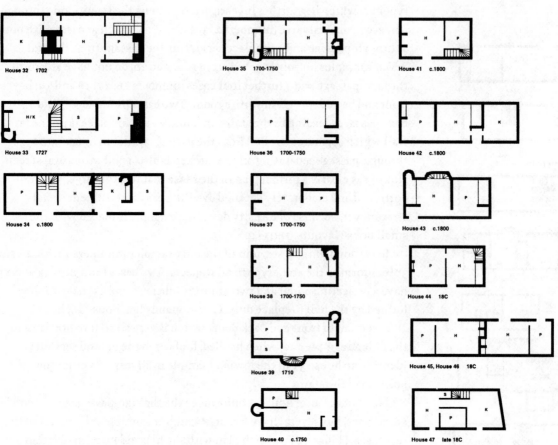

Formal 3 + 2 unit plans   Archaic 3 + 2 unit plans

Transcribing the plans

The first step for configurational analysis is to transcribe each of the house
plans shown in figures 2.2, 2.3 and 2.4 into the form of an access graph, in
order to clarify the disposition of the rooms and the pattern of permeability among them. Each effective space – a room or clearly differentiated area
supporting a household function – is represented by a circle and each transition or circulation space – passageways, lobbies and stairs – is shown as a
point. Doorways and other openings between adjacent spaces and circula-

tion routes passing through transitions are shown by lines linking circles or points.

The transcription begins from the outside of the dwelling, that is from the house plot, which is shown as a circle with a cross to differentiate it from the interior spaces, and works step-wise into the building so that each space or transition is represented above the point of origin according to its depth within the complex. The justified graph which results, records the minimum number of spaces or transitions which must be passed through in order to reach every space on the ground floor. Figure 2.5 shows the justified graphs for the houses in figures 2.2, 2.3 and 2.4, arranged in syntactic size order from those with the fewest numbers of spaces and transitions to those with the most spaces. Examples which are based on a simple linear sequence of rooms are to the left, houses with branching room arrangements are in the centre, and houses with entrances to several ground floor transitions and rooms are shown on the right.

The first point to be made about these simple houses is that the layout of the ground floor is considerably more complex than is dictated by structural necessity. Although the majority of the houses have an average of two to three structural bays, the average number of spaces and transitions these define is four or five spaces. This permits more variety in the real plans than is acknowledged in the 'ideal' through-passage and porch plans. The most striking feature of the sample as a whole is the predominance of sequential relations which add depth, over bushy relations which maintain shallowness in the domestic interior. Where the access graph branches, this tends to be into two arms rather than several. Sometimes, the graph forks close to the root and sometimes deeper into the interior, but the principle is clear. A more formal way of saying this is to note that, as the houses grow from small cases to large ones, the 'mean depth' of the complex increases. The mean depth at two cells is 1.5, at three cells 1.7, at four cells, 1.86, at five, 2.25, and at six to eight cells, 2.56. A good deal of depth is accounted for by the fact that only the smallest houses have rooms directly joined together in sequence and, in the sample as a whole, there is a strong tendency for rooms to be separated from one another by transitions. At the same time, even in the larger houses, the deepest spaces in the interior occur at a maximum of five steps from the entrance.

The next step in analysis is to eliminate syntactic redundancy by extracting all cases of houses with an identical room configuration, to reveal the extent of configurational variety in the plans and to highlight

Figure 2.5
Justified graphs, arranged in size order

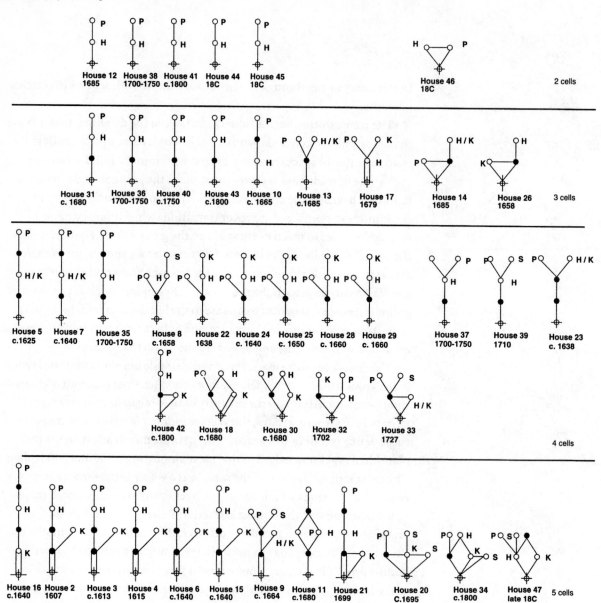

the principles for growth from the smallest to the largest houses. Faced
with a similar problem in settlement typology, Hillier and Stansall have
found it helpful to regard 'synchronous sets of evolving settlements in
different stages of development as though they were an evolutionary
sequence'.[4] If the collection of plans is based on any principles for patterning and relating spaces together, this will show as consistencies in the
data. It is best to do this first without taking account of room uses,
since these are not always known.

At two cells, for example, five out of the six cases take the form of two
rooms in a sequence. There is only one shallow room arrangement, which
takes the form of a ring. To get from two cells to three, there are two possible moves. Either the third cell can be placed in a sequence with the first
two, or it can be added to the shallower of the pair. Of the nine examples,
four cases are pure sequences, with a transition at the point of entry. A fifth
sequence shows a variation where entry is directly into a room. Two cases
are variants on a tree with symmetrical arms, and two more elaborate the
two-cell ringy form, by adding a cell to one side. In both cases, a transition
separates the deeper room from the shallower room and from the outside.

At four cells, only three cases take the form of an unilinear sequence.
Three more cases branch deep. The most common variant, with six identical cases, is to add the fourth cell so that the complex has a shallow and a
deep arm, springing from the shallowest point in the complex. In all six
examples, the fork is a transition. Five cases are ringy. Unlike the previous
cases, each ringy graph is configurationally speaking unique. By five cells,
the pattern is clear. Of the twelve cases, only one example is a pure
sequence. Five cases are based on a tree-like room arrangement with a deep
and shallow branch, in which the role of the extra space is to extend the
deeper branch. One case branches twice, and one more has a small internal
ring in an otherwise sequenced plan. The final four cases explore the
shallow, ringy theme, but each does so in a different way.

There is only one example at six, seven and eight cells, so no general
points can be made about these more complex interiors. However, all can
be interpreted as elaborations of a branching tree with a shallow and a deep
arm. One has a shallow and a deep arm, but the extra cells go to make a
ring through the shallow arm to give an alternative route to the outside.
The second has a shallow and a deep arm, with the extra cells making an
internal ring within the deeper arm. The third has a shallow and a deep
arm, both of which acquire an extra branch.

To put it another way, the majority of the Banbury houses have in common a 'seed', which is based on a branching sequence with a shallow and a deep arm. The seed is clear at four and five cells, where the largest number of examples are concentrated including many replications. Nearly all of the smaller examples are sequences, which can be interpreted as embryonic versions of this configuration. Adding a terminal space to form the shallow arm, would immediately bring this about, whilst in the case of the shallow branched plans adding a terminal space to one arm would have the same result. All but three, the ringy cases, of the two and three cell plans could therefore in theory extend to make the seed. Larger cases are frequently more elaborate versions of it. Of the thirty-two cases at four or more cells, eighteen contain this seed within their overall space configuration.

Among those cases which could not possibly 'morph' into the seed through a process of syntactic growth, quite distinct varieties are found. Four cases are straightforward unilinear sequences. Three cases are based on a sequence, but one with deep branches. These are clearly related to the seed and are a variation on the theme of two and three cell sequences. The remaining seven cases are based on a shallow ringy plan which is quite unlike any of the previous examples. To begin with, all these ringy cases are a maximum of two cells deep. Although the ringy access graph gives them a superficial family resemblance to one another, which is reinforced by the fact that any spaces which are not on a ring are only one step away, each configuration is very much an individual. There are no duplicates at all among these ringy plans.

Up to this point, the set of plans have been looked at without taking into account the labelling of spaces. If we now look at the labelling of the plans, then further refinements can be made to the argument. No matter how the other major spaces – that is the hall, kitchen and service rooms – are arranged within the domestic interior, the room called the parlour is frequently as deep as, or deeper than any other effective space in the complex. Only one case, House 26, does not have a labelled parlour, thirty-seven cases locate the parlour in a deepest space, eight cases reverse the kitchen parlour labelling and one case, House 11, has a parlour on a ring with the kitchen and the service room beyond. In nearly all cases, the parlour is a terminal space, rather than part of a ring. The exceptions are as instructive as the cases which comply, for in the cases where the parlour is not the deepest space it is located in the shallow arm of the access graph and the kitchen or service room is in the deepest space. Parlours may be linked to the hall as is the case in eleven of the examples shown here, but they are never directly connected to the kitchen or other service rooms and with only two exceptions – Houses 46 and 14 – they are not linked directly to the outside.

Halls tend to be well-linked to other parts of the house but, where space permits, they are seldom directly accessible from the outside. House 20 does not have a labelled hall, and in four cases (numbers 9, 14, 23 and 26) the hall is a terminal space, but the hall is normally a thoroughfare. At the same time, in all but the very smallest houses there is normally at least one way to reach the hall formally by means of an entrance lobby. Few houses are sufficiently prestigious to have both a kitchen and service rooms. Indeed Wood-Jones seems to use the terms interchangeably. Of all the effective spaces, kitchens are most likely to be directly permeable to the exterior, with the exception of those cases where the kitchen is the deepest space of all.

Time is, of course a label, and if this is added to the other information about these yeoman homes, then a new typology is suggested by the combination of space configuration and labels (see figure 2.6). Early in the seventeenth century, up to about 1640, Banbury houses tended to be deep and sequenced, made deeper by the insertion of transitions between the effective living spaces of the home. The dominant type is indeed a through-passage plan – defined syntactically rather than by construction – in that it has both front and rear entry to a transition. This type usually has a deep and a shallow arm, with a parlour in the deepest space strongly insulated from kitchens and other service rooms, which tend to be shallow. All the cases are drawn from Wood-Jones' through-passage type.

In the mid seventeenth century, a new and very strongly uniform morphology made its appearance in the region, which retained certain characteristics of the previous house-form, but put the complex together in a new way. This form of domestic space organisation retained the principle of a pair of arms, one shallow and the other deep, but reversed the position of the kitchen and the parlour, so that the kitchen is in the deepest space of the house and the parlour is in the shallow arm of the complex. This house type has a single entry leading to a transition, but again defined syntactically rather than by reference to construction. This 'single-entry' plan is characterised by only one main door, and has nearly all its examples in common with Wood-Jones' lowland or porch plans, but

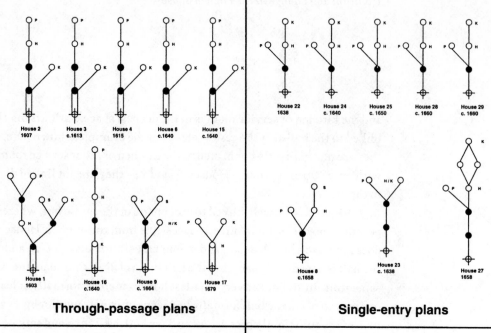

Through-passage plans

Single-entry plans

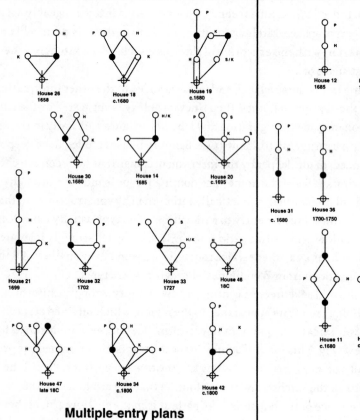

Multiple-entry plans

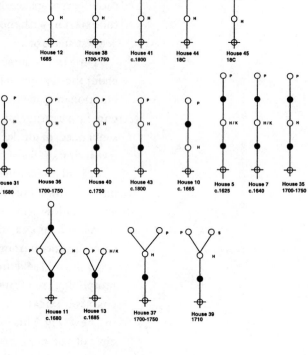

Sequenced plans

Figure 2.6
Configurational house types
in the Banbury region

one of his upland houses is included in the type. The earliest is 1638 and the latest 1660.

In the last few decades of the seventeenth century and continuing throughout the eighteenth century, a third syntactic type came into being, the 'multiple-entry' plan. This contains all those houses which have a shallow, ringy morphology, usually with a parlour as deep as any space and accessible through a transition, which separates it from the remainder of the ringy complex. However, the exceptional cases where a room bearing the label parlour is directly connected to the outside are also found in this grouping. Three of the houses clearly retain earlier morphological features but open up a second ringy route to the exterior. In most cases, it is the kitchen and service rooms which become directly permeable to the outside. The hall is well-connected, and often on a main ring. In one or two cases, it too is entered directly from the plot. As the plan becomes ringy, this seems to be accompanied by a decrease in the insulation within the domestic interior. Rooms tend to become directly permeable to each other, and the ratio of effective spaces to transitions decreases. All Wood-Jones' categories are found here. The earliest example of this 'multiple-entry' plan is dated 1658, and the latest is from about 1800.

Finally, and in complete contrast to these innovative and highly idio-syncratic ringy morphologies, an alternative form of dwelling based on a pure unilinear sequence is also found mainly after about 1660 and through-out the eighteenth century. All thirteen pure sequences are small but internally elaborate houses. Another four houses, again nearly all very small and late, are also based on a sequence with deeper branches. The entrance may be through a lobby or directly into the hall. The parlours in these houses tend to be deep terminal spaces. Kitchens and service rooms are rare. Examples come from all parts of Wood-Jones' original typology, but none resembles his archetypal through-passage or porch plans. They will be considered together as variants on a 'sequenced' plan.

Rich and poor households

Unfortunately, Wood-Jones gives few clues as to how these Banbury houses were used as a setting for everyday life, nor indeed of the composi-tion by age, sex and status of the average Banbury household. In this sense, his original study is more akin to an archaeological survey than a record of

family and household in past times. However, he does provide some clues
as to the social and economic pressures which were impinging on village
life at the time. Firstly villages, always nucleated, were growing denser. A
combination of rising populations and the need to preserve agricultural
land meant that, in the second half of the seventeenth century, 'new
houses had to be contrived in any open space within the village, encroach-
ing on the green or on the street itself, and producing a more compact
grouping'.[5]

At the same time, the general level of prosperity within the region was
in decline. At the beginning of the seventeenth century, Banbury was a
prosperous area, producing wool and dairy products. Home industry flour-
ished in the region, manufacturing stockings, plush, gloves and spun
thread. Most of the population were well-to-do yeoman farmers. By the
end of the century, the region had declined from second to seventeenth
place in the rank order of English counties in terms of wealth, and the
region never recovered its former affluence. As a result the population
began to polarise into rich landowners and poor tenants, as 'many of these
later cottages were tied to the lands of larger landowners, who had grown
wealthy with the enclosures at the expense of the cottagers'.[6] The social
climate in the Banbury region was one in which increasing density of
dwellings was accompanied by increasing differentiation in social status.

This was undoubtedly in Wood-Jones' mind in arriving at the categories of formal and archaic houses, for those built in the latter part of the
seventeenth century and on into the eighteenth century, but there seems
to be an even more powerful morphological distinction built into houses
after 1660, which is that between the multiple-entry plan and the
sequenced plan. It is striking that all the larger houses recorded after 1660,
whether or not they bear the stamp of fashionable sophistication or appear
to cling to regional building practices, are ringy configurations.
Characteristically, in the multiple-entry plan, kitchens and service areas
give directly into the grounds, but the house also has a more formal
entrance leading into a parlour by way of an entrance lobby. This entrance
also provides an alternative access to the ring, or rings, of principal living
rooms including the hall. Within this overall scheme of things, the actual
configuration of domestic space varies greatly from case to case. It would
seem that the ringy and shallow forms of domestic space organisation
which are characteristic of the multiple-entry plan can be associated with
the minority of more wealthy Banbury yeoman farmers.

Sequenced plans from the same period seem to have been the homes of poorer peasants who were impoverished by the economic decline of the region. Whilst none of these houses may be described as a through-passage plan in terms of its construction or mode of entry, these simple dwellings retain the syntactic principles of growth (depth, sequencing and branching) which were identified earlier as the touchstone of regional style in the Banbury area. These earlier houses tend to resemble each other more closely, both in their space configuration and in the assignment of labels to spaces. All have shallow halls and deep parlours. These principles of growth persist among the houses of the poor long after the widespread adoption of shallow, ringy plans by their wealthier neighbours. Wood-Jones' observation that it is particularly among the poorer villagers that conservatism and adherence to local traditions are found, may be pertinent and seems to be supported by syntactic analysis, which suggests that small houses had a tendency to cling to an earlier pattern of domestic space configuration.

Royalists and Puritans

But this is not all there is to be said, for it still remains to be explained why the houses of the yeoman farmers of Banbury were configured as deep, tree-like through-passage layouts in the early part of the seventeenth century but as shallow, ringy layouts in the latter part of the century, let alone how it came about that the positions of the kitchen and the parlour were reversed for the brief period of time when the single-entry plan became popular. To understand these changes, it is necessary to look more closely at the pattern of everyday life and social relationships in households of the period, and particularly at the values and beliefs which underpinned family life.

In his book *The Family, Sex and Marriage in England, 1500–1800*[7] Lawrence Stone attempts to describe the characteristic patterns of family life during the period, and to trace the process of evolution from one form of household organisation to another. Although not directly concerned with domestic space organisation, Stone makes frequent reference to architectural data and he describes many aspects of family life and village organisation in an intrinsically spatial way. Stone identifies three distinct forms of household organisation during the period, the 'open lineage family', the 'restricted patriarchal nuclear family' and the 'closed domesticated nuclear family', each with its characteristic way of relating household members together and interfacing them with a wider society.

According to Stone, the open lineage family was one in which relationships within the household were characterised by a lack of well-defined boundaries. He describes the relationship of a married man or woman to their respective parents, kin and neighbours as being almost as close if not closer than those of the husband and wife to each other and their children. The two most striking characteristics of the family at this time were its 'permeability to outside influences' and its members' 'sense of loyalty to ancestors and to living kin'.[8] Within the family, privacy like a sense of individuality and personal freedom, was neither possible nor, Stone suggests, desired. The authority of the kin group was vested in the male head of the household, but his authority was based not so much on his personal attributes for leadership as his positional power, emanating from his patriarchal role. He was therefore subject to the internal pressures entailed within the role of household head, and his behaviour at home was monitored by the external scrutiny of his neighbours and the powerful presence of church and priest.

Between households, the climate seems to have been dominated by gossip and close personal scrutiny. The maintenance of an untarnished reputation was essential to smooth social relationships. This was the era where denunciations of one family by another were common, particularly if anyone was seen to have offended against the social mores. At the same time, many cross-cutting links between neighbours were maintained, not on a household-to-household basis but on the basis of common interests. A member of such an open lineage family might feel emotional ties to 'other members of the kin, to fellow members of a guild, or to friends and neighbours of the same sex whom [he] met daily in the ale-house'.[9] The boundary of the household was therefore loosely drawn, and the social networks of family members were open-ended and inclusive. Stone dates this pattern of family life as running from 1500 to 1640.

In the last few decades of the seventeenth century and throughout the eighteenth century, beginning with the restoration of the monarchy under Charles II, Stone notes a decisive shift in household organisation, to a form in which the family was 'organised around the principle of personal autonomy, and bound together by strong affective ties'.[10] This closed domesticated nuclear family was associated with what Stone calls the 'companionate marriage' in which a measure of hitherto unprecedented equality and mutual regard was maintained between men and women. Stone himself points out that this period seems to have been marked by a shift of emphasis in domestic space organisation, to take account of the greater autonomy which was granted to, or seized by wives, children and even servants. Thus, according to Stone, during the latter part of the seventeenth century 'houses of all classes down to that of yeoman and tradesman, became more varied, more sub-divided, and more specialised in function'.[11]

Writers on this period suggest that women in particular benefited by these changes in family life. They gained in economic status and in social significance. For example, the size of a woman's marriage portion increased significantly during this period and it became common to write into the marriage contract the manner in which this money was to be distributed amongst her heirs in the event of her death. Women were increasingly allowed 'pin money', an independent fixed income to be used at their discretion. Finally, it became more common for women to inherit property, and for her rights of inheritance to be safeguarded in the marriage contract. Among the upper echelons of tradesmen, shopkeepers and yeoman and tenant farmers, more and more wives were being educated, were emulating the social graces of the aristocracy and were withdrawing from active participation in household production and farm labour. Instead, they were spending their time on the rearing of children, supervision of servants, marketing of produce and what Stone refers to as 'a round of status-enlarging activities',[12] including taking tea with the neighbours, indulging in light conversation, attendance at the local theatre, borrowing the latest novels from the new circulating libraries, playing at cards and other pastimes, or in doing good within the local community. During this period, women were both entertaining more at home in their parlours and were going out more into the wider society.

Intervening between these two periods, and reaching its climax in the mid-seventeenth century, was a transitional period that Stone terms the restricted patriarchal nuclear family. This period ushered in a sharp decline in loyalties to the traditional forms of family structure, patronage and local community. Instead people were beginning to experience more universalistic forms of allegiance to the concept of the nation state and its head, or to a particular religious denomination or sect. At the same time, both church and state actively promoted the influence of the patriarch within the family home. The father in the domestic setting provided an apt analogy for the ruler's relationship to his subjects. As a result, the power of the husband and father over his wife and their children was enhanced by legislation, turning him into a 'legalised petty tyrant within the home'.[13]

This was particularly the case among those parts of the country which were sympathetic to the Puritan cause. In these areas, the informal public life of the parish was completely annihilated, and was replaced by a strict household regime. No longer could people gather at the local church for a wide range of village events which included the spreading of news, the public castigation of disobedient servants and children, political meetings, and even cockfighting, roistering and gambling. Instead, they were expected to remain at home, engaged in an unending round of domestic labour, family prayers and household catechism. Stone suggests that, during this period of intensification in household life, the family became increasingly impervious to outside influences. The 'boundary awareness' of the family increased, and the influence of the wider circle of kinship and alliance correspondingly decreased. The moderating influence of the wife's relatives in particular was eliminated. The status of women declined markedly whilst this family pattern was in evidence, and women were expected to bear a 'crushing burden' of housework yet at the same time were kept in a 'thoroughly subservient position'.[14]

In the light of this material, it is tempting to view the through-passage configuration as one way in which the open lineage family was given a spatial form and embodied in the layout of vernacular houses. The latest unambiguous examples of the plan type pre-date 1640, none were constructed during the Commonwealth. The type had more or less died out by the Restoration, though similar organising principles based on a sequence continued to be used in the smaller houses of poor Banbury yeomen after the Restoration.

The configurational properties of the interior of the through-passage plan in the Banbury region, with its tree-like permeability graph, its emphasis on the depth and insulation of rooms from one another, and its strong tendency to segregation, does seem to support a loose but authoritarian way of life. The through-passage, separating front and back and therefore formal and informal entry to the dwelling, provides a subtle modulation of interior–exterior relations well-suited to a social climate where curiosity, gossip and denunciation between relatively egalitarian households is the norm.

Within the house, the well-connected hall is indicative of a lack of privacy and individualisation amongst members of the household, but the deeper and separate parlour would be an appropriate spatial mechanism to express the greater status and enhanced privacy of its occupants. According to the inventories of the day, this room was reserved for the household head, particularly in his declining years as he became less actively involved in the practical activities of the household, for old people were venerated by association with the ancestors.

Likewise, it is tempting to view the house configurations of the latter part of the seventeenth century and the whole of the eighteenth century as a vernacular interpretation of the companionate marriage, which is a lifestyle most likely to have been adopted by those farmers and landowners whose wealth was increasing with the accession of Charles II. Certainly, the later Banbury houses are more varied, and their spaces are shallower to the outside, more interchangeable and more symmetrically laid out within the configuration. Above all, the houses are ringy in their internal organisation and have several ways in and out from the house plot, so that the inhabitants have a choice of routes into and through the dwelling. This move in spatial configuration logically might be expected to go hand-in-hand with a shift in social relations from an overtly authoritarian to a more equal arrangement.

It seems reasonable to view shallow and through-permeable kitchens as an expression of the enhanced status and relative autonomy of women, children and servants, since the enhanced permeability would have the effect of freeing-up daily routine and making it less subject to spatial and behavioural controls. The shift in the physical position of the parlour from deep to shallow in the complex also relates well to the shift in its social role from an intra-household withdrawing room to an inter-household meeting space. In these Restoration houses, the position of the parlour is much more idiosyncratic than before, and much less subject to controls on access or even visual supervision from the other parts of the home. The location of parlours in these ringy houses therefore permits immediate but discreet access to selected parts of the domestic interior, whilst maintaining a degree of separation from the working life of the house. This would be appropriate to the new patterns of visiting and household entertainment enjoyed by the mistress of the house. Inventories of the day suggest that the parlour did indeed begin to accommodate more genteel pastimes and was used more for entertaining at about this time.

Finally, it is possible to view that group of Banbury houses which occurred only between 1640 and 1660 as an expression of the dominance, both locally and nationally, of Puritan ideals. The restricted patriarchal nuclear family might be expected to find its spatial expression in some form of deep, tree-like domestic interior which would incorporate highly prescriptive patterns of use. The substitution of a single point of entry for the through-passage increases control over the entrance to the home, whilst leaving the remainder of its spatial relations intact. However, it is not the syntax of these houses which differs markedly form the earlier examples, though they do resemble each other more strongly. It is in the labelling of spaces that the most telling differences occur. In all cases, the parlour and the kitchen exchange places. This simple move ensures that the functions are differently embedded in the overall space configuration. It therefore calls for an interpretation which takes the effects of this different embedding into account.

We have already seen in the Tallensi society whose family compounds were discussed in the Introduction that where women are subject to an authoritarian regime based on patriarchy, their living quarters and kitchens tend to be located deep in the homestead. The more general study of societies suggests that this is a common pattern where pronounced social inequalities between the sexes are found. It may therefore be the case that, in the Banbury sample, the deep position of the kitchen during this period can be linked with moves in society at large towards the subjugation of women, and the unlinking of wives from their natal kin. Finally, the shallow parlour in these houses may be a spatial resolution of the shift from church worship to household prayer meetings, which are known to have taken place in Puritan households during this period. Inventory evidence identifies 'Bible boxes' among the contents of parlours of this period. Furthermore, in contrast to the parlour in the Restoration period which is known to have been the domain of women, visitors to the family home during the Commonwealth were much more likely to have been male, meeting together in private to discuss religion and politics, and in this instance the shallow parlour is analogous to the 'men's room' in Muslim societies.

From archaeology to society

The configurational changes which took place in Banbury houses during the seventeenth century are more a matter of fact than of interpretation, since they are a product of careful detective work by Wood-Jones, which amounts to a spatial archaeology. The inferences which can be drawn from historical sociology are more a matter of social interpretation than of fact, since no one can ever know for certain how people in seventeenth-century England perceived their social world. Even if we could share their attitudes and values, then it is likely that individuals with different roles and statuses may have held different, even contradictory perceptions of their social situation. It is even possible that at least some aspects of people's world view were inaccurate or downright deceptive. Finally, it would be foolish in the extreme to expect all aspects of society to imprint themselves directly on space in a simple 'cause and effect' relationship.

However, it is not being suggested that domestic architecture determines how people live their everyday lives, but simply that there are fewer spatial means than there are cultural ends. If the layout of space is patterned so as to embody and structure changing social and cultural relationships, it can only do so according to the laws of space itself. In real space-time, as opposed to the multi-dimensional space of the mind, mathematics or a computer, things can be put next to one another or they can be placed inside one another. Things can be put together or they can be kept apart. Barriers can be erected between things or they can be made directly accessible to one another. Links can be asymmetric, in the sense that they are not reversible, or they can be symmetrical in the sense that A is to B as B is to A. Activities and objects can be manifested to one another or they can be hidden away. The most complex configurational structures are built out of these elementary spatial gestures.

Human spatial behaviours reflect the workings of rather fewer social forces than there are cultural phenomena to be accounted for. Such forces include differentiating individuals or groups with different statuses, roles or categories, and generating and controlling the possibility for encounter and avoidance among them. If a relation is not socially significant then, as often as not it is spatially 'left to chance', that is not specified or even randomised. Houses are sensitive to social relations only insofar as they construct and constrain interfaces between different kinds of inhabitant, and different categories of visitor.

Relations of category and control are mapped into space in a pattern constructed out of depth and rings. Depth among a set of spaces always expresses how directly the functions of those spaces are integrated with or separated from each other, and thus how easy and natural it is to generate relations among them. The presence or absence of rings expresses the degree to which these relationships are controlled, or marked by an absence of choice, forcing permeability from one space to another to pass through specific intervening spaces. It is these spatial potentials which are used to make a culturally-intelligible pattern of space within the domestic interior.

However, the pattern itself is usually capable of more than one interpretation. Consider the two versions of the early Banbury house based on a tree-like access graph with a deep and a shallow arm. In the first case, it was suggested that the deep position of the parlour indexed the status of its inhabitants, in the second case, that it acted as a control on the women, children and servants using the kitchen. Conceivably, the discourse could argue that a deep kitchen expresses the high value placed on women as home-makers, indeed this case is eloquently made in respect of the deep kitchens in many modern homes. Likewise, placing the old folks in a deep parlour could be interpreted as a form of control over their movement, rather than an expression of status.

The same ambiguity is inherent in the meaning of the shallow arm of the plan. In the first case, it was interpreted functionally, as a convenient place to prepare and cook food. In the second instance, it was assigned a symbolic value, as a separate but shallow place appropriate to the celebration of special and therefore more formal events, such as the celebration of family prayers, and to the reception of (male) guests.

It all depends on how you look at it. The simplest of space configurations can support complex, many-layered and evolving meanings which can be assigned and reinterpreted by different individuals and groups, be they located within the culture or commenting on it from the outside. These inherent ambiguities in the interpretation of human spatial patterning set limits to what can ultimately be known, but also open up a universe of what can be expressed through design. The problem of ambiguity encapsulates both space's greatest limitation and also its most liberating experiential dimension.

The evolution of family life during the seventeenth century, with its attendant changes in the relationships between husband and wife, adults and children, and household members and visitors to the home, seems to provide suggestive parallels to the physical changes which have been observed in the Banbury data. If houses are in any sense cultural products, it seems reasonable to place the changes which were undoubtedly taking place in Banbury yeoman houses during the seventeenth century, in the context of the social changes which were reshaping contemporary concepts of family life and community relations. The interpretations which we place on space will never be absolute, can never be certain. The best we can offer is internal coherence of an argument which is consistent with the world as it presents itself to us – but this, after all, is the stuff of theory.

Notes

1 Raymond Wood-Jones, *Traditional Domestic Architecture in the Banbury Region* (Manchester University Press, 1963).

2 M.W. Barley, *The English Farmhouse and Cottage* (London: Routledge & Kegan Paul, 1961), pp. 3–4.

3 Wood-Jones, *Traditional Domestic Architecture in the Banbury Region*, p. 72.

4 Bill Hillier and Paul Stansall, 'The Morphology of Small Settlements in the South of France', unpublished manuscript of the Unit for Architectural Studies, the Bartlett, University College London (1978), p. 3.

5 Wood-Jones, *Traditional Domestic Architecture in the Banbury Region*, p. 10.

6 Ibid. p. 12.

7 Lawrence Stone, *The Family, Sex and Marriage in England, 1500–1800* (London: Weidenfeld and Nicolson, 1977).

8 Ibid., p. 4.

9 Ibid., p. 7.

10 Ibid., pp. 7–8.

11 Ibid., p. 225.

12 Ibid., p. 656.

13 Ibid., p. 7.

14 Ibid., p. 655.

Chapter three

Ideas are in things

(with Bill Hillier and Hillaire Graham)

Summary

The previous chapter provided a mainly visual and qualitative analysis of relatively simple house plans, which showed that superficially similar domestic space arrangements can hide quite distinctive lifestyles which seem to relate to different forms of household organisation and community life. This study of a sample of seventeen more complex farmhouses from the Normandy region of France, uses a mainly quantitative and statistical analysis to uncover 'genotypical' similarities in houses which apparently have quite different floor plans. Patterns of spatial integration and segregation suggest two types of Normandy farm-house, one organised around the salle commune *and the other around the entrance hall. Thus, a careful exploration of the relative integration or segregation of different household functions demonstrates that cultural ideas may be objectively present in artefacts as much as they are subjectively present in minds. As before, the configurational types seem to relate to lifestyle variables, including shedding fresh light on an intriguing distinction in the historical record, which draws a contrast between a female-centred and a male-centred view of the interior of the dwelling.*

La maison rustique

In his recent book on the French rural house, Cuisenier[1] developed a theme originally taken from its namesake, *La Maison Rustique* by Charles Estienne, published in 1564. In his exposition, Cuisenier proposed that Estienne's account of the *maison rustique* – as opposed to the château or the manorial domain – can be clarified by reference to an underlying model with three elements. The first, *orientation*, regulates the general orientation of the farm and its built elements in relation to each other and to the outside world. The more specific concept of *frontalité* is seen to regulate the distinction between the front and back of the farmhouse, and to organise its associated functions. Finally, *latéralité* is deemed to regu-late the arrangement of the functions both inside the dwelling and in the farm as a whole, by disposing them to the left and right of the 'master' as he stands at the main entrance to his dwelling, welcoming his guests (see figure 3.1).

The concept of *latéralité* is of particular interest to any spatial analysis of the domestic interior, since it specifies not only a principle for the arrangement of rooms, but also a male-centred view of this arrangement. Such 'microcosm effects' are well-documented in the anthropological record, but instances from the advanced societies are both rare and con-tentious. However, Cuisenier's thesis is a product of what promises to be the most comprehensive regional survey of the surviving forms of tradi-tional and vernacular domestic architecture of a nation. This undertaking by the Musée des Arts et Traditions Populaires has not only drawn atten-tion to the possibility that French rural housing may embody feelings and sentiments based on a male-dominated domestic ideal, but has also ensured that sufficient data are available to test the model, and thus to confirm or refute it.

The primary data for this study of space and gender in traditional French houses, is a sample of seventeen vernacular farmhouses from the Normandy region of France, originally assembled by Brier and Brunet in 1984.[2] The data on Normandy is one of the first volumes to emerge from the French national survey, and it was clearly instrumental in prompting Cuisenier's formulation of the concept of *latéralité*. It is therefore an ideal sample with which to investigate configurational variables and gender roles in French rural architecture.

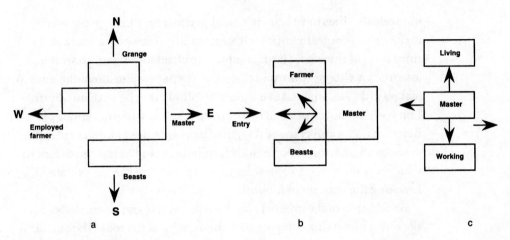

Figure 3.1
Three elements of a model farmhouse:
(a) orientation, (b) *frontalité*, (c) *latéralité*

The data and the method

Initially, the data appear heterogeneous, and immediately raise a
methodological difficulty in that some examples show only the farmhouse, whilst others are more elaborate farm complexes containing a
number of barns, outbuildings and animal houses which are linked
together externally by farmyards, courtyards and gardens. It is obvious
that some standardisation is necessary if analysis is to proceed in a consistent way. Three levels of analysis are therefore distinguished from the
outset: first, the level of the *minimum living complex*, defining this as
the least set of continuous interior spaces which link together the main
ground-floor living spaces of the house, including any major functions
which form part of that complex but excluding all those rooms that can
only be reached by way of the farmyard; second, the minimum living
complex plus a single space representing the exterior of the dwelling; and
finally the whole farm complex, including any outbuildings and major
differentiations in the exterior space into yards and gardens.

   The research reported here is confined to the most detailed level of
domestic arrangements which have to do with the spatial embedding
of the concept of *latéralité*. It therefore deals with the analysis of the
minimum living complex, with and without its exterior. The complex
with its exterior is always dealt with in the first instance. When the
exterior is 'discounted' in the analysis, the reader may assume that all

numerical values have been re-calculated just for those spaces which make up the domestic interior. Occasionally, reference is made to the third level of the whole farm complex, to check the extent to which assumptions about this more extensive spatial system affect the numerical results. The analysis is carried out 'blind', that is, with no information which is not contained on the plan, labelled with its various functions. The aim is to see if regularities can indeed be detected in the space configuration of Normandy farmhouses, and to test the extent to which any underlying consistencies which emerge can be 'explained' by invoking the concept of *latéralité*.

In addition to the original plan, justified access graphs are shown for the minimum living complex with the exterior as the root. The outside is treated as a single space, in the first instance, because the study is concerned first and foremost with the interior pattern of space, including its relations to the farmyard, but not with the external differentiation of space.

As with the Banbury sample that was considered in chapter two, these dwellings are looked at first as pure space arrangements, without considering the labels or functions assigned to particular spaces. Then the space patterns are analysed in terms of functions, to see how different functions fit into the spatial pattern as a whole. Unlike the previous chapters, a key feature of the analysis which is presented here is the measure of relative depth, 'integration', which was referred to in chapter one and which is a more developed and quantitative form of depth than the justified graph. The integration value of a space expresses the relative depth of that space from all others in the graph. It therefore captures numerically a key aspect of the shape of the justified graph from that space. A more complete description of the measure was given in chapter one. The set of integration values for the seventeen houses which make up the Normandy sample are shown in figure 3.2, and will be referred to throughout the chapter.

In most samples of real houses, integration values will be different for different spaces, and justified graphs will express this visually, as was the case with the four idealised courtyard houses which were illustrated earlier in chapter one. This study goes further in quantitative analysis by looking closely at the distribution of integration values in each house and in the sample as a whole, to see if the different household functions or activities are consistently assigned to spaces which integrate or segregate the minimum living complex to different degrees. In other words, to

Ideas are in things

Figure 3.2
Ranked order of integration of functions,
house by house

House Number	Integration Order Integration Value									
1	sc< 0.60	co< 0.68	ex=v< 0.83	v< 0.90	la< 1.06	s< 1.21	d< 1.28	l< 1.51	gs< 1.58	b 1.88
2	m< 0.34	ex=s=l< 0.68		c< 1.01	d=a< 1.13	d=d 1.47				
3	ex=2=1< 0.58		3=6< 1.01	a=5=4 1.45						
4	sc< 0.30	ex=s< 0.68	lla=a< 0.75	sbr< 0.82	ca< 0.98	d< 1.13	a< 1.21	d< 1.43	l 1.51	
5	sc< 0.31	co< 0.45	c< 0.57	ex=la< 0.83	s=s< 0.96	c=1=c< 1.08	lx< 1.21	l 1.34		
6	v< 0.56	s< 0.68	sc< 1.13	la< 1.24	ex=a< 1.35	gs< 1.47	lla< 1.92	d 2.03		
7b	sc< 0.47	2< 0.95	ex=c< 1.89	c 2.37						
8	ex< 0.13	c=sm=co=cu< 0.51		9=5=sr=sm< 0.57		c 0.70	br< 0.89	c 1.09		
9	sc< 0.29	la< 0.86	ex=sr< 1.15	c< 1.43	l 2.00					
10	v=sc< 0.58	ex=v< 0.87	s=ca=1< 1.45		cu 1.74					
11	v< 0.67	ex< 0.70	cu< 0.77	d< 0.96	11< 1.02	7=sc< 1.09	c< 1.15	4< 1.34	c=a< 1.40	re 1.60
12	ex< 0.45	v< 0.53	la=v< 0.75	sc< 0.83	la< 0.90	gs< 0.98	9< 1.06	cu< 1.21	sm< 1.51	1 1.58
13	sc=v< 0.57	l=ex< 0.86	la< 1.15	s 1.72						
15	v< 0.59	s< 0.79	sc< 1.18	ex< 1.59	la=br< 1.77	sb 2.16				
16	v< 0.47	ex=s< 0.95	gr< 1.42	sc 1.89						
17	a< 0.45	s< 0.56	ce< 1.01	sm=5< 1.24	ex=d=d< 1.35	8 1.80				

establish whether there is an integration inequality 'genotype' for Normandy farmhouses.

One further measure plays a significant part in this study. How strong or how weak these inequalities are in a layout, or a sample of plans, is also of great importance in establishing whether any candidate genotypical effects may have arisen by chance, or are so strongly and consistently built into the pattern of space as to be clearly and unambiguously articulated in space. To measure this, we have developed an entropy-based measure

House	Integration with exterior			Difference factor	integration without exterior			Difference factor
	mean	min	max		mean	min	max	
1	1.12	0.60	1.88	0.76	1.36	0.73	2.00	0.81
2	0.95	0.34	1.47	0.66	1.23	0.44	1.80	0.68
3	1.02	0.58	1.45	0.84	1.74	0.98	2.75	0.80
4	0.93	0.30	1.51	0.60	1.22	0.45	2.09	0.62
5	0.89	0.31	1.34	0.66	0.97	0.37	1.58	0.66
6	1.30	0.54	2.03	0.71	1.45	0.73	2.18	0.79
7b	1.52	0.47	2.37	0.61	2.00	1.00	3.00	0.78
8	0.60	0.13	1.09	0.42	1.52	0.90	2.41	0.82
9	1.15	0.29	2.00	0.49	1.52	0.47	2.37	0.61
10	1.12	0.58	1.74	0.78	1.40	0.59	2.16	0.72
11	1.10	0.67	1.60	0.86	1.71	0.90	2.71	0.78
12	0.96	0.45	1.68	0.69	1.67	0.91	2.73	0.78
13	0.96	0.57	1.72	0.76	1.33	0.47	2.37	0.59
15	1.40	0.59	2.16	0.72	1.62	0.86	2.58	0.78
16	1.14	0.47	1.89	0.68	2.00	1.00	3.00	0.78
17	1.15	0.45	1.80	0.68	1.23	0.44	1.89	0.66

Figure 3.3
House-by-house difference factors
for mean, minimum and maximum
integration values, with and without
the exterior

called difference factor to quantify the degree of difference between the
integration values of any three (or more, with a modified formula) spaces
or functions. This measure was discussed briefly in chapter one, in relation to the four theoretical courtyard houses. It is essentially an adaptation
of Shannon's H-measure for transition probabilities, in which we sub-
stitute the integration value of a space over the total integration for the
three spaces for the transition probabilities in Shannon's original equa-
tion[3] (see chapter one for further details).

This can then be 'relativised' to give figures tending towards 0 for
strong differences between integration values and 1 for weak differences.
To give a feel for this measure, the difference factor for, say 0.4, 0.5 and
0.6 is 0.97, that is, close to 1 or very weak, whereas that for 0.3, 0.5 and
0.7 is 0.84, or considerably stronger. The difference factor for 0.1, 0.5 and
0.9 is 0.39, which is even stronger than before. The difference factors for
the maximum, mean and minimum integration values of each house
with and without its exterior are given in figure 3.3, and will be set

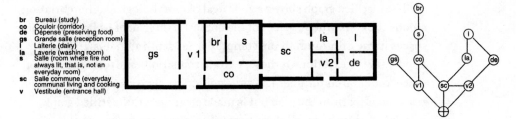

br Bureau (study)
co Couloir (corridor)
de Dépense (preserving food)
gs Grande salle (reception room)
l Laiterie (dairy)
la Laverie (washing room)
s Salle (room where fire not
     always lit, that is, not an
     everyday room)
sc Salle commune (everyday
     communal living and cooking
v Vestibule (entrance hall)

Figure 3.4
La Bataille, plan and justified graph

against the difference factors for triads of key function spaces in each
of the houses. These will, of course, differ from example to example,
depending on the precise layout and labelling of the minimum living
complex.

Each stage of analysis generates 'genotypical' statements about the
sample as a whole, as well as 'phenotypical' statements about individual
dwellings. The presentation which follows will follow this logic. First,
each house will be commented on as an individual case, drawing on three
types of information: that contained in the visual representations, quantitative analysis and interpretative frameworks. Then the sample as a whole
will be reviewed, again using all three types of data.

La Bataille, a typical Normandy farmhouse

La Bataille (see figure 3.4) is a typical long, single-pile Normandy farmhouse. It appears at first sight to be a simple linear plan, with an entrance
hall giving onto a formal reception room *(grand salle)* to the left and a farm
office *(bureau)* and *salle* to the right. The salle could possibly be translated
as 'parlour' since it is a room where the fire is not always lit, that is, it is
not an everyday room but a space for special occasions but, since it has no
natural and direct equivalent in English, the French term will be used. A
corridor leads past these rooms to the everyday living and cooking space,
the *salle commune*. This room also will be referred to throughout by the
French term, which has no direct English equivalent. Living room is the
nearest equivalent term, but it is insufficiently specific to merit its use in
translation here. A second lobby to the outside also separates this room
from the *dépense* (a room for preserving food, best translated as pantry),
the dairy *(laiterie)* and wash-room *(laverie)*.

The justified graph shows a good deal of morphological differentiation among the constituent spaces of the domestic interior of La Bataille. Three spaces in the minimum living complex are at depth 1, that is, linked directly to the exterior. Of these, two are transitions and one is a function space, the *salle commune*. The *salle commune* also has a property that is not at all clear from the plan but is made clear from the justified graph, which is that it lies on all three non-trivial circulation rings; that is, rings which involve more than two spaces. Of these three rings, two pass through the exterior and one is purely internal. The internal ring passes through several work-related spaces, including the wash-room and the dairy. Of the two external rings, one simply links the *salle commune* to the exterior by way of a lobby, but the other is the main link from the *salle commune* to the other living functions including the salle, reception room and office. The *salle commune*, in effect, acts as a kind of hinge linking and separating the two functionally differentiated circulation rings devoted to housework and more formal domestic activities, including the entertainment of guests.

Figure 3.2, which sets out the integration values of all the spaces in each house, in rank order of integration from the most integrated to the most segregated household function, shows that the *salle commune* is also the most integrating space, and by far the most integrating of the function spaces. A strong inequality thus exists among the main living spaces, with the order *salle commune* < exterior < salle < reception room: meaning that the *salle commune* is more integrating than the exterior, which is more integrating than the salle, which is more integrating than the reception room. All this remains the case when the exterior is discounted, although in this case the corridor linking the two parts of the house takes on an equal value to the *salle commune* as the most integrating space. The *salle commune* thus has a striking set of syntactic properties: it is the most integrating space, it lies on all circulation rings, it is shallow to the exterior, and it links and separates the two main functionally differentiated zones of the house, It will be of interest to see how far these properties are reproduced in other cases.

The three other main living spaces – the salle, the reception room and the office – all have quite different syntactic characteristics. All three are non-ringy spaces, being either end points or on the way to end points. The office is both at the end of a sequence and also the deepest space in the complex from the exterior. It is also the most segregated space if the exterior is included, and equally most segregated if the exterior is discounted. The reception room is also an end point, and the second most segregated space in the complex if the exterior is included, and equally the most segregated space with the office if the exterior is discounted. Unlike the salle and the office, however, the reception room is shallow in the complex. The salle is a both relatively deep and a relatively segregated space, both with and without the exterior, but less segregated than either the office or the reception room.

Of the remaining spaces, all the work-related spaces – wash-room, dairy and pantry – are segregated, but all are less so than either the reception room or the office. If the exterior is discounted, the wash-room is a little less segregated. Among the transitions, the corridor is a strong integrator with and without the exterior, but the entrance hall and lobby are much less so.

It is also useful to look at the degree of differentiation among the integration values of the different functions in La Bataille. Figure 3.4 shows that the basic difference factors for the maximum, mean and minimum integration values of the minimum living complex are 0.76 with the exterior and 0.81 for just the interior spaces. These values provide a benchmark against which to measure the amount of configurational difference the layout produces among the main living functions. For example, the three main living spaces – the salle, *salle commune* and reception room – have a mean integration value of 1.13, but a difference factor of 0.83. This last figure indicates a strong degree of differentiation among the integration values for the three spaces. In fact, this differentiation among the living spaces is almost as great as it could theoretically be in the interior of this particular configuration because, unusually, the most and least integrating spaces in La Bataille are both living spaces. If the office is substituted for the salle, then the difference factor is stronger even than the benchmark figure, at 0.77.

If, on the other hand, we take the three main work-related spaces – the wash-room, dairy and pantry – then the mean integration of these functions, at 1.28, is only a little higher than for the living spaces. But the difference factor for these spaces is very weak, at 0.97. For the three transitions – the corridor, entrance hall and lobby – the mean integration value is 0.80, but the difference factor at 0.98, is even weaker than for the work-related spaces. Both of these difference factors are weaker than the value we obtain by taking the mean integration values of the three types of space

– living, working and transition – which is 0.95, even though this averages out the differences between individual spaces.

These difference factor results are striking and unusual. It is not common to find such strong differences between living spaces, nor for these functions to take up so much of the possible configurational differentiation in a spatial complex. It will be of interest to see how far the strength and the order of these differences which are embedded in the layout of La Bataille, are reproduced elsewhere in the sample of Normandy farmhouses.

Exploring the dimensions of regional style

Le Manoir, from the hamlet of Maquemonts, visually seems a much smaller and more compact plan than was La Bataille (see house 2 shown in figure 3.5). However, it has a justified graph which has certain striking resemblances to that of La Bataille. Most notably, there is a space which has all four syntactic properties of the *salle commune*: it is the most integrating space, it is shallow, it lies on all rings (though in this case there are only two, and both are external) and it links and separates living from work functions. In this case, however, the space is labelled *maison*, but there seem to be strong functional and syntactic grounds for regarding this space as equivalent to the *salle commune*. Indeed, in the original text the two terms are often used interchangeably.

There are also a small number of differences. Le Manoir has no reception room. The salle links directly rather than indirectly to the most integrating living space. The work-related spaces to the right of the maison are terminal spaces rather than linked together in the form of a ring. There are no transitions, and no farm office. There is, however, a *chambre de commis*, a bedroom and office for a clerk, on the ground-floor. The plan is thus in certain respects less spatially complex and less functionally differentiated than La Bataille. Nevertheless, the justified graph shows a striking syntactic resemblance.

This resemblance is reinforced by numerical analysis. The order of integration of the living spaces is maison < exterior < salle < bedroom, and the difference factor for the three living spaces is again strong, at 0.79, much stronger than for the three work-related spaces at 0.89, though neither is as strong as the benchmark difference factors, which are 0.66 for

Figure 3.5
Plans and justified graphs of minimum
living complexes in Normandy farmhouses

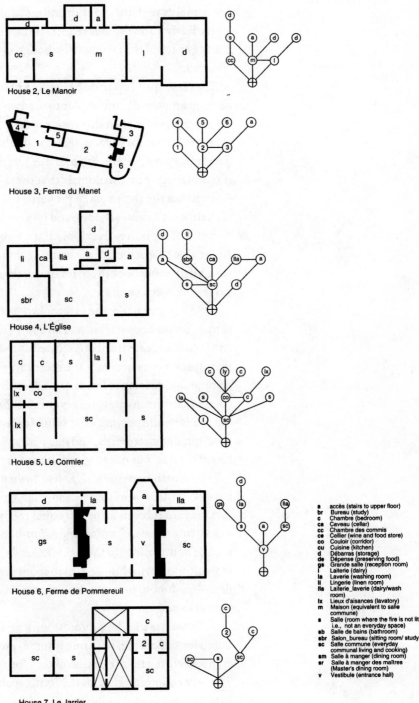

House 2, Le Manoir

House 3, Ferme du Manet

House 4, L'Église

House 5, Le Cormier

House 6, Ferme de Pommereuil

House 7, Le Jarrier

a	accès (stairs to upper floor)
br	Bureau (study)
c	Chambre (bedroom)
ca	Caveau (cellar)
cc	Chambre des commis
ce	Cellier (wine and food store)
co	Couloir (corridor)
cu	Cuisine (kitchen)
d	Débarras (storage)
de	Dépense (preserving food)
gs	Grande salle (reception room)
l	Laiterie (dairy)
la	Laverie (washing room)
ll	Lingerie (linen room)
lla	Laiterie_laverie (dairy/wash room)
lx	Lieux d'aisances (lavatory)
m	Maison (equivalent to salle commune)
s	Salle (room where the fire is not lit, i.e., not an everyday space)
sb	Salle de bains (bathroom)
sbr	Salon_bureau (sitting room/ study)
sc	Salle commune (everyday communal living and cooking)
sm	Salle à manger (dining room)
sr	Salle à manger des maîtres (Master's dining room)
v	Vestibule (entrance hall)

the complex with the exterior and 0.68 for the interior room arrangement. These fairly strong values reflect the fact that the dairy is a relatively integrating space in the farmhouse, though much less so if the exterior is discounted.

The L-shaped Ferme du Manet is a plan without function data as well as being geometrically dissimilar to the two previous examples (see house 3 shown in figure 3.5). In this case, analysis is limited to what can be inferred from the artefactual or archaeological information which resides in the domestic space pattern. Even so, the justified graph does suggest certain resemblances. Most striking is that there is a space – marked 2 on the plan – which has the three spatial properties of the *salle commune* or maison: it is shallow, it lies on all rings, and it is the most integrating space in the complex. This is, however, only if the two small spaces 4 and 5, which lie either side of space 1 and are seemingly too small to count as rooms, are ignored. If either or both are included, then it equalises the integration values of spaces 1 and 2.

On the other hand, the external space of this farm is divided into a front garden, an inner courtyard and an approach road leading to the side door, and it cannot realistically be treated as a single space. If this is corrected, then space 2 does becomes the most integrating space. There is also a comparable difference factor of 0.78 for the three main spaces, and a comparable mean integration value for the layout of 1.02. However, if space 2 is a *salle commune*, it is unclear how the other spaces are to be functionally interpreted, and it is perhaps safer to note the syntactic resemblances, but not to speculate too far on the assignment of functions.

The fourth farmhouse, L'Eglise, is visually a much more elaborate plan, two rooms deep (see House 4 shown in figure 3.5). The front of the house is divided into three more or less equal rooms. The room on the left doubles as a sitting room and office *(the salon-bureau)*, the *salle commune* is in the middle and a salle is to the right. Behind these principal rooms lie a range of work-rooms, including a linen room *(lingerie)*, cellar *(caveau)*, dairy–washroom *(laiterie–laverie)*, storage *(débarras)* and stairs to the upper floor.

L'Eglise has a *salle commune* with all four defining characteristics noted for La Bataille, with one internal and two external rings, and a comparable mean integration of 0.93 for the minimum living complex. The order of integration for the living spaces is, as before *salle commune* < exterior < salle < salon-bureau. The difference factor is very strong for the maximum, mean and minimum integration values (0.68 and 0.62) and for the triad of living rooms above it is still quite strong, at 0.82. In this case, however, the salle is both shallow and on an exterior ring, while the salon–bureau is deep and on a dead-end sequence. Internal work functions are again on a deep, independent ring linked to the exterior.

The next house, Le Cormier, again has a geometrically central *salle commune*, flanked by a bedroom *(chambre)* and a salle (see house 5 shown in figure 3.5). The range of rooms at the back of the farmhouse include more bedrooms, a lavatory *(lieux d'aisances)* a second salle and a wash-room and dairy.

The *salle commune* of Le Cormier has all four defining characteristics of the previous Normandy farmhouses, with one internal and one external ring. It has two salles, both of which are end points, and a relatively inte-grating bedroom lying on an internal ring. The mean integration is 0.89, and the order of integration is *salle commune* < bedroom < exterior < both salles. The benchmark difference factors are 0.66 both with and without the exterior, while the difference factor for the *salle commune*, bedroom and salle is comparatively strong at 0.76. The dairy is the most integrating work function, at 0.83. As before, work-rooms lie on an independent ring passing through the outside.

The next example, the Ferme de Pommereuil, is spatially unlike any previous case, although the kinds of household function which it appears to perform are similar, in that the *salle commune*, salle, and reception room are the main spaces in the layout. Attached to the rear are the usual spaces for storage and farm work, including a dairy and a linen room (see house 6 shown in figure 3.5).

As the justified graph shows, the spatial form of the configuration is a tree, springing from a single entrance space. The layout has no rings, either internal or external. The *salle commune* is, however, relatively seg-regated, at 1.13, and the salle is the most integrated of the living spaces, at 0.68, reversing the previous order. The mean integration of the minimum living complex is 1.31, substantially more segregated than previous cases, and the order of integration for the living spaces is salle < *salle commune* < exterior < reception room. The exterior is substantially more segregated than any of the previous farmyards, at 1.35, whilst the most integrating space of all is the entrance hall, at 0.56. The benchmark difference factors are 0.71 and 0.79, but the difference factor for the *salle commune*, salle and reception room is weaker than previous cases, at 0.89, and only by including the entrance hall can strong difference factors be found within the spaces of this house interior.

Le Jarrier is a special case, though it does not appear so at first sight. However, closer inspection of the ground-floor plan reveals that this is made up of two separate premises at ground-floor level, separated from one another by a large storage room and stairs to the upper floors and linked only through the exterior of the building. Each minimum living complex has its own *salle commune* (see house 7 shown in figure 3.5). The one on the left is very simple: a *salle commune* and a salle, connected directly to each other and to the outside, meaning that this area of the domestic interior is maximally shallow, maximally integrating, and minimally differentiated. Little can be said of typological interest except, perhaps, that the *salle commune* does preserve the spatial characteristics previously noted of being shallow, integrated and on all rings, but obviously not uniquely so.

The right-hand complex is a simple tree form, with the *salle commune* shallowest and most integrating, and controlling access to two bedrooms one directly and one indirectly. The complex as a whole is relatively segregated, at 1.52, but the *salle commune* is a strong integrator, at 0.47. This gives the very strong difference factor of 0.61 for the living spaces. The benchmark figure for this house is unaffected by the exterior and is weaker, at 0.78. In spite of its simplicity, the living areas to the right of the farm do reproduce the order of integration, *salle commune* < exterior < bedrooms. In spite of their differences from previous examples, therefore, the left and right-hand complexes can both be said to reproduce at least some of the spatial characteristics found in La Bataille.

The next farmhouse, La Ferme Neuve, is a thin, attenuated building visually reminiscent of the farm at La Bataille (see house 8 shown in figure 3.6). However, La Ferme Neuve is spatially and functionally quite unlike any other house so far. Every space, barring the office and one bedroom, is directly linked to the outside, creating a ground-floor living arrangement with nine external and two internal rings. The complex is highly integrated, at 0.60, if the exterior is included and very segregated, at 1.52, if it is discounted. In this case, it is again unrealistic to treat the house plot as a single space since it divides sharply into a rear walled garden, inner courtyard and outside approach. However, even when the garden is treated as a separate space, the mean integration of the ground-floor rooms with the exterior is 0.64, and the complex behaves in a very similar way whether the exterior is disaggregated or treated as a whole.

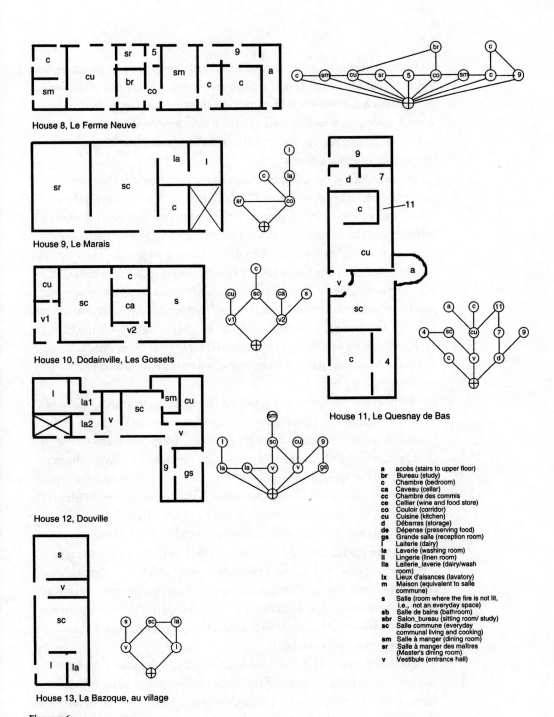

House 8, Le Ferme Neuve

House 9, Le Marais

House 10, Dodainville, Les Gossets

House 11, Le Quesnay de Bas

House 12, Douville

House 13, La Bazoque, au village

a   accès (stairs to upper floor)
br   Bureau (study)
c   Chambre (bedroom)
ca   Caveau (cellar)
cc   Chambre des commis
ce   Cellier (wine and food store)
co   Couloir (corridor)
cu   Cuisine (kitchen)
d   Débarras (storage)
de   Dépense (preserving food)
gs   Grande salle (reception room)
l   Laiterie (dairy)
la   Laverie (washing room)
ll   Lingerie (linen room)
lla   Laiterie_laverie (dairy/wash room)
lx   Lieux d'aisances (lavatory)
m   Maison (equivalent to salle commune)
s   Salle (room where the fire is not lit, i.e., not an everyday space)
sb   Salle de bains (bathroom)
sbr   Salon_bureau (sitting room/ study)
sc   Salle commune (everyday communal living and cooking)
sm   Salle à manger (dining room)
sr   Salle à manger des maîtres (Master's dining room)
v   Vestibule (entrance hall)

Figure 3.6
Plans and justified graphs of minimum
living complexes in Normandy farmhouses
(continued)

Inside, there is no *salle commune*, no salle and no reception room, but there is an office which combines the properties of being one of the two spaces which are two steps deep into the interior. This room is also the second most segregated function space if the exterior is included (one bedroom is more segregated), but the most integrated function space if the exterior is discounted.

Instead of the more common function spaces, there is a kitchen *(cuisine)*, a master's dining room *(salle à manger des maîtres)* and two other dining rooms *(salle à manger)*, one small, and directly linked to the kitchen, and the other large, separated from the kitchen by two intervening spaces and said to be '*d'apparat*', that is, for special occasions. The benchmark difference factor is very strong indeed with the exterior, at 0.42, but rather weak without it, at 0.82. Difference factors for the major spaces are maximally weak: 1.00 for the large formal dining room, kitchen and office without the exterior, and 0.91 for these spaces with the exterior, suggesting that even though the potential for spatial differentiation exists the major function spaces are homogenised within the layout of the minimum living complex.

Without the exterior, the corridor is the most integrating space, and with the exterior it is equally most integrating with the kitchen and the formal dining room. The order of integration changes with and without the exterior and, either way, it is unlike any previous case. With the exterior we find the integration rank order of exterior < corridor = large dining room = kitchen = small bedrooms < office < large dining room. Without the exterior, we find the rank order of corridor < office < large dining room < kitchen < bedrooms. Both with and without the exterior, the master's dining room is average in its integration value but, along with the office, it seems to divide the farm into two zones, one more integrating and the other more segregating. This echoes its visual and geometric position at the centre of the layout. Both functionally and spatially, the division suggests a fundamental distinction between masters and servants, rather than between living and working.

The ninth example, Le Marais, has a much simpler plan which returns, in a simplified form, to some of the earlier *salle commune* themes (see house 9 shown in figure 3.6). The *salle commune* at Le Marais is the most integrating space which lies on the only (external) ring. This is a shallow room which separates living from work functions. This time, however, the *salle commune* is described as '*des domestiques*'. There is neither a salle nor a reception room but there is a master's dining room, and this is much larger than in the previous case. Spatially this master's dining room seems comparable to the salle in some respects, in that it is less integrated than the *salle commune*, but more integrated than the bedroom. On the other hand, the master's dining room is shallow and it lies on the external ring, and in this it resembles a normal *salle commune*.

Mean integration for the living complex is normal, at 1.15. Difference factors are very strong: 0.62 for the *salle commune*, master's dining room and bedroom. This can be compared with a benchmark figure of 0.49 with the exterior and 0.61 for just the interior spaces.. The order of integration is: *salle commune* < exterior < master's dining room < bedroom. The farm office at Le Marais is external and independent, and does not form part of the minimum living complex.

The farm of Dodainville, in the village of Les Gossets, introduces some new features into a pattern that nevertheless continues to resemble the *salle commune* type (see house 10 shown in figure 3.6). The first, deep in the plan, is a small kitchen which has not so far co-existed with the *salle commune*. The second is a pair of entrance lobbies – one resulting from the same partitioning that created the kitchen – which unlink the *salle commune* from the exterior.

Even so, at 0.58, the *salle commune* remains the most integrating function space when the exterior is included, equal to the central entrance hall which also gives access to the upper floor. It is easily the most integrating space, at 0.59, if the exterior is discounted. The kitchen is the most segregated space both with (1.74) and without (2.16) the exterior. The salle is also strongly segregated. Mean integration is average, at 1.12, and the order of integration for the living spaces is *salle commune* < exterior < bedroom < salle < kitchen. Difference factors are strong, with 0.83 for the *salle commune*, salle and bedroom, and 0.79 for the *salle commune*, salle and kitchen nearly as strong as the comparable benchmark figure of 0.72 (0.78 with the exterior).

Le Quesnay de Bas is another rare case where a kitchen co-exists with a *salle commune*, though in this case the kitchen has become, with or without the exterior, the most integrated function space, at 0.77 (see house 11 shown in figure 3.6). This should be compared with a value of 1.09 for the *salle commune*. With the exterior, the rudimentary entrance lobby to the *salle commune*, clearly an afterthought, is the most integrating space of all, though without the exterior the kitchen takes over.

Spatially, Le Quesnay de Bas is characterised by two deep rings passing through the house plot, but the farm has no purely internal rings of circulation. Mean integration is average for the Normandy sample, at 1.10, but the spaces of the farmhouse become much more segregated on average, at 1.71, without the moderating influence of the exterior. The order of integration for the living spaces is exterior < kitchen < *salle commune* < bedroom. Difference factors are weak, with a value of 0.92 for the kitchen, *salle commune* and the larger of the two bedrooms as against the benchmark of 0.86 and 0.78 for the maximum, mean and minimum values with and without the exterior.

The next example, Douville, is architecturally a more elaborate L-shaped plan (see house 12 shown in figure 3.6). Douville has more functional differentiation among the living spaces than any other case to date, with a *salle commune*, kitchen, dining room and a formal reception room. Even so it reproduces some – but not all – of the features of the dominant *salle commune* type. With the exterior, the *salle commune* remains the most integrating function space, but the exterior is much more integrating, as are both the central entrance hall and one of the two dairies, this being brought about by the strong integration effect of the exterior. Discounting the exterior, the *salle commune* becomes uniquely the most integrating space.

The integration order of the principal living spaces at Douville is *salle commune* < reception room < kitchen < dining room with the exterior, and without the effect of the exterior it is *salle commune* < dining room < kitchen < reception room. The mean integration is 0.96, but this too is largely because of the integrating effect of the exterior. Without the exterior, this rises to 1.67. Difference factors for living spaces are weak with the exterior, with 0.92 for the living, reception and dining rooms. The differentiation among rooms becomes stronger when the exterior is discounted, with a value of 0.88 for the same three spaces. With the exterior, strong difference factors are only produced if the entrance hall is one of the three spaces considered. Finally, all four rings in the domestic space pattern at Douville are external, but the *salle commune* does perform the classic role for these Normandy farmhouses of linking and separating the living and work functions.

House 13 is the farm of La Bazoque, which is yet another case of the dominant *salle commune* type in a simplified form (see house 13 shown in figure 3.6). The *salle commune* at La Bazoque, in spite of being unlinked from the outside by an entrance hall at the front and the wash-room to the rear of the premises, is the most integrating function space (equal to the entrance hall, at 0.57) when the value is calculated for the configuration with the exterior, and is by far the most integrating space of all, at 0.47, without the exterior. The *salle commune* also lies on both rings, one internal and one external, and it links and separates the living areas from the work-related functions of the farm.

The mean integration value of La Bazoque is average, at 0.96, going up to 1.33 when the exterior is discounted. The order of integration is *salle commune* < exterior < salle, following the dominant pattern. Difference factors are strong, 0.76 and 0.59 for the maximum, mean and minimum values with and without the exterior, and 0.78 for the three functions of *salle commune*, salle and wash-room, but there are not enough living spaces to compute this for living spaces as a separate category of use.

The next house, Le Domaine, is a very small dwelling in which the minimum living complex has only one space, so it cannot therefore be analysed (see house 14 shown in figure 3.7). Even so, the fact that this space must by definition be shallow and integrating but also happens to lie on a ring, is not without typological relevance. This space, which is called the *salle commune*, clearly functions as a typical *salle commune* we have come to associate with the Normandy type. It could be argued that the complex would only have to develop in a way which preserves those features which are already present, to arrive at the dominant *salle commune* type.

Le Tourps has a *salle commune*, but it clearly does not conform to the dominant type (see house 15 shown in figure 3.7). Spatially the complex is split by the entrance hall into two branches of a tree, with the *salle commune* on one branch and the salle on the other. The lavatory is on the salle side and the bathroom on the *salle commune* side. Because there is one extra space, the office, on the salle side, the salle appears as the most integrating function space, though with the rather poor value of 0.79, compared with 1.18 for the living room. The entrance hall is the most integrating space, at 0.59, and the exterior is strongly segregated, at 1.57. Mean integration is 1.40 with the exterior and 1.62 without. The office at Le Tourps is strongly segregated, at 1.77, and it is also deep in the complex.

The order of integration for the living spaces is salle < *salle commune* < exterior < office. The difference factor for the main living areas is fair, with a value of 0.87 for the salle, *salle commune* and office, but this is more a

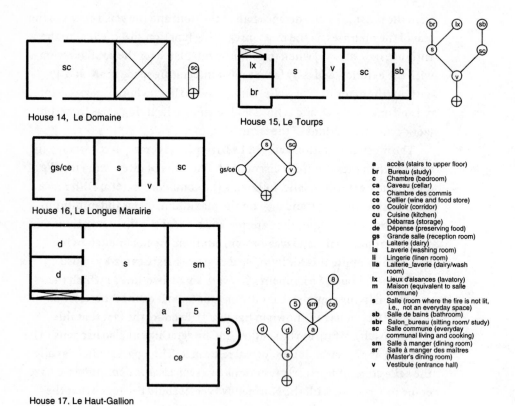

House 14, Le Domaine

House 15, Le Tourps

House 16, Le Longue Marairie

House 17. Le Haut-Gallion

a	accès (stairs to upper floor)
br	Bureau (study)
c	Chambre (bedroom)
ca	Caveau (cellar)
cc	Chambre des commis
ce	Cellier (wine and food store)
co	Couloir (corridor)
cu	Cuisine (kitchen)
d	Débarras (storage)
de	Dépense (preserving food)
gs	Grande salle (reception room)
l	Laiterie (dairy)
la	Laverie (washing room)
ll	Lingerie (linen room)
lla	Laiterie_laverie (dairy/wash room)
lx	Lieux d'aisances (lavatory)
m	Maison (equivalent to salle commune)
s	Salle (room where the fire is not lit, i.e., not an everyday space)
sb	Salle de bains (bathroom)
sbr	Salon_bureau (sitting room/ study)
sc	Salle commune (everyday communal living and cooking)
sm	Salle à manger (dining room)
sr	Salle à manger des maîtres (Master's dining room)
v	Vestibule (entrance hall)

Figure 3.7
Plans and justified graphs of minimum living complexes in Normandy farmhouses (continued)

result of the segregation of the office than of the strong integration value of any of the main spaces of the domestic interior. The benchmark figures are unremarkable, at 0.72 and 0.78 respectively. It is perhaps worth noting that several of the properties of the dominant *salle commune* type would be restored if the – apparently added – partition between the bathroom and a large storage area to the right, and now completely separate from the minimum living complex, was removed.

La Longue Marairie is another simple plan (see house 16 shown in figure 3.7). Although it could, in theory, approximate a simplified version of the *salle commune* type, in practice it inverts it by having the *salle commune* as the most segregated space, at 1.89, and the only end point. The salle both integrates more than the *salle commune* and lies on the single exterior ring. Even so it integrates less than the entrance hall. Mean integration for La Longue Marairie is normal, at 1.14 with the exterior, but if the exterior is discounted from the calculation the complex become a single sequence of spaces with a mean integration of 2.00, that is, as segregated as it could possibly be. Difference factors for function spaces are very weak, in spite of the strongly segregated *salle commune*, but the factor becomes very strong if the entrance hall is considered as one of the spaces – for example, the *salle commune*, salle and hall have a factor of 0.65. The benchmark figures are 0.68 with, and 0.78 without the exterior.

The last case, Le Haut-Gallion, is a large, L-shaped farm complex, with a large number of outbuildings attached to the dwelling (see House 17 shown in figure 3.7). Spatially, it is another tree form, without a room labelled *salle commune*, but with a salle as the most integrating function space, at 0.56, and a deep lobby as the most integrated space of all, with a value of 0.45. Mean integration is average, at 1.15 with the exterior, and 1.23 without it. This shows that integration values inside the dwelling are very little affected by circulation routes passing through the house plot. The order of integration for the living spaces is salle < dining room < exterior. Difference factors for Le Haut-Gallion are weak unless the internal lobby is taken into account, in which case we find a value of 0.75 for the lobby, dining room and salle.

The problem of type in Normandy farmhouses

The house-by-house review has suggested that, although no obvious single regional house type can be identified in the sample – 'type' being defined here as a more or less standard way of constructing the house and arranging its rooms – there is evidence of at least one underlying spatial-functional genotype – 'genotype' being defined in terms of some set of underlying relational and configurational consistencies which show themselves under different 'phenotypical' arrangements. However, sometimes this dominant genotype is realised strongly, in the sense that all the spatial-functional themes are present, and sometimes more weakly, in that some themes are present and others are missing. In yet other cases, these themes seem to be totally lacking, or even inverted.

The questions to be addressed in this section are: 'can the idea of a dominant genotype be formally demonstrated?' and 'is there also a second type, and can this too be formally demonstrated?' The first step in trying to answer the first question is to consider the spatial and functional properties of the sample as a whole. Figure 3.8 sets out each main named use-type

Figure 3.8
Numbers, mean depths and mean
integration values for key functions
in the Normandy data set

Function	Number of cases	With exterior		Without exterior
		mean depth	mean integration	mean integration
Exterior	16		0.93	
Salle commune	13	1.47	0.74	0.79
Chambre	13	2.07	1.21	1.67
Salle	11	1.91	1.01	1.13
Vestibule	9	1.00	0.68	0.95
Laverie	9	2.20	1.15	1.42
Laiterie	8	2.00	1.33	1.76
Cuisine	4	1.75	1.06	1.52
Salle `a manger	4	2.00	0.96	1.45
Grande salle	3	2.00	1.34	2.00

of space that occurs in the sample of farmhouses, the number of times it occurs, and its mean depth and integration value averaged for all those cases when it does occur. This shows that the commonest types of function in these Normandy farmhouses are *salles communes* and bedrooms, with thirteen occurrences each, followed by salles, then transitions of all kinds and the various types of work space. Kitchens are rare, as are reception rooms.

There are also clear across-the-board differences in the way in which these various functions are spatialised. *Salles communes* occur in the sample with a mean depth of 1.47 and a mean integration value of 0.74 (0.79 without the effect of the exterior). Salles have a mean depth of 1.91 and a mean integration of 1.01 (1.13 without the exterior). Reception rooms have a mean depth of 2.00 and a mean integration of 1.21 (1.67 without the exterior). These differences are sufficient to give a difference factor of 0.93 for the mean values for the *salle commune*, salle and reception room. This would be considered weak in an individual case, but it is relatively strong in a sample.

Among the less common spaces, kitchens are rare, but where they occur their mean depth is 1.75 and their mean integration value is 1.06 (1.52 without the exterior). Kitchens, in effect, only appear occasionally and in deep and segregated spaces. The generality of dining rooms is similar, but the two master's dining rooms which occur in the set of farms are both found in shallow and relatively integrating spaces. Offices or studies, on the other hand, are normally strongly segregated, at 1.34. Work functions are, in general, considerably more segregated than living functions, and there are fewer quantitative differentiations among them. Wash-rooms are both the deepest of all the function spaces from the exterior and the most integrating of the work functions, at 1.15. Transitions are common, and are usually shallow and strongly integrating. The overall mean integration for all spaces in the Normandy data is 1.08 and, broadly speaking, one might say that the living functions are found on the integrated side of the mean whilst the work functions lie to the segregated side.

These strong trends across the sample of farms are in themselves convincing evidence of an underlying spatial culture for the Normandy region, which expresses itself through the spatial form of the houses. However, this spatial culture expresses itself in spite of numerous inversions and oppositions that were noted earlier, in the house-by-house review. It seems likely, then, that if more than one genotype could be identified, these spatial cultures would show through and be expressed even more strongly.

A common sense, conjecture-test procedure seems appropriate here. The house-by-house review suggested a dominant type based on the existence of a *salle commune* with the four dominant properties of being shallow, most integrating, lying on all rings, and linking and separating living from work functions in the domestic interior. La Bataille seems to be a clear case in point. Le Manoir can be admitted since the labels of maison and *salle commune* are used interchangeably elsewhere. The Ferme du Manet is unlabelled and must be omitted from any conjectures on the use of rooms; but L'Eglise and Le Cormier are both clear examples of the *salle commune* type. No such case can be made for the Ferme de Pommereuil. Le Jarrier seems a reasonable case, but perhaps should be omitted as being too small. La Ferme Neuve is clearly not of the *salle commune* type, but Le Marais and Dodainville reasonably are. Le Quesnay de Bas is not an example of the *salle commune* type but Douville is. A case can be made for La Bazoque, Le Domaine is too small, and Le Tourps, La Longue Marairie and Le Haut Gallion are clearly not examples of the candidate regional genotype. Disregarding all the houses that are too small, we have eight possible cases of the dominant *salle commune* genotype, and six cases which clearly do not conform to this type.

Figure 3.9 therefore divides the sample into two, along these lines, showing the mean integration with and without the exterior, the use function and integration value of the most integrated space, the difference factor for the main living spaces and the integration value for the exterior. The table shows a number of interesting results.

First, the mean integration of the genotype examples is very stable, at around 1.0. The houses that strongly deviate from this mean value are all

Decoding Homes and Houses

Figure 3.9
Data on the Normandy sample organised
into the two proposed house types

House number	Mean integration		Most integrating space				Difference factor	Integration value
	with exterior	without exterior	with exterior		without exterior		main functions	exterior
Genotype								
1	1.12	1.36	sc	0.60	sc	0.79	0.83 (sc, s, gs)	0.83
2	0.95	1.23	sc	0.34	sc	0.44	0.79 (m, s, c)	0.68
4	0.93	1.22	sc	0.30	sc	0.45	0.82 (sc,s,sb)	0.68
5	0.89	0.97	sc	0.31	sc	0.37	0.76 (sc, s, c)	0.83
9	1.10	1.52	sc	0.29	sc	0.47	0.62 (sc, sm, c)	1.15
10	1.12	1.40	sc	0.58	sc	0.59	0.83 (sc, s, c)	0.87
12	0.96	1.67	ex (sc	0.45 0.83)	sc	0.91	0.88 (sc, gs, sm) (0.92 with ext)	0.45
13	0.96	1.33	sc	0.57	sc	0.47	0.78	0.86
Mean	1.01	1.37	sc v all t	0.48 0.64 0.80	sc	0.56	0.79	0.79
Nongenotype								
6	1.30	1.45	v (sc	0.56 1.13)	s,v (sc	0.73 1.31)	0.89 (sc, s, gs)	1.35
8	0.60	1.52	ex (co	0.13 0.51)	co, v	0.90	0.91 (sm, cu, br) (1.0 without ext)	0.13
16	1.14	2.00	v (sc	0.47 1.89)	s, v (sc	1.00 3.00)	0.91	0.95
11	1.10	1.71	v (sc	0.67 1.09)	cu (v	0.9 1.13)	0.92 (sc, c, cu)	0.70
15	1.40	1.62	v (sc	0.59 1.18)	s, v (sc	0.86 1,43)	0.87 (sc, s, br)	1.57
17	1.15	1.23	a, v	0.45	a, v	0.44	0.88 (s, sm, ce)	1.35
Mean	1.12	1.59	v sc all t	0.55 1.32 0.54	v sc	0.84 1.81	0.90	1.01

in the non-genotype part of the sample, which also has a slightly higher mean of means. Second, if the exterior is discounted, then the mean integration of the genotype examples remains relatively integrating, at 1.37. Eliminating the exterior from the non-genotype examples has a more segregating effect, raising the mean to 1.59.

If we now look at the mean integration for *salles communes*, the defining room in the genotype examples, this is 0.48 with the exterior and 0.56 without. For the non-genotype examples, the mean of this room is 1.32 with the exterior and 1.81 without it. The *salle commune* is the most

•

integrating space of all throughout the genotype examples. The only exceptions are at Dodainville (10) and Douville (12). Dodainville is the farm
where the entrance hall is equally most integrating if the exterior is
included, but the *salle commune* is the most integrating room if the effect
of the exterior is discounted. At Douville, the exterior is the most integrating space of all and the *salle commune* is only the most integrated living
space, but as at Dodainville, the *salle commune* becomes the most integrating space if only the relations among the interior spaces are considered.

A quite different but equally consistent pattern of most integrating
spaces is found in the non-genotype part of the sample. In the Ferme de
Pommereuil (6), the entrance hall is most integrating, although the *salle* is
equally so if the exterior is discounted. In La Ferme Neuve (8), the exterior
is by far the most integrating space, but the corridor follows, and becomes
most integrating if the effect of the exterior is discounted. In Le Quesnay
de Bas (11), the entrance hall is most integrating, though it becomes second
to the kitchen if the exterior is discounted. The entrance hall is also the
most integrating space at Le Tourps (15), though here too the *salle* has an
equal value if the effect of the exterior is disregarded. The same is true of
La Longue Marairie, (16). Finally, in Le Haut-Gallion (17), the internal
lobby is most integrating, remaining so when the exterior is discounted.
The mean integration for all the transition spaces in the non-genotype
examples is 0.54 with the exterior, and 0.84 without. The comparable
figures for transitions in the genotype examples are 0.80 and 1.02 respectively. In other words, *salles communes* and transitions change places
in the two parts of the sample.

Difference factors then reflect this change. The mean difference factor
for living spaces in the genotype examples is 0.79, whereas for the non-
genotype examples it is 0.90. In the non-genotype examples, strong difference factors are only found when transitions are included among the
spaces considered. The opposite is the case for the genotype examples.
Lastly, the mean integration of the exterior of the genotype examples is
0.79, whereas for the non-genotype examples it is 1.01.

In other words, two distinct genotypical tendencies can be demonstrated by splitting the sample of Normandy farmhouses into two. The
first centres on the highly integrating *salle commune*. This configurational type creates strong spatial differences among living spaces,
incorporates the exterior into its pattern of strong integration, has a more
integrating interior, and a more integrating exterior. The alternative type

which has now emerged centres on transitions; that is, on entrance halls and lobbies. This type creates more internal segregation amongst living spaces and less configurational differentiation among them. It separates the inside more clearly from the farmyard, and has a segregated exterior. These genotypes do not appear to be correlated either with size or with the overall geometry of the building. On the contrary, they appear to be two distinct spatial-functional tendencies, each of which expresses itself through several different built forms.

An interpretative speculation

In considering these two genotypes against the background of the concepts drawn from Cuisenier's interpretation of Estienne, the concept of *latéralité*, implying the division of the dwelling into living and working zones on either side of a central space, seems particularly apposite. It is a pervasive theme throughout the Normandy sample, though with great variation in the way it is realised and the degree to which it is realised in each farmhouse.

However, when it is related to the two genotypes, a more complex picture emerges. Cuisenier's model specifies a *latéralité* with three strong properties: it has a geometric left-right element; it is organised around a central transition space; and it is based on the point of view of the male master of the house. None of these properties can be left without further comment.

On the geometric dimension, or the left-right question, it is clear that this does sometimes apply, as for example at La Bataille or Le Marais. But in other cases, the *latéralité* is just as strongly realised in the syntax of the spaces, but it takes on either a front-back geometry, as at L'Église or Le Cormier, or a more indeterminate form, as at Douville. It seems reasonable on the basis of this evidence to think of *latéralité* as a primarily syntactic property which sometimes takes on one geometric form and sometimes another. It is pervasively present, but its form seems more to do with the cultural arrangement of practicalities than with an exogenous conceptual model.

On the question of the organising feature of a central space it is clear that, although *latéralité* is sometimes organised around a central transition, more often than not it is organised around the dominant function space, the *salle commune*. Which alternative is selected seems to be the principal choice that leads to one genotype or the other. This raises an important question: 'does *latéralité* organised around a transition mean the same thing as *latéralité* organised around a main function space? Or does it arise in different social circumstances?'

This, in turn, raises the question of the male-centred view of *latéralité*. The *salle commune*, with its conjunction of cooking and everyday living, seems to be a space in which women might be expected to be dominant, the more so since the work functions which the *salle commune* typically separates from other living functions are those associated with female roles – washing the laundry, making dairy produce and so on. It is difficult to avoid the inference that the form of *latéralité* which is centred on the *salle commune* is, in fact, organised around the female functions of the household. One is almost tempted to the view that the transition-centred form of *latéralité*, following Cuisenier's interpretation of Estienne, is associated with a male view of the household and the *salle commune*-centred form with a female view.

However, the attractions of this simple 'explanation' of the two genotypes must at least be put in question by an awkward fact: the distinction between transition-centred and function-centred domestic space organisation has been made before in quite different explanatory circumstances. For example, chapter four of this book will associate the distinction between room-centred homes and corridor-centred homes with differences between social class fragments rather than gender differences, whereas Glassie associates such a distinction with social changes over a period of time, linked to changes in house locations and changes in privacy needs.[4] Robin Evans[5] has gone so far as to point to different psychological tendencies towards gregariousness or seclusion, as the underlying generator of social preferences for room-centred or corridor-centred layouts.

In all of these studies, however, a similar view is taken of the social mechanisms underlying domestic space patterning, which emphasises the importance of considering the house not only in terms of the relations among its inhabitants, but also in terms of the relations between inhabitants and visitors. Domestic space cannot be understood without understanding the dynamics of both types of relationship, and the house can only be understood as a device for managing both types of interface. In both studies, the house is thus seen as a spatial and symbolic means to

Figure 3.10
A comparison of visual fields from the
salle commune

a. La Bataille

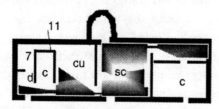

b. Le Quesnay de Bas

social and communal solidarities, as much as an instrument of family and
individual privacy.

In pursuing these ideas, we can explore what we might call the experiential dimensions of space and, in particular, the changing experience of
the house as one moves from one space to another. A key aspect of this is
often the relationship between permeability and visibility. The permeability structure of a complex is essentially a matter of how the relations of
spaces to their immediate neighbours build into a system of possible
routes. It defines where you can go, and how to get there. The visibility
structure, on the other hand, tells you how much space you are aware of
without moving. In a sense, it tells you where you already are.

The relations with visibility are often, it seems, a means by which the
basic permeability syntax of a complex is fine-tuned into a more effective
device for interfacing or distancing different kinds of relationship. This
certainly seems true of the Normandy sample. If, for example, one looks at
the *salle commune* of La Bataille (assuming that doors are open) there is a
line of sight and direct access that originates in the pantry, crosses the *salle
commune*, passes through the corridor controlling access to the *salle* and
the farm office, then through the front-back entrance hall and finally
through the reception room (see figure 3.10a). Another such line crosses
the *salle commune* then passes through the lobby to the outside. Another
crosses the *salle commune* and passes through both the wash-room and
the dairy. In a sense, all the major spatial relations in the complex are gov-

erned visibly from the *salle commune*. Included in this panoptic view are the interfaces between the *salle commune* and the other living functions, the interior world of work, and the relation to the outside world.

In total contrast, in Le Quesnay de Bas the visibility relations from the *salle commune* are hardly more than to the immediate neighbouring permeabilities, and even these are highly restricted (see figure 3.10b). None of the three interfaces of visibility that are so evident at La Bataille are realised to any degree at Le Quesnay except, arguably, that with the outside world. To be in that space is only to be in that space, not to be visibly part of a complex system of spaces involving both interior and exterior. Similar differences are found if one compares, say, Le Cormier with the Ferme de Pommereuil.

In contrast, the most striking cases of visual relationships in the houses which have a genotype organised in relation to a well-integrated transition occur in the transition itself. The Ferme de Pommereuil, Le Quesnay de Bas, Le Tourps, and La Longue Marairie, for example, all have the strongest visual relations from their entrance hall. La Ferme Neuve has a seven-space enfilade with the corridor at its centre. Le Haut-Gallion does not have this property, but even there in a less strong sense, the interior lobby at the hinge of the L-shaped plan is the strongest visual integrator.

These distinctions are, it seems, reinforced by the ring structure. In the *salle commune* type, the eight *salles communes* lie on a total of fifteen rings, or 1.87 per *salle commune*. In fact, with the exception of Douville, where the *salle commune* lies on only one of three rings, the *salles communes* lie on all rings in the complexes. On the other hand, if the external rings are cut, then in each case the *salle commune* becomes a controlling space which must be passed through to move from one part of the house to another. In contrast, of the four *salles communes* in the transition-centred genotype, only one lies on a ring, and that a single ring. In this type, the transition becomes the controlling space which must be passed through to move from one part of the house to the other, with a correspondingly much more restricted opportunity to use the exterior for alternative routes. The *salle commune* in the *salle commune* genotype is, it seems, a controlling space for the interior – its control of certain aspects of interior permeability is pervasive and unavoidable. But it is only a strategic space for the interior–exterior relation – it is powerful, but avoidable. The transition in the transition-centred genotype is, on the other hand, more often a controlling space for both interior and interior–exterior relations.

It is hard to avoid the inference that these relations are linked to the ways in which domestic space creates and structures the possibility and form of encounter among inhabitants, and between inhabitants and visitors, and that the differences between the two genotypes express some profound difference in the forms of social solidarities. The *salle commune* type seems to suggest a pattern that works by creating spatial differences between functions, strong interior integration with everyday living at the centre, and a permissive rather than controlling relation to the outside world. The transition-centred type works by more uniformly segregating the interior functions, through a central transition which controls both interior relations and relations with the exterior.

The first might be seen as a constitutive or spatial model in which the social role of space is expressed directly through the way in which the space pattern is lived. The second might be seen more as a representative or conceptual model, in which individual function spaces are assigned a spatial identity more through separation and control than through the organisation of complex inter-relations. Such a distinction may, however, be related to the different ways in which gender relations can express themselves through space. The suggestion has been made before[6] and there seems perhaps a possibility that we may be dealing with a pair of 'genotypical' tendencies of some generality. But their further exploration would require non-archaeological forms of data, and thus lie beyond the scope of this chapter.

Notes

1 Jean Cuisenier, *La Maison Rustique: logique sociale et composition architecturale* (Paris: Presses Universitaires de France, 1991), pp. 29–63.

2 Max-André Brier and Pierre Brunet, *Normandie*, Berger-Levrault *(ed.)*. *L'Architecture Rurale Française, corpus des genres, des types et des variantes*, (Paris: Musée national des arts et traditions populaires, 1984).

3 C. Shannon and W. Weaver, *The Mathematical Theory of Communication* (Chicago: University of Illinois Press, 1948), p. 125.

4 Henry Glassie, *Folk Housing in Middle Virginia: a Structural Analysis of Historic Artifacts* (Knoxville: University of Tennessee Press, 1975), pp. 114–22.

5 Robin Evans, *Translations from Drawing to Building and Other Essays* (London, Architectural Association, 1997) p. 88.

6 Bill Hillier and Julienne Hanson, *The Social Logic of Space* (Cambridge University Press, 1984), pp. 239–40.

Two domestic 'space codes' compared

(with Bill Hillier)

Summary

Throughout the 1960s and 1970s, design guidelines for social housing laid great emphasis upon the functional design of the domestic interior, and for the need for a clear hierarchy of space between the dwelling and the street. However, studies of contemporary lifestyles in small terraced houses in the residential areas of inner London provided evidence for the existence of two common forms of 'non-architectural' domestic space organisation, neither of which seemed to be internally purely functional nor externally hierarchical. Rather, each way of configuring domestic space embodied the dominant cultural practices of a different socio-economic group. This chapter describes these two 'codes' of domestic space organisation, and argues that they are based on socio-spatial principles which are, in some senses, the inverse of each other. More awareness of these organising principles for domestic space would seem to be required, if guidance is not to lead to insensitive, standardised design.

Community and privacy as a paradigm for design

During the 1960s and 1970s government-sponsored guidelines for the design of new social housing stressed the basic requirement for a clearly expressed hierarchy of spatial domains, ranging from public circulation spaces at one end of the spectrum, to the private interior of the dwelling at the other. This trend was supported by more formal proposals from leading architects and social reformers[1] to reconcile the imperative for individual privacy to the necessity for community life, in the context of the design of residential areas. The paradigm was supported by an appeal to socio-biology. Man's territorial instincts, it was argued, required that space should be organised in such a way as to ensure that people should feel secure at home and able to relate sociably to each other. A strong 'privacy gradient' guaranteed that the integrity of the family group would not be compromised by indiscreet visual, audible or bodily intrusions among close neighbours or by passing strangers, whilst appropriate behaviours in group situations were stimulated by environmental clues and cues. Anyone who studies this design guidance today might be forgiven for inferring that there was, at that time, an explicit and shared view of the way in which people should live; a set of objective principles which amounted to a 'right way' of designing.

Whether these principles were set out in the form of standard plans or in more abstract checklists, the scheme of ideas was undoubtedly attractive in its simplicity and its completeness. It seemed to offer the architect clear and unambiguous solutions to the challenge of housing design. It certainly influenced a whole generation of housing projects, including the comprehensive redevelopment of low-income, terraced housing in many inner city areas throughout Britain. Its only serious disadvantage was that it failed to account for the variety of ways in which people were actually living at the time. Contemporary literary and sociological studies of people's homes were unearthing a wealth of evidence that space configuration featured in British society in surprising, and often unexpected ways, as a means of social and cultural identification. The manifest variety of ordinary people's lifestyles seemed to point away from behavioural universals and basic human needs and towards a view that, if space had a purpose, this was to encode and transmit cultural information.

This chapter seeks to lay bare the principles underlying just two, apparently polar types of 'space code', which could be found co-existing in large numbers in the residential streets of Fulham, Chelsea, Camden Town and Islington throughout the 1960s and 1970s. In these areas of Inner London, the nineteenth-century street pattern of small, narrow-frontage two and three storey terraced houses had remained largely untouched. Over the years, this type of house had proved itself to be versatile, and it had been adapted to serve the needs of quite different sectors of the local housing market. The ways in which it did so were quite systematic, so much so that the comedians of the day made jokes about how people organised and decorated their houses, as a way of identifying to their audience who their characters were, and the values they aspired to socially.

One fact, which was apparent from the outset, made these London terraced houses a particularly attractive vehicle through which to explore the proposition that domestic space organisation might be governed by cultural conventions at least as much as by behavioural universals: neither space code was significantly hierarchical in the way in which the domestic interior was related to the street outside. Indeed, both could be described as 'street-cultures' in the sense that they both depended, though in different ways, on maintaining a direct physical relation to the street. They offered, therefore, a direct challenge to the view that strongly hierarchical forms of space organisation would be adopted where people were free to express their preferences. These polar cases, co-existing in close proximity often as next-door neighbours on the same street, provided tangible evidence that architects should beware of espousing a 'natural' philosophy of basic human needs or shared norms and values, and particularly in determining a spatial form for such nebulous concepts as those of 'community and privacy'.

These domestic space codes, which were prevalent a generation ago, are no longer an aspect of the urban London scene. The houses still exist today, but people's tastes have changed and new forms of behaviour have supplanted the previous ways of living. This suggests that some aspects of culture are relatively ephemeral, and that we need to distinguish the more fashionable from the durable elements of domestic space organisation. At the same time, the spatial gestures which were permutated in these houses are recognisable to us as a fertile substrate from which cultural variety has the potential to grow. The account which follows, describes how the houses were originally built and were subsequently transformed. It is based on first-hand observation, but it also draws upon novels,

Figure 4.1
A comparison of house types **a** and **b**
before and after conversion

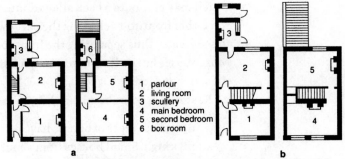

1 parlour
2 living room
3 scullery
4 main bedroom
5 second bedroom
6 box room

Figure 4.1a Typical examples of traditional working class terraced housing

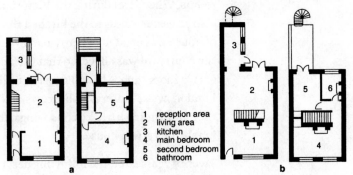

1 reception area
2 living area
3 kitchen
4 main bedroom
5 second bedroom
6 bathroom

Figure 4.1b Conversions of types **a** and **b** by new middle class owners

historical and sociological studies, research reports, design guidance and
architectural publications to flesh out the detail.

The raw material

Both space codes use, as raw material, the same standard London house.
The period at which the house was first built is immaterial, varying from
early Georgian to late Edwardian, since apart from the decorative features, all conform to the same basic plan (see figure 4.1a). Both cultures
are associated with a small, narrow-frontage terraced house. Typically,
such a house is two or three, and occasionally even four storeys high, with
two living rooms on each floor. There may be a basement, with steps
leading down to a separate entrance in a small, railed light-well, or the
house may lead directly onto the street. Both are normally entered
through an entrance hall, and have a yard or small garden at the back,

which may give onto a back alley running behind the terrace. The stairs run either front-to-back along the party wall, or across the house, parallel to the facade, thus separating the front room more strongly from the back. Most houses have a lean-to rear extension containing a scullery, bathroom or box room.

Rasmussen describes them thus, as they appeared to him in the 1930s:

> The smallest types of houses have no basement and are only two storeys high. Small houses from about 1820 had sometimes even four storeys, including the basement, and on each floor there were only two rooms. When later during the Victorian era a lavatory was required, and also an easier access to the kitchen than up and down stairs, a new type of house was created, where a narrower side-building projecting into the courtyard was added, so that each of the two storeys now consisted of two rooms and 'a half'. From the railroads intersecting the suburbs of London, we see interminable rows of these swarthy little houses, with their protruding little kitchen wings. It is the most compact type imaginable for a street house.[2]

Twenty years later, the following description of an untransformed example of the house type is found in *Family and Kinship in East London*:

> Mr. and Mrs. Barton and their two young children live at present in a four roomed house in Minton Street in the middle of the borough. The other houses (but not the two pubs, obviously newer) were all built in the 1870s of brick which has become a uniform smoke-eaten grey. They are nearly all alike in plan: on the first floor two bedrooms, and on the ground floor a living room, a kitchen and a small scullery opening onto a yard which has a lavatory at the end of it and a patch of earth down one side. Many of the yards are packed with clothes hanging on the line, prams, sheds, boxes of geraniums and pansies, hutches for rabbits and guinea-pigs, lofts for pigeons and pens for fowl. The only difference between the houses is the colour of the curtains and the door steps, which the wives redden or whiten when they wash down the pavement in front of their doors in the morning.[3]

This house, as are many of the untransformed examples, is inhabited by a 'traditional' working-class family, perhaps the family of a skilled or better-paid artisan, and indeed precisely the sort of people for whom the houses were first built, by small speculative builders throughout the nineteenth century. Many of these aggregations of working-class dwellings were originally occupied by porters, market workers, building tradesmen, dock hands, tailors, jewellers and the casually employed. At that time, the majority were first-generation town dwellers, migrant rural workers. Nonetheless, it is clear from contemporary reports that the sort of life-style described over a century later by Willmott and Young, quickly established itself amongst a certain section of the working class (the 'respectable poor' rather than the 'degenerate classes' – a distinction still reflected in today's social studies) for whom this sort of house afforded 'the desired separation between washing in the scullery, eating and living in the kitchen (often referred to as the living room or sitting room) and display in the parlour'.[4]

However, this sort of house is not only occupied by members of the traditional working classes. Nowadays, when a house of this sort is sold, it is frequently purchased by a member of the 'new' middle class, who deals in the symbolic and representational aspects of culture.

> Their professions are vaguely, entrepreneurially 'cultural': academics, journalists of a literary turn, television directors and producers, actors, copywriters, publishers' agents, with a few lawyers, accountants and business executives. For them, the purchase of a house has become an act of conscience, and they have left the old strongholds of their class behind them (believing that their education and judiciously left politics have declassed them anyway) and searched out 'unspoiled' areas in the city where they can live conspicuously cheek-by-jowl with the polyglot poor.[5]

In the two polar types of domestic space code, which form the subject of this chapter, the variable of built form is held steady, and its organisation by a traditional working-class family, on the one hand, and a new middle-class household, on the other, are directly contrasted. It is clear, however, that these codes do not exhaust the possibilities for the spatial embodiment of sub-cultural and class identities.

Domestic space transformed

Once the member of the new middle classes – Raban terms him a 'frontiersman' – moves into his newly acquired terraced house, he begins to make alterations to the place. He will undoubtedly paint both the exterior and the interior of the house, and make technical improvements, inserting a damp-proof course, rewiring, replumbing and replacing cracked panes of glass and broken sashcords, and perhaps insulating the roofspace. These alterations are, however, insignificant compared with the 'improvements' in internal organisation which are also made, for:

> Decoration is the least important part of the style, and it is done with caution and embarrassment. Its dominant features are bare rectangles and circles, natural materials, a colour scheme in white paint and unstained wood surfaces, a lust for light and air and a horror of fuss, embellishment and chi-chi. A house converted on these principles has an atmosphere of passionate neutrality.[6]

So much so, that it is likely that within the space of a few months even if it were dark so that a passer-by could not see the new paintwork, it would be possible to walk down the street and state, without doubt, which house had been moved into by the representative of the new middle classes (see figure 4.1b).

The most obvious improvement to the internal organisation of the house is that well-known phenomenon 'knocking-through':

> Destruction is its whole point. The first stage of conversion is 'knocking-through', tearing down internal walls so that each room is turned into an extended patio, hardly a room at all, except as it is protected (by double-glazed picture windows) from the weather. Out come staircases and balustrades: in go feathery key-hole steps in wrought iron.[7]

Conran offers a list of possible ways of combining rooms within the scope of the new regime: 'hall and living room and dining room, kitchen and dining room, lavatory and bathroom or utility room, living room and morning room, kitchen and scullery'.[8] Whatever their proposed uses, it is inevitable that the result will eliminate the wall between the two ground-floor rooms, and also possibly between the two rooms in the basement. This may entail major structural alterations, or alternatively the pair of doors separating the two rooms will be removed and put in a shed at the bottom of the garden.

It is also likely that the wall between the hall and one of the major living rooms on the ground floor will be removed. This will have the effect of bringing the stairs into the living room. At the same time, a new flight of

external wrought iron stairs may be added, to link the first floor rooms
to the back garden. Here the pigeon coops and old sheds are cleared away,
and the garden is commonly reorganised as a series of outdoor rooms, an
extension of the children's playroom, the kitchen or the indoor living
rooms.

A new kitchen will almost certainly form a part of the improvement
scheme, possibly in a place where eating did not occur before. The old back
scullery, where the chores were formerly done, will be pulled down or con-
verted into an utility area, and the new kitchen may be moved into the
basement front room, or onto the ground-floor living area where it can be
seen from the street outside. This is not all that will happen. Part of the
kitchen improvement scheme will entail removing cupboards, and removing existing fittings which are replaced by shelves full of glass jars with
bright labels.

Concurrent with these transformations in the physical appearance of
the house are new forms of behaviour, affecting the relationship of the
house to the street, the degree of control over the door, the placing of
objects within the interior, the relationship of specific activities to rooms
and eating behaviour: all of which casts doubt on the conceptual separation which is normally made between people and buildings. In this case
they seem to be aspects of the same phenomenon.

The relation of the house to the street

In a traditional working-class house, the interior of the house is usually
concealed from the street by net curtains, which remain closed even at
mid-day. The interior is often further screened from the outside by symbolic objects, a specimen plant or a prized piece of china. This trait clearly
pre-dates modern net curtains, since it is described by Victorian observers
as typical of 'respectable' or 'superior' homes that the parlour window
facing onto the street was covered by a lace or muslin blind. Even in some
of the poorest hovels, the window was covered with a calico blind or even
with paper.[9] On his arrival, the member of the new middle classes will
take down the net curtains at the window of the house and replace them by
shutters of blinds. These will only be shut late at night. Instead, the interior of the room will be arranged so that a casual passer-by can look into the
room, to see what a wonderful place it is.

Raban offers a graphic description of the result:

> Waiting for a taxi on the pavement one night, I saw a bow-windowed
> room full of humming birds. Lit from low down, they hovered bril-
> liantly among the potted ferns and rubber plants, and I heard a
> Monteverdi record on the gramophone inside. In another house nearby,
> I saw a whole room converted into an aluminium cage for a monkey
> (and this in an area where human beings claw for a few square feet,
> enough to unroll a sleeping-bag in). The monkey's only companion
> was a huge stuffed ape in a glass case outside its cage.[10]

Walking down the street is like visiting an exhibition of interiors, each
wonderfully different from its neighbours. Lights are left on for effect, even
when the room is not in use. Spotlights highlight the arrays of objects,
gleaming white paintwork and walls, pine furniture and glass and paper
accessories, rocking horses, harps and antique spinning wheels and the
library shelves lined with impressive displays of books. Even the people
inside become a part of the display. Instead of being concealed, the interior
of the house is manifested boldly to the street. From the point of view of
visual contact with the street, the old code is entirely reversed.

Control of the entrance

At the same time as this change occurs, the new middle-class occupants
will polish the door furniture, which will probably be of brass or bronze. If
it is painted over or wood-grained, as it often was in the old culture, many
hours will be spent in scraping off the old paints. Burglar alarms may be
installed, knockers and bells added and the number of the house proclaimed on a crisp French enamelled plate. Everyone enters the house formally by the main door. Indeed the back entrance may well be blocked off,
or the plot at the bottom of the garden may be sold as a site for a 'mews
house' in order to finance the transformation.

   In the untransformed order, however, control over the door, especially
the back door, is light. Members of the family and close neighbours, especially women, 'pop round the back'. The front door is frequently left
slightly ajar, closed but on the latch, or even wide open, especially in the
mornings. A key may even be attached by a string to the inside of the letter
box, so that relatives are able to let themselves into the house if the family

is out. Clearly the concept of the closed door does not fit into traditional working-class culture in quite the same way as it does in the transformed order, for:

> On the warm summer evening of the interview, children were playing hop-scotch or 'he' in the roadway, while the parents, when not watching television, were at their open window. Some of the older people were sitting in upright chairs on the pavement, just in front of their doors, or in the passages leading through to the sculleries, chatting with each other and watching the children at play.[11]

This easy-going and informal relation between the door and the street is not found in the transformed house where, on the whole, the new door furniture sits firmly upon a well-closed door. Once again, the relation of the inside to the outside is reversed, this time not for visual contact but for direct, physical accessibility.

It is clear from these observations that the relationship of the house to the street and the degree of control over the entrance are direct in both cases. Both codes are predicated upon this relation. However, the relation is made in different ways. It is a puzzle to see how an alleged 'basic need' for privacy would feature in this scheme of ideas. Is it to do with seeing into the interior of the dwelling, or controlling access to that interior? Clearly there are cultural differences between the two codes, but these are not arbitrary. On the contrary, one set of spatial behaviours appears to be a curious inversion of the other. Some sort of order is present, but it has nothing to do with a clearly expressed hierarchy of spatial domains controlled by 'barriers and locks', which has been advocated by Chermayeff and Alexander.[12]

The placing of objects within the interior

Inside the transformed house of the new middle-class family, it is usual to find that a great deal of the apparatus of day-to-day living is manifested in the space. One of Malcolm Bradbury's characters from *The History Man* epitomises the understated style of new middle-class living:

> Flora's room is long and dark with a white Indian rug and a few scattered furnishings. In her white blouse and black skirt, she goes

around, switching on table lamps and spotlights. The lights reveal the straight lines of plain modern furniture, and the texture of unpatterned fabric. Flora's room is a room of shapes and colours, rather than of things, though there are a few things that, carefully chosen, do stand out: a blue Aalto chair by the bookcase, a Hockney print on the wall, an Epstein bust on the teak coffee table. The galley kitchen is a construct in oiled wood at the end of the room, and looks straight out into it.[13]

This is in contrast to the untransformed working-class code where, with one notable exception which will be referred to later, things are normally put away in cupboards, sideboards or drawers.

Collections of objects frequently, although not invariably, do feature largely in the new middle-class scheme of things. Books, pictures, bottles and boxes, plants, kitchen equipment and toys are the standard raw material of such object arrays. Curiously, however, collections often consist of objects which are not in themselves valuable either in monetary or sentimental terms. Often they are not even useful, 'toast racks of the white china sort, keys from long-forgotten doors, wood blocks that were used in Edwardian printing works, all good on their own, but infinitely better in an organised mass'.[14] The order within the array tends to be subtle rather than obvious, in some instances designed to make a purely intellectual point – a visual pun – for 'a real birdcage closely associated with a picture of another makes a telling unit on the wall'.[15]

Collections of this type are not to be kept, but to be rearranged or thrown away. As Bernstein observes:

> The Hampstead room is likely to contain a small array which would indicate strong classification (strong rules of exclusion) but the objects are likely to enter into a variety of relationships with each other. This would indicate weak framing. Furthermore, it is possible that the array would be changed across time according to fashion.[16]

Nonetheless, there is order in the most apparently motley of arrays and the principles on which the collection is based are capable of being violated. Generally speaking, collections in working-class interiors, where they do exist, are more directly related to everyday life – photographs of the family, mementoes of holidays, prizes – and they remain stable in composition over relatively long periods of time.

The relationship of specific activities to rooms

Where collections of objects are displayed in the interior of a working-class house, it is more than likely that they will be associated with a specific room – the front parlour. The ubiquity of this special space in traditional working-class homes is, perhaps, an indication of an even more funda-mental difference between the two space codes, indeed it is one which was used by Victorian writers to define the respectable artisan as opposed to the degenerate idler.[17]

Many of these older houses are used for multiple occupancy. Quite often, a daughter and her husband live for a period of time after their mar-riage with the older parents.

> Their houses hardly ever contain more than two or three bedrooms, and they are sometimes so small that as one woman put it 'when one breathes out, the other has to breathe in'. The parents clearly have not got room, in houses of this kind, for four married children as well as for their husbands and wives. One married child is, as a rule, the most they can accommodate.[18]

Frequently, working-class families live in severely overcrowded condi-tions, but are likely to be replaced by one middle-class family with fewer children. The same amount of space is used in the transformed house to accommodate fewer people. Nonetheless, in the untransformed home there is likely to be one special room, the front room on the ground floor facing the street, which does not form part of the everyday living accommodation. Although the parents 'have not got room' for married children, they still reserve a separate space for all the symbolic equipment of the household. Here is kept the best furniture, piano, family photo-graphs, plaster ducks and company clock. This room is hardly ever used. It is only opened on formal and ceremonial occasions, to entertain the vicar or to lay out the dead. In other words, the parlour is categorically impor-tant, almost amounting to a sacred place which contrasts sharply with the more profane use of the remainder of the accommodation, which is the domain of family and close friends – if 'kith' are met in the street, and 'kin' are found in the living room, then 'strangers and outsiders' are received into the parlour.

Of all the spaces in the Victorian working-class home, the parlour is perhaps that for which the most documentary evidence is available,

simply because the ethnographer was shown into the best room and rarely
gained access to the remainder of the accommodation. The sort of possessions which Willmott and Young noted a century later in Bethnal Green,
also featured prominently in early accounts of the parlour. The walls
occasionally were papered, there was a carpet, linoleum or at least a
hearthrug on the floor, the mantleshelf over the black-leaded grate was
adorned with brass ornaments, tumblers, glasses, commemorative plates,
the best tea service or a looking-glass, and there were engravings, litho-
graphs, prints or samplers of needlework on the walls. The furniture was
solid, if old-fashioned, 'indicative of taste, elegance and commendable
self-respect'. In short, it was a 'state room', used only occasionally for
entertaining or to celebrate important life career events, and as such 'not
the focus of family life but the ideal, which proclaimed to the world
through its lace curtained window and revealed objects (then, as now, a
plant in a china pot) the cult of respectability'.[19] In the latter half of the
nineteenth century, seven out of ten dwellings possessed such a space.
Old customs die hard, and most respectable working-class households in
post-war Britain still retain a front parlour as a prominent feature of the
domestic interior.

However, members of the new middle-class family do not have a 'state
room'. In fact, no space is supposed to be particularly significant in their
scheme of things. The house is, in some sense, homogenised and neutral-
ised, as Bradbury describes in this extract from *The History Man*.

> After a while, Howard leaves the kitchen and begins to go around the
> house. He is a solemn party-giver, the creator of serious social theatre.
> Now he goes about, putting out ashtrays and dishes, cushions and
> chairs. He moves furniture to produce good conversation areas, open
> significant action spaces, create barriers of privacy. . . . Now he goes
> upstairs, to pull beds against the walls, adjust lights, shade shades, pull
> blinds, open doors. It is an important rule to have as little forbidden
> ground as possible, to make the house itself a total stage. And so he
> designs it, retaining only a few tiny areas of sanctity: he blocks with
> chairs the short corridor that leads to the children's room, and the steps
> that lead down to their basement study. Everywhere else the code is
> one of possibility, not denial. Chairs and cushions and beds suggest
> multiple forms of companionship. Thresholds are abolished: room
> leads into room . . . the aim is to let the party happen rather than to

make it happen, so that what takes place occurs apparently without
any hostly intervention, or rather with the intervention of that higher
sociological host who governs the transactions of human encounter.[20]

One of the basic assumptions of the decategorising of space in the new
middle-class home is that activities are unlinked from spaces, and even
from positions in the house – 'if there's a better view from the upstairs
window, why not live up there and enjoy it, and sleep downstairs?'[21]
Bedrooms double as a study, den, workshop or playroom, to be used
during the day and not just at night for sleeping. The garden is treated
in the transformed house as part of the homogenised space, an outdoor
version of the flexible living-space, to be taken advantage of in good
weather.

In the working-class household, space is more carefully mapped onto
the social events which can take place there. Bedrooms are upstairs, and
are used only at night or in cases of dire illness; everyday living is limited
to the back, downstairs room – children battle against the noise of the television to do their homework – whilst the parlour is used only on social
occasions and perhaps on a Sunday. The relative position of rooms is an
important 'constant' in the traditional working-class code.

Along with the strong imposition of categories and relationships in a
working-class house, there is strong insulation of rooms from each other.
Doors are kept shut for most of the time, particularly the parlour door.
Cupboards and the staircase frequently isolate the parlour even more
firmly from the back room. It is not even possible to see into the interior of
the front room from the street. Those objects which are most highly prized
are precisely those which are least seen, yet it would be perfectly possible
to manifest the interior of the parlour to the street. On the other hand, the
new middle classes do not just manifest special objects, but rather their
everyday lifestyle is also put on display. It is possible to look into the house
and see them eating their breakfast, playing with the children or watching
television.

In the traditional working-class example, there appears to be a great
deal of order in space: order which is nonetheless hidden away. In the case
of the new middle-class household, there is very little order inherent in the
layout and decoration of rooms, but this lack of order is put on view. It is
indeed paradoxical that the members of one sub-culture should show off
their untidy lives, whilst the others precisely reproduce the same spatial

and social relationships, but at the same time hide their conformity from others.

Eating behaviour

Members of the traditional working classes rarely invite people, kin excepted, into their houses. Willmott and Young stress that their study of social encounters refers mainly to what happens outside the home: 'Most people meet their acquaintances in the street, at the market, at the pub, or at work. They do not usually invite them into their own houses. This attitude of exclusiveness in the home runs alongside an attitude of friendliness to people living in the same street'.[22] More specifically, people do not visit each other at mealtimes. This is a family occasion: 'people live together and eat together – they are considered part of the same household'.[23] However, for members of a traditional working-class household, the term 'family' takes on a different significance to the more usual meaning of 'nuclear family'. A person's family, especially if that person is a woman, will include female relatives living in the nearby streets and a few close women friends who, though unrelated, are treated as kin. During the day, women visit each other's houses and take a cup of tea, and maybe share lunch together – the households are temporarily 'merged'. Children eat with female relatives in the same way, sometimes returning home only to sleep. Non-kin are excluded from this easy-going informality. Entertainment, especially by men, takes place outside the home, at the local pub.

In the new middle-class house, eating takes on a different significance. It is the one occasion when friends are invited into the home. People are asked to dinner, and at such an occasion it is considered important to 'put on a show'. Entertaining and party-giving are one of the primary means of social integration within this social stratum. In the transformed house, space or spaces are assigned as eating areas – whether room is found in the kitchen, in a living room or work area, at a 'bar' or on the floor, in a formal dining room, indoors or in the garden, or in any combination of these possibilities, is largely an individual choice, but the new middle-class code invariably includes at least one 'relaxed place where good food and conversation can be enjoyed by guests and host alike'.[24] Part of the ritual of the meal may involve moving from space to space as the evening progresses.

'Potential' and 'effective' environments

People make these houses their own in systematically different ways. They convert the 'potential' environment of the dwelling into an 'effective' environment, or habitat.[25] All these kinds of individual behaviour are not the product of universal organising principles. They cannot be, because they appear to be fundamentally different ways of organising the same basic house, linked by a system of unwritten rules for transforming one set of spatial behaviours into the other. So far, these organising principles have been described in terms of the properties of the evidence for their existence as revealed through spatial behaviour. It is possible to order this evidence at a rather more abstract level – half way between pure description and fully abstract thought – to show the dimensions underlying the two sets of manifested behaviours (see figure 4.2). Whilst this diagrammatic way of presenting the evidence is rudimentary, it is perhaps a more convenient way of thinking about the properties of space than is offered by the appeal to basic needs. The diagrams are made for the two sub-cultural groupings, the new middle class (NMC) and the traditional working class (TWC) out of three pairs of spatial variables: (i) visibility/permeability, (ii) insulation/sequencing and (iii) categoric differentiation/relative position, and out of two kinds of spatial relation: (i) within the domestic interior and (ii) between the interior and the exterior of the home.

Visibility/permeability

Visibility refers to whether or not the interior of the dwelling can be seen from the street, or to whether it is possible to see clearly from one part of the domestic interior into another. A plus score means that it is possible to see into the interior or from room to room, and a minus score that the interior is concealed. Visibility is about whether space is used to manifest objects and behaviours or to conceal them. It tells us about the relative transparency or opacity of the domestic setting, a highly 'architectural' characteristic. This variable is set against *permeability*, which refers to the amount of control exercised over the way in which it is possible to move from one space to another. If doors are kept shut or locked, then permeability is minus. If openings are left between rooms, or the door is left ajar or 'on the latch' so that people may enter freely, then permeability

Figure 4.2
Dimensions of the two domestic space codes

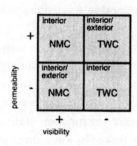

a. visibility-permeability

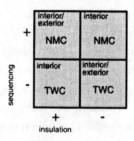

b. insulation-sequencing

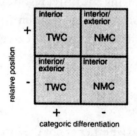

c. categoric differentiation-relative position

has a plus score. It is worth noting that the property of visibility is different to and independent from that of permeability. Visibility is immediate and unmediated by rules, but permeability depends on both spatial properties and the presence or absence of rules governing behaviour, which may be different according to the categories of people involved (see figure 4.2a).

For the *interior* relation, the new middle-class code scores a plus on both visibility and permeability. Rooms are combined by 'knocking through' so that the interior becomes a continuum of space in which it is possible to observe everything that is going on. It is possible to 'flow' freely from one space to the next, since spaces are knit together into new room sets, often between floors. For the *interior/exterior* relation, the new middle-class code scores a plus on visibility, the interior is boldly manifested to the street, but a minus on permeability, it is necessary to pass through an elaborate door which is kept locked.

Conversely, for the *interior* relation, the traditional working-class code scores a minus on both visibility and permeability. Both are strongly controlled. The interior is made up of separate rooms, the doors of which are kept closed and, in order to pass from one space to another, it is necessary to go out of one room, into a transition space, the hallway, and then into the adjacent room. Rooms are knit together not by spaces but by passages. However, for the *interior/exterior* relation, the working-class code scores high on permeability; the door is left on the latch or ajar, but minus on visibility; net curtains shield the exterior from the street.

Insulation/sequencing

The second pair of variables sets insulation against sequencing (see figure 4.2b). By *insulation* is meant the degree of discontinuity, that is, the strength of the boundary, between rooms. Where insulation is plus, rooms may be separated by a partition, or perhaps face each other across an intervening space. Cupboards or stores may be used to add mass and to emphasise the boundary wall. Where insulation is minus, spaces are adjacent without any intervening barriers, perhaps delineated by a railing or line of columns, a change of floor level or ceiling height, or even by differences in surface appearance. *Sequencing* refers to the way in which spaces are connected together into chains, frequently into rings so that it is eventually possible to return to the point of origin by another way, but also into dead ends so that it is not possible to go out at the far end, in which case the only course of action is to retrace the route back to its starting point. Where sequencing is plus, it is always necessary to go through one space to reach another, and minus sequencing means that spaces are one cell deep from a central circulation space.

For the new middle-class code, both insulation and sequencing are high for the *interior/exterior* relation. The house is frequently insulated from the street by a well at the front, set about with railings and connected only by a narrow path and flight of front steps – the change in level increases insulation. (Paradoxically strong insulation is accompanied by strong visibility.) Where this cannot be achieved, the area in front of the entrance is delineated by a change of surface, and elaborated with plants set in pots to deepen the threshold. Sequencing is likewise plus. It is necessary to go through a series of barriers and transition spaces to gain entry from the exterior to the interior of the home – there is no 'popping round the back' in this code, even for close relatives. For the *interior* relation, the new middle-class code is minus on insulation, no barriers at all, but plus on sequencing. When the partition between the two major living rooms is taken out, it is normal to lock one of the doors and to turn the pair of linked spaces into an unipermeable sequence. Frequently spaces are connected together into deep rings made within and between floors. These are not trivial rings. Many key spaces participate in several rings, each of which leads round a large sequence of spaces before returning to the point of origin. It is this property which is exploited when visitors are entertained within the family home, but it also introduces a measure of flexibility and choice into everyday life.

In the traditional working-class code, however, the *interior* relation scores a minus on sequencing; spaces are not knit together into deep internal rings or dead ends, but form a simple star on each floor centred on the hallway and landing. Insulation within the working-class interior has a plus score. Walls, boundaries, halls and passages are preserved, and the doors leading off them are kept closed. On the *interior/exterior* relation, the traditional working-class code is minus on insulation and on sequencing. The front door normally opens directly onto the street without any intervening spaces. Where these do occur, the wall at the front may be broken down. Likewise, the back door opens directly into a (sometimes shared) yard.

Categoric differentiation/relative position

The final pair of variables deals with categoric differentiation and relative position, aspects of spatial organisation which are not so much morphological – to do with the internal logic of the physical arrangement – as microcosm effects – to do with the way in which spaces acquire particular social identities (see figure 4.2c). *Categoric differentiation* refers to the extent to which particular functions are assigned unambiguously to specific spaces within the home. A plus means that spaces are associated with particular activities and a minus means that space is homogenised and seen as a neutral container for any and every activity. Rooms are multi-functional. *Relative position* deals with the way in which spaces are related to each other and to the outside world through a conceptual scheme based on the cardinal points, or some such scheme of reference. A plus score means that great emphasis is placed upon aspect and orientation of the dwelling, or on the way in which rooms fit together within the home. A minus score means that no specific relations are required to hold within room arrangements or in the orientation of the dwelling.

For the traditional working-class code, categoric differentiation and relative position are both plus in the *interior* of the dwelling. The positions up/down, front/back are important, and linked to the categories night/day, sacred/profane respectively. As a result, there is a tendency for interiors to resemble each other closely, with little individual deviation. The order which exists in any particular house is exogenous, that is, imposed from the outside by tradition, custom and usage, rather than arising out of the preferences of particular occupants. Conversely, both variables are of low importance in the new middle-class *interior*. All spaces are homogenised and position is relatively unimportant. The result of this lowered intensity of space categories is to turn the inside living area into an individual expression of preferences in lifestyle – the order is endogenous, it arises from what particular occupants do.

On the *interior/exterior* relation, however, the new middle-class code is plus on relative position and minus on categoric differentiation. Whilst the space outside is not assigned but appropriated in the same way as the indoor living areas, relative position in the form of location, aspect and orientation is seen to be of great importance. The house is orientated to the street, on the one hand, and the garden, on the other (an east/west position is preferable). The 'ideal' house has a panoramic view over some section of its neighbourhood. Finally, in the new middle-class code, location is all-important, spelling out the social difference between being 'at the frontier' and 'in terra incognita'. Conversely, relative position is minus in the case of the *interior/exterior* relation in traditional working-class culture (it is important only for internal relations). What goes on outside the dwelling is all profane everyday activity. It is of no significance whether the car is repaired in the street in front of the house or in the back yard. 'Prospect' and 'area' are not a part of working-class vocabulary. What is valued is the maintenance of close kinship and friendship ties, and it is these considerations which feature largely in the selection of a home. Nevertheless, categoric differentiation is plus with respect to the relation of the house to the street – the interior is reserved for private family activity and the street for public social encounter.

Integration/segregation

Quantitative analysis of the space configurations adds an intriguing layer of complexity to the hitherto more sociological comparison (see figure 4.3). In the traditional working-class home, the three principal spaces on the ground floor have quite markedly different integration values. The space which is invariably the most segregated is the parlour, in spite of this room's being next to the front door and at the front of the house. The scullery kitchen has a value in the middle of the range, whilst the living room is the most integrated activity space of all. The main integrators of the home, however, are the transitions between rooms – lobbies, halls and stairs – rather than the spaces where domestic activity actually takes place. The exterior is slightly more integrated than the average for all the spaces in the dwelling; the back yard is a little to the segregated side of the mean. The most segregated parts of the domestic interior are the bedrooms and the toilet.

Despite the fact that the two space codes reverse just about every aspect of domestic life, the integration order of the principal living functions survives the transformation into a new middle-class home, and the reassignment of activities to spaces. New middle-class homes do not have a parlour, but a part of the living room usually doubles as a 'best' room, in the sense of being a reception area into which visitors are shown. Surprisingly, this is considerably more segregated than the remainder of the living area, even though the two spaces appear to 'flow' into one another with no perceptible boundary. The integration value of the kitchen lies between the two, in spite of the complete alteration of the permeability relations which hold among these spaces. Bedrooms and bathrooms remain strongly segregated.

As the mean integration values for the four complexes shows, almost all the values in the transformed houses are considerably more integrated

Figure 4.3
Justified graphs for types **a** and **b** before
and after transformation

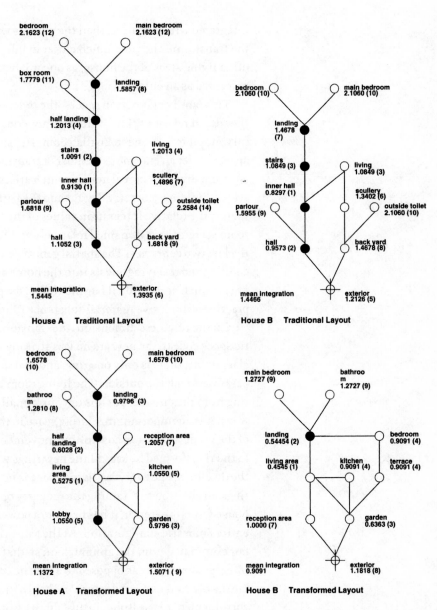

than before. However, there is one striking exception of a function which
actually increases in segregation against the general trend, and that is the
exterior. This space goes from being one of the most integrated spaces of all
to one of the most segregated. The change is therefore more marked than it
might appear to be at first sight, especially as the new house is much more

integrated with its garden than the old was with its yard, for the garden of
the transformed home is much closer in integration value to those for the
other living areas of the house, as one might expect for a space which is
perceived as an outside room.

This family of function spaces, the order of their integration values and
the spatial relations those values imply, constitute an immensely powerful genotypical theme in English domestic space organisation and re-
appear under an enormous number of transformations. Underlying the
apparent diversity of real houses which arises from such factors as market
sector, building geometry, layout and the pattern of permeability between
rooms, the relative integration values of the living room, kitchen and 'best'
room seem to have remained relatively stable in English houses for at least
the last two centuries. The spatial genotype which relates everyday living,
cooking and receiving guests into the home seems to provide a sociogram,
not so much of individual families but of deeply ingrained and enduring
practices which give material substance to an entire social system.

On the ringiness dimension, the transformations from the old domestic space code to the new are no less striking. In the traditional working-
class home, there is only one ring, and that is not internal to the house but
passes through the outside. The living room is the deepest space on this
ring from the outside, but it is only minimally connected – that is, two
ways. It is an important mediating space in the interior/exterior relations
of the home, but not in controlling movement about the domestic interior.
In the transformed house, all the new rings which are added are internal to
the dwelling. The everyday living space is now the hub of a set of internal
rings. In addition to retaining the property of controlling the relation of the
house with its exterior, it has become a powerful organising space for the
entire domestic configuration. At the same time, transitions have been all
but eliminated from the ground floor, so that the house is now a *space-
integrated* complex as opposed to a *transition-integrated* complex; a
'nexus of interconnected rooms' rather than a 'compartmentalised
corridor plan' to use Robin Evans' distinction.[26]

Collection and integration codes

The two domestic space codes appear to operate by means of symmetries
and inversions on a basic field of possibilities. However, they are not

equivalent ways of ordering space, since they appear to fit into the underlying configurational model in different ways. In the traditional working-
class code, spaces are collected together, but each participant in the
collection retains a strong identity, which is clearly distinguished from all
others. The order which exists in the collection is exogenous. The traditional working-class code appears to be a form of *collection code*.[27] In the
new middle-class example, spaces are not simply collected together but
are subordinated to a new *relational* idea, 'style', which depends largely
on an individual's conception of what the good spatial life should be.
There is no 'right way' of doing things: 'the most important thing about
your house is that it should be yours, and not a kit picked up lock, stock
and barrel from a book, magazine or designer'.[28] In this sense, the code is
analogous to what Bernstein calls an *integration code*.[29] If Bernstein is
correct in his view that collection codes tend to transmit the existing
social order and that integration codes transform existing knowledge into
new knowledge, it is surely no accident that the main protagonists of the
new middle-class code are those very people who are engaged in capturing, externalising and representing society to itself.

Ultimately, the two codes may even be bound up with the way in
which the two class fragments relate to the structures of power and
authority within society, for collection codes tend to be associated with
forms of *positional power*, where the social actors derive their authority
mainly from their social role rather than from their individual competen-
cies. Integration codes, on the other hand, are associated more with forms
of *personal power* that are legitimised by practical performance and enactment. In a family situation, decision-making in a positional family is
invested in people's formal statuses as a father, mother, grandparent, child,
whilst, in a person-orientated family, decisions and judgements are associated with the psychological and social qualities of the individuals
involved.[30]

In the traditional working class home, space can be interpreted as supporting positional social roles by building them into the bricks and mortar,
thus rendering them invisible. This might at first sight appear somewhat
repressive, since phenomena which are hidden are arguably difficult to
surmount or even to raise to the level of conscious thought, but if we consider how power manifests itself in the transformed domestic space code,
we might begin to suspect that here too the physical milieu may provide a
setting in which insidious but penetrating and intrusive forms of social

control are able to flourish. In the former case the social pressures embodied in organised space seem to support conformity to social norms and values, whereas in the absence of rooms, walls and doors, the whole of the integrated, open-plan interior potentially can be dominated by the most powerful personality in the household. Paradoxically, the compartmentalised corridor planning of the traditional family home may be intrinsically no more constraining for its occupants than the nexus of connected rooms.

Nurture not nature

If an analysis of domestic space organisation takes as its starting point some concept of 'basic human needs' it is likely that these needs will prove to be so basic and otiose – like the need for shelter from a hostile environment – so as not to yield useful information. An analogy may be made here with eating. Of course man needs to eat, in order to ensure his *biological* survival, but this is not what makes the study of human eating habits interesting. What is of significance is how eating behaviour is made part of that knowledge which is necessary to being a member of a *society*, through rules restricting diet, governing the preparation of food and timing of meals, and prescribing the customary forms of etiquette and 'table manners'. All this information is shared and taken-for-granted by the members of a society or sub-culture, so that it appears entirely natural to behave in this way.

This analogy suggests that it is society and social behaviour which is reproduced in everyday life, and it is not the case that society is made up of an aggregate of individual behaviours. The order which exists in the interior of the dwelling and the way in which that interior is related to the exterior is predominantly an aspect of social relations. Furthermore, there may be fundamental differences within as well as between societies in the way this is done. Indeed, the contrasts and inversions within patterns of space and behaviour in a single society may be far more pervasive than the differences between societies which are revealed by cross-cultural comparisons, which can disclose rather striking genotypical similarities between superficially dissimilar cultures.

This chapter has examined the order which exists in two polar subcultures, the traditional working classes and the new middle classes. These polar types do not exhaust the possibilities, although they perhaps indicate the nature of the 'game'. Traditional middle-class families and new, upwardly mobile working-class 'spiralists' may choose to live in quite other ways which are beyond the scope of this chapter, though we may gain some insights as to how these social groupings give a spatial form to their aspirations and values in the next chapter. More awareness of these strong cultural factors in shaping domestic space would seem to be required if design guidance is not, unwittingly, to obliterate the richness and diversity of social practice in favour of a spurious biological uniformity.

Notes

1 Serge Chermayeff and Christopher Alexander, *Community and Privacy* (Harmondsworth: Penguin, 1963), Christopher Alexander, *A Pattern Language* (Oxford University Press, 1978) and Oscar Newman *Defensible Space* (London: Architectural Press, 1972).

2 S.E. Rasmussen, *London the Unique City* (Harmondsworth: Penguin, 1934), p. 220.

3 Peter Willmott and Michael Young, *Family and Kinship in East London* (Harmondsworth: Penguin, 1957), pp.37–8.

4 John Burnett, *A Social History of Housing* (Newton Abbot: David and Charles, 1978), p. 158.

5 Johnathan Raban, *Soft City* (London: Fontana/Collins, 1974), p. 85.

6 Ibid., p. 85.

7 Ibid, p. 87.

8 Terence Conran, *The House Book* (London: Mitchell Beazley, 1976), p. 50.

9 David Rubenstein, *Victorian Homes* (Newton Abbot: David and Charles, 1974), p. 118.

10 Raban, *Soft City*, p. 109.

11 Willmott and Young, *Family and Kinship in East London*, p. 38.

12 Chermayeff and Alexander, *Community and Privacy*, p. 167.

13 Malcolm Bradbury, *The History Man* (London: Arrow Books, 1975), pp. 183–4.

14 Conran, *The House Book*, p. 334.

15 Ibid., p. 338.

16 Basil Bernstein, *Class, Codes and Control* (London: Routledge and Kegan Paul, 1975), p. 141.

17 Rubenstein, *Victorian Homes*, p. 115.

18 Willmott and Young, *Family and Kinship in East London*, p. 33.

19 Burnett, *A Social History of Housing*, p. 77.

20 Bradbury, *The History Man*, p. 71.

21 Conran, *The House Book*, p. 44.

22 Willmott and Young, *Family and Kinship in East London*, p. 108

23 Ibid., p. 47

24 Conran, *The House Book*, p. 213.

25 Herbert Gans, *People and Plans* (New York: Basic Books, 1968), pp. 4–11.

26 Robin Evans, *Translations from Drawing to Building and Other Essays* (London: Architectural Association Press, 1997), pp. 55–91.

27 Bernstein, *Class Codes and Control*, p. 233.

28 Conran, *The House Book*, p. 9.

29 Bernstein, *Class Codes and Control*, p. 235.

30 Ibid., pp. 176–92.

Chapter five

Shaping the taste of middle England

Summary

At its inception, Milton Keynes recruited the best young architects to plan and design its housing, with the explicit intention of offering all the city's inhabitants the chance of a better standard of living. This was to be achieved through a high quality and well-designed environment, for the vision of the policy makers and town planners was to bring the benefits of architecture to everyone who lived there. Twenty-five years on, in the commercially dominated housing market, only two out of thirty developers claim that their houses are 'architect-designed'. Whilst architects and designers advocate flexible, open and well-connected domestic interiors, the houses in Milton Keynes are laid out in a much more compartmentalised and segregative manner, at every level of the market. To the extent that the speculative housing market can be viewed as an expression of popular taste, the domestic space of Milton Keynes suggests that the lifestyles to which ordinary people aspire have little in common with the concepts which architects use when they theorise about the relation between house form and family life.

From housing the masses to homes for the managers

The *raison d'être* for Milton Keynes is its housing. Milton Keynes was formally designated as a new town in January 1967, and building began on site in 1970. The new town was originally conceived of as a place to house a population of one quarter of a million. Many of the city's new residents were to be drawn from among London's clerical and manual workers and, in offering them a chance to escape from what were portrayed at the time as overcrowded and insalubrious Inner London neighbourhoods, opportunity and freedom of choice were placed at the top of the housing agenda. The site allocated to the new town was a 'huge pocket handkerchief' covering about forty square miles of the undulating North Buckinghamshire landscape, about fifty miles to the north of London. The intention from the outset was to create a low-density city whose inhabitants would not need to 'live like rabbits'.

In sheer numerical terms Milton Keynes is a housing success story. The target for new homes was set at two thousand five hundred a year in the Development Plan and throughout the 1970s the town's Development Corporation was building about two thousand houses a year in public ownership. This was the dominant form of housing in the new city, and only a small minority of homes were built by speculative house builders for sale to private clients. The second decade, however, saw a marked change in government housing policy from one which was broadly in favour of subsidised social housing to one which believed that housing provision should be dictated by market forces. Government subsidies continued to be given to home owners through tax relief on people's mortgages, and special incentives were introduced in order to widen home ownership by encouraging people on low incomes to move out of the rented sector and to invest in a home of their own. Cuts in public spending ensued, precipitating a sell-off of the housing stock in public ownership. A new form of shared-ownership, the 'housing association' in which groups of tenants co-operated to finance homes for private rental, began to attract government assistance.

The effects of government policy on the housing stock in Milton Keynes were immediate and pronounced. Public sector house building petered out during the 1980s, whilst in the same period owner-occupation rose from about fifteen thousand to nearly forty thousand homes. Private developers took over smoothly from the public housing sector and, despite a recession in the British economy in the late 1980s, they were able to maintain housing completions at about a thousand per year. By the beginning of the 1990s the proportion of the total housing stock in the Milton Keynes development area was 39,343 (69%) in private ownership, 3,076 (5%) in housing association shared-ownership and 14,953 (26%) in public sector ownership.

New home completions for the first year of the 1990s reveal that nearly one thousand new homes were built for owner-occupation, almost three hundred for private housing association rental, whilst no new homes at all were built in the public rented sector. The Development Corporation was formally wound up in 1992, but there is still a considerable amount of work to be done and house building is set to continue throughout the 1990s. The town is planned to have in excess of eighty thousand dwellings on completion, and it is likely that all of the homes yet to be built will be in private ownership. Approximately 1% of all new homes in the country have been built here in recent years.

It was always hoped that significant numbers of professionals and managers would be attracted to the new town. The planners acknowledged that incomers to the town would most likely be from a working-class and lower-middle-class background but, at the time that the master plan was conceived, living standards generally were forecast to rise. Moreover, it was hoped that the town would appeal particularly to people who aspired to better themselves by joining the ranks of the middle classes. In the early days, professional and managerial workers tended to seek out older properties in the surrounding villages and small towns.

However, the town now seems to have overcome the stigmatisation of being a brash, new environment. In recent years the houses which have been built for sale have included a greater proportion of more expensive properties, and there is an increasing emphasis on individually designed houses for professionals, managers and business executives. If we compare the proportion of dwellings in each of the council tax bands for the whole of England, produced by the Department for the Environment in May 1991, based on the assessed capital value of the property, with the proportion of dwellings in Milton Keynes falling within each band (see figure 5.1) then we can discover that the city is over-represented in the middle, and under-represented at the extremes.

The last figure, which shows the proportion of the sample of 120 house types surveyed here which falls within each tax band, indicates that the

Figure 5.1
Distribution of tax bands in Milton
Keynes compared with the national
averages and the proportion of houses
within the overall sample

Tax Band	Value	National	Milton Keynes	Sample
Band A	£40,000	19%	5%	4%
Band B	£52,000	16%	15%	16%
Band C	£68,000	20%	24%	23%
Band D	£88,000	17%	22%	13%
Band E	£120,000	13%	23%	25%
Band F	£160,000	8%	6%	10%
Band G	£160,000+	7%	4%	9%

sample on which this research is based is also broadly representative of all bands except D, which is under-represented. The upper ranges are over-represented, suggesting that in Milton Keynes today there is an up-market trend in the newest houses built for sale. Set against national trends, the current population of about one hundred and sixty thousand is solidly middle of the road and middle class.

The city is also more diverse in composition than the planners could have foreseen at its inception. Longevity, divorce, a rise in the numbers of young single people and one-parent families, the declining birth rate, the smaller size of families and shifts in household composition have joined forces to produce a situation where, to meet the present and future needs of its residents, the city's housing stock must offer balance and variety. 'Starter homes' for childless couples have widened the base of the housing pyramid, whilst at the top of the market developers are building homes with an annexe for the extended or expanded household. It is now standard practice for a house builder to include at least some dwellings which will accommodate grandparents, unmarried adult children or even a resident home-help. Compared with the public sector, privatisation apparently offers more choice not less, at least for those people who have the resources to buy at all.

Architectural antecedents

Early Development Corporation housing was explicitly dedicated to exploring new ways of living appropriate to the city of tomorrow and, during the 1970s, the 'young turks' of British architecture including Norman Foster, Richard Rogers, Edward Cullinan, Jeremy Dixon, Richard MacCormac, Peter Phippen and Ralph Erskine, to name but a few, were recruited to the city to enhance its architectural character through good design in housing. At the time, good design meant 'international style' and housing meant 'social housing'. The design and layout of the space between dwellings was, if anything, more important than the organisation of the domestic interior. A neighbourhood was held to be successful if it visually shaped the relation between dwellings and street to reflect the needs of community and privacy.

At the same time, architects were exploring the potential of open-plan living, functional flexibility and interchangeability to widen the lifestyle choices on offer to council tenants. Split-level plans and *piano nobile* living produced a variety of interesting sections, and in its first decade Milton Keynes Development Corporation produced some of Britain's most innovative – and some would argue most problematic – housing. Exhibition layouts like Homeworld and Energy World have ensured that Milton Keynes' reputation as a sponsor of experimental architecture has survived the decline in public housing.

Taken at face value, it would seem that the reputation which Milton Keynes enjoys for offering an almost unlimited choice of homes and a wide variety of lifestyle opportunities is well-deserved. The 1992 directory of housing for sale in the city, published by Milton Keynes Development Corporation's Homefinder Centre, contains sixty-six entries, exclusive of retirement homes. If we also exclude developments which are at inception, between phases of release onto the housing market or are substantially complete, the number of developments which are actively being promoted by sales offices and show homes in the development area is thirty schemes by twenty-two separate house builders. This represents some 2400 houses in 226 house types, of which 120 are currently available for private purchase and have a show home which can be visited. This last group, which covers all sectors of the market from bedsitters and one-bedroom starter homes to five-bedroom executive houses, forms the basis of the account which follows.

Individuality, and the image of home

Observation of housing development sites quickly establishes that most visitors to show houses spend only a few minutes in each home, and are rarely observed standing outside discussing the architecture. People rely heavily on the sales brochure to 'jog their memory' about the appearance of houses, especially in the initial stages of selection. To assist their recall, all brochures feature the principal elevation of each house type. A manifest variety of decorative and stylistic features is exhibited in the thirty brochures which illustrate homes on sale across the town today. None look modern and few are memorable, but the overwhelming impression is that developers try hard to counter the accusation that their houses all look the same.

However it can be argued that, in some senses at least, individuality is no more than skin deep. All 120 house types have pitched and tiled roofs, and are built predominantly in brick, with accented string courses, cills and lintels. All but eight have an open porch with a pitched and tiled roof to mark the entrance, and 30% of the houses have a bay window to the principal living room on the ground floor. Although bay windows are found in all price brackets, they tend to be associated with more expensive homes. In 1992, the average price of houses with a bay is £110,000, whilst the average price of those without is £83,000. Whilst their use in larger houses seems to be mainly for dramatic effect and room dimensions in the accompanying brochures are quoted exclusive of the bay window, their use in small houses seems to follow economic logic, not aesthetic concerns. Bay windows make small houses seem larger, and enhance the dimensions of the rooms which nearly always include the depth of the bay.

Chimneys are even more firmly associated with 'up-market', more expensive and ostensibly more desirable properties, even though all the houses in the sample are equipped with central heating. In the 28% of homes which have a hearth, the average property price is £140,000 against £72,000 for those without. Nearly half the houses in the sample have a symmetrical facade, but unlike other features, symmetry is favoured by 'down-market', lower status properties. The average price of dwellings with a symmetrical facade is £60,000, while those without average £117,000. Architects tend to read symbolic meanings into these features, but their inclusion by speculators seems financially driven. The precise relationship between the additional capital costs of these details and the 'added value' which is deemed to accrue to the property in terms of its subsequent sale price remains unclear but, whatever the origin of elements within the design vocabulary, their inclusion does seem to constitute a form of conspicuous consumption. The aesthetic and emblematic significance which architectural critics and historians often read into the shaping and massing of the principal volumes and facades of the house and the architectural detailing of the building envelope may, in popular culture, be secondary to their value as a status-symbol.

The not-so-open plan

Architects tend to explore space in shaping their designs, and their houses frequently propose novel living patterns. Developers seem to favour more conventional living arrangements. Despite the modernity of the town, most designs would be equally appropriate to a suburban development almost anywhere in the country. There is a clear bias in the sample towards two-storey houses with a 'proper' upstairs, and a marked prefer-ence for detached houses. Of the 120 house types, two are flats, two are bungalows, there are two pairs of single-aspect houses placed back-to-back, three maisonettes, nine terraced houses, four types are found in both terraced and semi-detached versions, twenty-seven are semi-detached houses, there are six link-detached houses and sixty-five are detached houses. A complete absence of large town houses in the sample already makes the housing profile in Milton Keynes unlike that found in most towns of a comparable size. As might be expected, price and plot size rise steadily with the degree of non-contiguity, but this simple relation also disguises a more complex interaction which seems to take place between the purchase price and the plot size, gross floor area and number of habit-able rooms of houses within the sample as a whole.

Most contemporary English households begin to search for a suitable new home by reference to the number of bedrooms they require to ensure the perceived, culturally given decencies between parents and children, and among children of different ages and genders. The information con-tained in the brochures and show houses therefore uses this as the main criterion to classify and categorise the types of new homes which are offered for sale. However, the price which speculative builders ask is only loosely related to bedroom provision particularly in the upper price ranges, with an overall correlation of 0.759 between price and bedroom provision for the sample of one hundred and twenty house types. The total number of separately identifiable spaces in the home gives a more reliable guide to the asking price, with a correlation of 0.884, but the variables which predict price most accurately, with a correlation of 0.914 and 0.926

respectively, are the total area and total number of the principal ground floor living rooms. The purchase price of a Milton Keynes property is clearly related to its size, but in the form of separate rooms not as metric area. The extra rooms in more expensive houses are not just more bedrooms, but rooms for activities which occur within the waking hours of family life. The dominant domestic space culture of the city is one in which the interior is compartmentalised into separate rooms, rather than knit together into open-plan living arrangements. Houses which organise the interior in this way tend to attract a higher price than equivalent examples which have fewer but larger rooms.

What is less obvious, is the extent to which space is set aside for circulation in even the smallest homes. An ordinary Milton Keynes house has its complement of entry, hall, stairs and landing, but the larger ones have up to nine of these transitions between rooms, which serve to separate functions more thoroughly than the mere provision of walls and doors. For every space in the house which is intended to be occupied and used, there is on average 1.462 transitions which are provided just for people to circulate through. In the speculative houses of Milton Keynes etiquette demands where money allows, that circulation be separated from rooms and groups of rooms be separated from each other by chicaned halls and landings, so that small houses appear large and large ones labyrinthine.

The sample of eleven one-bedroom house types is made up of two flats, two bungalows, three semi-detached houses and four terraced houses. Even the smallest starter homes for single people and married couples with no children living at home provide adequate space for living, eating, cooking, washing and sleeping, allowing between twenty square metres and twenty five square metres per person. Only one manages to separate all five functions whilst, at the other extreme, the sample contains one 'bedsitter' where most of the functions take place in a single multi-purpose space. Space is at a premium, and the living room is used for circulation to the kitchen (eight cases), to the upstairs (four cases) or to an inner hall (three cases). Yet despite this, only three houses favour an open-plan arrangement on the ground floor. Even starter homes have porches, but a separate, internal entrance lobby is also the norm. Entering directly into the living room is unpopular, and occurs only once.

If we compare the plans of these small dwellings to their access graphs from the front door, then the graphs reveal clear stereotypes which are difficult to discern from the brochures. There are only two ways of planning these basic starter homes. The dominant plan, with seven examples, is a sequence, with an integrating living/dining room on the main circulation route leading from the front porch to the bedroom, and a small kitchen and bathroom branching one step deeper away from the main tree (see figure 5.2a). The alternative, with four examples, branches immediately on entry into two separate sequences, for living downstairs and sleeping upstairs (see figure 5.2b).

At two bedrooms, a preference for detached, two-storey dwellings shows clearly, and the sample of twenty-two two-bedroom house types is made up of three maisonettes, two terraced houses, two pairs of single-aspect houses placed back-to-back, four houses available in both terraced and semi-detached versions, ten semi-detached houses and one detached house. There is a little more variety in the layouts, but two stereotypes still show up in the access graphs. Eleven houses are variants on an uni-linear sequence, the defining feature of which is that the living room lies on the main circulation route through the home (see figure 5.2c). As this morphology grows, there is a tendency for integration to gravitate towards the stairs which lie beyond the living room, but the living room is still the most integrated habitable space in the 'heart' of the home. Four are identical to the dominant one-bedroom version in all respects save for the additional bedroom. Eating is in the living room, and the kitchen is too small to serve a family meal. Seven more plans reserve the living room for relaxing. These have a separate kitchen/dining area in a shallow end-point off the living room (see figure 5.2d).

The remaining eleven two-bedroom plans branch immediately upon entry and are, in this sense, transition-centred homes. Five continue to connect the ground floor living functions directly in some form of living, dining, kitchen sequence. The final six two-bedroom examples have a separate living/dining room and kitchen off a common hall. In these homes, the living/dining room is an end point. If lack of space demands that functions must be put together, it is more common to associate eating with living rather than with food preparation, but open-plan arrangements which combine all three activities are never found (see figure 5.2e).

Of the forty-two three-bedroom houses, twenty are detached, six link-detached, thirteen semi-detached and three terraced. At three bedrooms, functional diversity is more in evidence. Only six dwellings now use the living room to circulate to other areas of the home. All these larger homes now have a separate dining area, either on the main route to the upper floor

Figure 5.2
A selection of typical Milton Keynes
houses

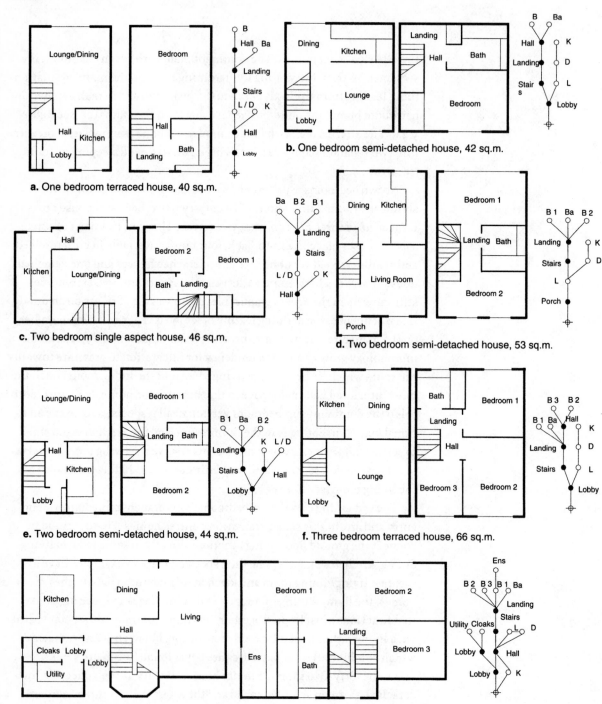

a. One bedroom terraced house, 40 sq.m.

b. One bedroom semi-detached house, 42 sq.m.

c. Two bedroom single aspect house, 46 sq.m.

d. Two bedroom semi-detached house, 53 sq.m.

e. Two bedroom semi-detached house, 44 sq.m.

f. Three bedroom terraced house, 66 sq.m.

g. Three bedroom detached house, 83 sq.m.

or in a shallow spur leading to the kitchen. Every house now has a proper entrance hall, and by far the most common plan type, found in thirty-six cases, uses this to control access to all the principal living rooms as well as to the upstairs bedrooms. The emphasis on transition-centred homes is overwhelming.

However, the houses do this in different ways. One quarter of three-bedroom houses (eleven cases), develop the shallow-branching, double-sequence noted earlier, of directly linked living rooms downstairs and bedrooms upstairs (see figure 5.2f). Twelve examples opt for a living/dining room and separate kitchen downstairs, whilst six houses combine dining with the kitchen, and preserve a separate living area. Four dwellings separate all three rooms connected by a common hall. In all cases, cooking, dining and living are allotted separate zones. In three houses, an external ring is created through a second kitchen entrance, and the living and dining rooms are directly linked so that it is possible to enter by one door and leave by another (see figure 5.2g).

Over half of the three-bedroom houses have a downstairs cloakroom (twenty-four cases) but a separate utility room is rare, and is found in only four cases. Upstairs, the choice has to be made between providing an ensuite to the main bedroom, and forming a more elaborate stair and landing which separates the main bedroom from the others in an embryonic bedroom wing. Twelve houses do neither (none of these have a downstairs toilet), sixteen homes have an ensuite bathroom to the main bedroom, thirteen examples elaborate the upper hall and just one house does both.

The four- and five-bedroom houses are almost invariably detached but resemble previous examples in most other respects. Of the forty-three four-bedroom houses, one is semi-detached and the remainder are detached. There are only two five-bedroom houses in the sample, both detached. Only one example, a bungalow, retains the living room as part of the main circulation route within the home, and only one example has a double sequence of downstairs and upstairs rooms, branching from a common hall. Over half the examples (twenty-seven cases) have completely separate kitchen, dining and living rooms entered from a downstairs hall, and in the majority of houses this, like the upper hall, becomes elaborate and articulated. Five houses retain a sequence between kitchen and dining room downstairs, and there is just one home with a living/dining room. In ten of these four- and five-bedroom dwellings, a small ring of internal circulation is created through the kitchen, dining and living room.

In most four and five-bedroom homes (thirty-eight cases) the kitchen acquires a utility room in sequence and a downstairs cloakroom is almost always provided (forty-three cases). A downstairs study is sometimes provided (thirteen cases). Three more have just a family room and another nine have both. These rooms normally have a separate access from the hall. A separate casual eating space, the breakfast room, is provided within the kitchen sequence in two cases. Conservatories are rare, and occur only twice, as a feature of the house. This is surprising in a city which prides itself on its green, leafy and pastoral image, whereas in the more polluted Inner London areas which many of the residents had left, conservatories were frequently a feature of the home. Upstairs, all examples have an ensuite to the main bedroom, and nine have a dressing room as well. Over half the four-bedroomed houses have an elaborate staircase and upper hallways which separate the bedrooms into smaller clusters. The access graphs are more varied than before, but all resemble a tree with two sets of branches, one shallow on the trunk and the other deep.

Two striking features are common to all sectors of the housing market. First, the justified access graphs show an overwhelming preponderance of deep tree-like forms. The incidence of rings passing through the exterior is low among the small houses: one third have a second door, usually a kitchen door giving separate access to the garden. In larger houses, an interior/exterior ring passing through the exterior becomes more common but this is by no means ubiquitous: 48% of three-bedroom and 82% of four and five-bedroom houses have a second permeability to the garden. There is a strong association between having a utility room and a secondary access: the correlation is 0.878 for the sample. Only thirteen of the 120 houses have an internal ring in the configuration.

Second, even in the largest houses where several living rooms are adjacent to each other, they are separated by walls rather than linked by openings and, where rooms are linked directly in a sequence, the opening strongly differentiates the constituent spaces. Domestic space in these speculative houses seems designed to separate household activities and even to insulate family members from each other. The mean integration values for the sample reflects this tendency. The average integration value for the one hundred and twenty houses is 1.423. Despite their more generous metric area and syntactic size, the up-market houses are on the whole slightly more integrated at 1.349 than the physically more compact but configurationally more tree-like down-market houses, which have a mean integration value of 1.497.

The way eating is handled is a crucial cultural factor in the design of homes in all price brackets and illustrates a fastidiousness in household management which is rarely acknowledged. Kitchens are not, on the whole, designed to incorporate a table for casual meals. In small homes, eating takes place in the living room, or in a separate but linked dining area. In larger houses, dining is given a separate space, preferably a separate room off a common hall. If this cannot be achieved, then doors are provided to shut off the kitchen. Visually linked kitchen/dining areas without this facility are rare. This flies in the face both of all the architectural design guidance since Tudor Walters and of the informal culture of eating and entertaining in the kitchen promoted by the home-making magazines. It implies that both family meals and entertaining are more formally conducted in Milton Keynes today than designers and social commentators allow.

In Milton Keynes even simple homes are complex, and the message they put across suggests that the liberal attitudes and values which are assumed to accompany open, fluid interiors have no place in popular domestic space culture. Houses, like other possessions, seem to provide an index of social status and purchasing power. Downstairs, the priorities are for a clear hall and entry sequence, a decent separation of living functions off a common circulation, a cloakroom and a utility room. Once these basic features have been incorporated, the priority is to separate noisy and quiet activities, particularly where this offers the potential for an office at home. As we shall see later, the imagery of Milton Keynes is derived from a rural 'country house' tradition, but adding a garden room is apparently not a strong selling point.

Upstairs, it is desirable that the main bedroom should have an ensuite bathroom and the prestige of the owners is further enhanced by the presence of a dressing room. The houses of the 'smart set' have elaborate stairs and appear larger than they are because of convoluted halls and passages. Astute Milton Keynes residents play the housing market, 'trading-up' every few years as their purchasing power increases. The average length of residence in a house in this part of the country is only two to three years, and it is taken for granted that residents maintain a home commensurate with their capital assets and earned income.

The innate conservatism of the layouts of speculative houses is reflected in the handling of volume and choice of materials and finishes. Where stairs are designed to separate zones within the domestic interior rather than to effect a dramatic entry, there is little scope for an architectural statement. Staircases are normally in turned wood, and the detailing draws on historical precedent. Bay windows and fireplaces are likewise simplified, mass-produced reproductions of their Georgian, Victorian and Edwardian counterparts which are applied as decoration, rather than integral to the form of house construction. Where form and volumetric sophistication are lacking, decoration tends to be applied to add visual interest within each room. Despite its vibrant image, most of the speculative houses on offer in Milton Keynes are variations on a limited configurational, architectural and decorative vocabulary.

These tendencies go against the trend in architect-designed homes which, through their wide publication and discussion, shape the standards by which 'informed' good taste is judged. The houses which feature prominently in this debate derive much of their aesthetic from building visually rich, permeable linkages between living areas, so that a visit becomes a voyage of discovery through an unfolding complex of ever-changing spaces and, even in repose, one is always aware of the larger volume of the house. By contrast, even the most expensive of the Milton Keynes houses are conservative in layout, and the choice offered to the prospective purchaser is largely illusory.

Neighbourhood homogeneity or heterogeneity

If private houses in Milton Keynes are designed to insulate family members from one another, the messages they convey about relations with the neighbours are no less striking. The legislative framework for new housing developments calls for the residential areas within each grid square to be designed with a mix of houses built around primary school catchments of about one thousand five hundred dwellings. Each neighbourhood should offer future Milton Keynes residents a choice in size, density, tenure and price of home, to suit the needs of individual families. The social philosophy underpinning these criteria is one which believes that a heterogeneous mixture of people locally promotes social understanding, which is thought to be preferable in a new town to designing like-minded enclaves living as communities of interest. No firm guidance is given on housing layout, other than a statement of general intent that new developments should uphold environmental quality, offer visual variety and promote a sense of place.

However, the way in which these design intentions are implemented permits considerable latitude in how each residential area is laid out locally. Roads in physically adjacent housing layouts need not connect to one another, and landscaped areas of grass, bushes and trees may be used to screen groups of houses from one another. It is equally possible for speculative builders to mix house types, or to separate houses in different price brackets into different sectors of the site. On the thirty developments which form this sample, it seems that the more exclusive the development, the smaller it is, the more strongly bounded and delineated it is physically, and the less it seems to matter that neighbouring houses are dissimilar in type and price. Conversely, estates which are aimed at first-time buyers and low-income households not only tend to be larger, but also these are the most conscious of the fine distinctions which purchasing power brings. Clear grouping by type and price within the overall layout is almost always to be found. Where a good cross-section of homes is found on one site, these are frequently grouped so that houses in the upper range are located together in the quieter cul-de-sac parts of the development.

The break-point between up-market and down-market developments can be diagnosed by the predominance within the layout of the three-bedroom, detached family home, which is smart enough to have pretensions, yet can be built at a price which is within most people's grasp. Ten of the developments surveyed are up-market, with three to five-bedroom houses and an average number of dwellings per site of thirty eight, an average price of £140,000 and with an equal split across all developments between mixing and separating small and large houses. Nine developments are down-market, with from one to three bedrooms per dwelling, an average number of dwellings per site of seventy eight, an average price of £54,000 and with an eight to one bias in favour of separating and grouping dwellings by type and price. Eleven schemes cross the range of housing provision, with from one to five bedrooms per house, an average number of dwellings per site of 116, an average price of £86,000 and a nine to two bias towards separating dwelling types. Heterogeneity in housing layout is, it seems, only partially implemented, and divisions are particularly marked at the bottom of the housing ladder where the economic distinction which

results from the number and arrangement of rooms in the domestic interior is at its sharpest.

A sense of place

A layout is a standard feature of all brochures, but the preoccupation with
images of the past does not, on the whole, extend to any attempt to recreate it through a cosy, village-style layout of houses grouped around a green.
The text of developers' sales brochures concentrates exclusively on the
location, both of Milton Keynes as a convenient place to live and of the
number and type of the local amenities in the new city generally and in
the local area immediately around the site, especially the variety of com-
merce, schools and leisure pursuits which are to be found there. Some
information is conspicuous by its absence, and surprisingly few brochures
specify the total number of houses which will eventually be built on the
site. Five small developments give this information, all stressing the select
nature of the scheme with the preface 'just'. Of the thirty schemes, only
fourteen show a north-point.

This does not mean, however, that there is nothing to be learned from a
visual comparison of residential layouts. Apart from the very obvious lack
of any focal point or overall planning in most of the layouts, almost all are
deep, meandering, curvilinear arrangements of dwellings grouped around
culs-de-sac: twenty-three out of thirty layouts have adopted a curvilinear
form, twenty-nine out of thirty group some dwellings around culs-de-sac
or courts and of those, twenty-six do this to a marked degree, so that more
dwellings are grouped around the courts than face out to the access roads.
To paraphrase Christopher Alexander,[1] if 'a city is not a tree', then Milton
Keynes is not a city.

Taken as a whole, the layouts appear to reflect divisions in economic
status and potential purchasing power. There is one development which
makes explicit reference to matters of status which amounts to an accomplished 'tongue-in-cheek' simulation of the social hierarchy of a mediaeval
village, in its allusion to barns, lodges and manor houses in its sales litera-
ture: 'the two bungalows at either side of the entrance to the cul-de-sac
represent barns that provide the privacy to the unfolding courtyards
beyond. The courtyards are flanked by the weatherboarded and dormered
two-storey farmhouses and headed by the impressive three-storey manor

houses.' The aesthetic is reproduced faithfully, and the relative price of the
constituent dwellings is accurately reflected in the architectural form and
layout of the development.

Objects of desire

Brochures are informative, not only for the pictorial content through
which they illustrate the proposed residential environment. They also
offer a more interpretative commentary, in order to assist the prospective
purchaser in recognising and appreciating the ostensible merits of the new
homes. Two thirds of Milton Keynes property developers choose to use a
rhetorical, persuasive style in the promotional material through which
they advertise their houses, and the copywriter's techniques of persuasion
are clearly intended to enhance self-confidence and appeal to the purchaser's sense of social prestige.

The ten most often used adjectives in the sample brochures were: spacious, which had a total of fifty citations, attractive (thirty-five), quality
(twenty-one), generous (twenty), stylish (nineteen), beautiful (fifteen),
well-planned (thirteen), luxury and superb (twelve citations each) and
impressive (ten). Of the ninety-six different adjectives used in all to
describe the houses, nearly half aim to persuade the reader that acquiring a
new home will impress the visitors. Attributes of convenience, practical-
ity and common sense are conveyed by only a quarter of building descrip-
tors, as are the warm, comforting qualities which we tend to associate
with home: forty suggest a dwelling's individuality and ability to impress,
twenty convey practical values, twenty warmth and homeliness, nine size
and seven excitement and modernity.

Solidity, tradition and craftsmanship are seen to be worth mentioning
in the text of sales brochures but not, it seems, so much as exclusivity.
Explicit reference is seldom directly made to the metric area of a home,
but it is implied by adjectives which stress its magnificence, opulence or
splendour. Modernity is eschewed in favour of tradition, and familiar
architectural buzz-words like modern, innovative, split-level or open-
plan occur on only seven occasions altogether.

Some copywriters market their properties by an explicitly adjectival
style of writing, with an average of between ten and fifteen evaluative
statements in a descriptive text which seldom exceeds two hundred words

per house type. Others adopt the alternative approach of awarding each design a signature adjective which seeks to encapsulate, in a memorable word or phrase, its promise to the prospective purchaser. One third of publicity brochures, including both starter homes and exclusive developments, elect not to use written text at all. The former produce simple, self-explanatory brochures with a clear, graphic message. The latter offer the prospective purchaser an apparently more objective technical specification of the dwelling. A strongly adjectival literary style seems largely to be confined to properties in the middle of the price range, where there are more schemes for a prospective purchaser to choose from, and where it may be assumed that competition for customers is keen between developers.

Only one developer claims a stylistic pedigree for his houses, thereby seeming to appeal to a more architecturally-informed client. Two more brochures refer to architectural detail by name. Principles of massing and layout are occasionally discussed in an architectural way, though without any explicit reference to architects or architecture, as the following extract shows: 'the development aims to reproduce many of the qualities associated with the "English Country House" of the Arts and Crafts era. The fragmentary plan form, with steeply sloping roofs, deep porches, corner windows and chimney stacks seeks to interpret the familiar forms of an earlier age, but in a contemporary manner'. In general, however, an appeal to imagery is preferred to any discussion of the finer points of the aesthetics of domestic architecture.

Architects, craftsmen and surveyors

Three further qualities of houses are referred to in the sales brochures. The first considers what might loosely be considered as the dwelling's 'design pedigree'. Irrespective of the fact that many schemes will have involved an architect, either in the design of house types or in the overall layout, only two speculative builders mention this in the accompanying sales brochure. At the same time, of the thirty sites looked at nearly two thirds mention the National House Builders Corporation guarantee as a strong sales point. It seems that the epithet 'architect-designed' is not considered by developers to be a strong selling point. This is in sharp contrast to current social attitudes to the value of 'good design', which seems increasingly to be a source of critical appreciation.

By contrast, 73% of developers highlight the reliability and longevity of the firm of builders used, even to the extent in one case of relating the external appearance of the dwellings, 'through the corporate signature of our external elevational treatment', to the sound investment policies of the flagship company. Few houses these days are, strictly speaking, traditional or built by skilled craftsmen. At the same time, fifteen brochures make explicit reference to tradition, traditional building methods and established practice, though craftsmanship as such is only thought worth mentioning by eight firms. However, there is an inverse relation between the intensity of the emotive sales-pitch and the amount of technical information offered to the prospective purchaser. A detailed technical specification is offered by thirteen of the sample, three of which also highlight special features, another nine list special features but nine more give no technical information whatsoever.

Rus in urbe

Developers' housing layouts in Milton Keynes are invariably given a name, by which each site is identified in pre-sales publicity and is subsequently enshrined in the postal address. It is perhaps surprising of a new town with pretensions to city status, that the names given to the new housing developments show a strong tendency to rural connotation. Of the thirty schemes, twenty-seven have names which are redolent with rural imagery – Woodcote, Swansdowne, The Lindens – and eight explicitly refer to the land – Watermeadows, Greenacres, Fresh Fields. A favourite source for estate names is by association with the homes of the English aristocracy or Royal Family as, for example, in names such as Balmoral or Badminton. A few developers call their layouts after squares in the West End of London, that is, after the 'great estates' built by the aristocracy during the eighteenth century. Others name their developments after local Buckinghamshire villages and towns.

Themed developments are the order of the day. Chequers attempts to convey a racing image with its racing car logo and chequered flag. The house types are named after racing circuits – Donnington, Daytona, Monaco, Monza. At Swansdowne the imagery is of birds, whilst at Berrystead Manor one can live as if 'to the manor born'. In another scheme, houses are themed for wild flowers in an estate named Summer Meadow.

The Willows plays on cricket imagery, with a bat and ball logo and house types named for famous pitches. Another development backs horse racing, known colloquially as 'the sport of kings' to sell its houses. On another estate, the placid, sealed monastic life is evoked by house type names like the Belfry, Cloister, Hermitage and Friar. However superficial these references may be, the rural connotations used in advertising may tap into a half-conscious desire for continuity, a search for a lost rural idyll and sense of community.

Selling the dream

Few developers offer just unfurnished dwellings on the housing market, thereby selling their homes solely on the merits of the architecture. Most employ a professional interior designer, invariably a woman, to simulate how family life might be lived out in the empty house. Ostensibly show-homes are furnished to give the prospective purchaser an idea of how everyday domestic artefacts will fit into the interior: an anthropometric and ergonomic exercise. However, the effort, expenditure and choice of objects used by interior designers suggests that the show house may also be conveying and reinforcing people's perceptions of 'home'.

At the bottom of the market the imagery is invariably 'cottage style'. The walls are painted in pastel pink, blue and apricot upstairs, with an occasional touch of yellow in the kitchen. Walls tend to be painted with emulsion rather than papered. Decorative paint techniques such as ragging, rolling, stippling and stencilling are not in evidence, but border wallpapers are invariably applied to the cornice and dado. Curtains and blinds are luxurious, frilly affairs in floral prints. Net curtains are not used as a window-dressing. The furniture is reproduction country pine with a small, inviting plump sofa in the living room. Pine wardrobes and chests complement the beds, which display patchwork quilts or crocheted bedspreads, suggesting that traditional crafts are to be valued and displayed.

Pictures on the walls are of flowers or, hinting at trips abroad, pastel views of Mediterranean villages. Small china animals and ornamental vases suggest that the future occupants of these houses will have collections of memorabilia, inherited perhaps or purchased as heirlooms for the children. The kitchen invariably has an object array consisting of copper pans, old fashioned scales, fresh herbs, spices and glass-bottled preserves.

The most striking impression is the smell of these show houses, for in most, bowls of pot-pouri permeate the interior with perfumes including apple blossom and lavender.

The more expensive the house, the more these homely qualities are likely to be replaced by more sombre solid furnishings which appear to reflect distinctions in the wealth and taste of prospective purchasers. Pastels are still in evidence in the bedrooms, but in the principal living rooms colours darken to shades of olive, maroon and royal blue. The elaborate curtains may be augmented upstairs by canopied bed hangings. The dining room furniture is reproduction Adam or Hepplewhite. The living room is equally formal, with upholstered and buttoned sofas suggestive of a 'country manor'. Standard lamps cast a warm, discreet glow. Pot-pouri is not set out in bowls, but potted plants are used as a room decoration. Ornaments are larger, and more obviously reproductions of antiques.

Few houses contain items of furniture which are recognisably modern. In only a minority of cases are the children's bedrooms decorated in bright, primary colours. Primary colours and bright shades are never used downstairs. The atmosphere in show homes is almost invariably retrospective. The sole counter-example was produced by the same developer who addressed architectural issues in his brochure. This builder explained that he wished for a neutral, modern feel to the interior, so he chose the furniture himself from Habitat, the stylish chain store which was made famous by the designer Terence Conran in the 1960s and 1970s. With this exception, judging by its show homes Milton Keynes is a futuristic city which goes in for collective nostalgia.

Victorian values

This chapter has argued that, in this town of aspirers and achievers, material success tends to be demonstrated by the elaboration of the house, but all are similarly configured, deep, tree-like and zoned. This tells us something about status, but a great deal more about family life. The historian Robin Evans has argued in a different context that open planning may be appropriate to a society which takes pleasure in sensuality and where gregariousness is the norm.[2] The speculative houses and housing layouts of Milton Keynes seem to eschew these liberal values, and to be more suitable for a culture in which human contact within the home and between neighbours is carefully orchestrated, and where individual privacy is valued.

Milton Keynes houses, perhaps, owe even more than they openly acknowledge in their furnishing and detailing to Victorian values, for Evans has also suggested that it was the over-arching concern for privacy and domesticity which produced the discrimination between route and destination, circulation and room, within the Victorian home. The separationist domestic arrangements of the Victorian middle classes have been interpreted as one way of facilitating polite entertaining across the social divide, whilst others have argued that it may have been a mechanism to prevent the family from falling apart. Perhaps this is no less true in Milton Keynes today, and it is certainly the case that spatial segregation increases as houses – and household size – become larger.

Many of today's architects and designers advocate experimentation with an open, domestic space organisation which recognises the passion and sensuality which draws people together. If these developers' houses are anything to go by – and these houses are bought in large numbers by apparently satisfied customers – ordinary English people may not want to live in this way. The all-too-open plan can become the stage for petty social drama just as easily as it can express an egalitarian domestic harmony. Privacy can be interpreted as generalised social neurosis, but if space takes the strain out of everyday social interaction perhaps the family can survive the irritations which living in close proximity invariably brings. Entertaining in the kitchen depends on a mastery of cuisine and a lofty disregard for dirty dishes. In that we can choose our friends but not our relatives, the social significance of a home which will simultaneously impress the former and protect us from unsolicited familiarity with the latter is, perhaps, to be appreciated, not sneered at.

Notes

1 Christopher Alexander, 'A city is not a tree', *Architectural Forum* 122 (April/May 1965), pp. 45–55.

2 Robin Evans, 'Figures Doors and Passages', *Architectural Design* (April 1978), pp. 267–71.

Chapter six

Configuration and society in the English country house

Summary

The country houses of the English aristocracy are so noted for their architectural diversity that it is difficult to see how a morphological analysis of the plans could add anything of value to a descriptive account of the particular historical and social circumstances which gave rise to each individual establishment. Yet this chapter seeks to shed new light on the layout and life of the English country house by bringing together four archetypal English country houses, Hardwick Hall in Derbyshire (1590–6), Coleshill House in Berkshire (c.1650), Mereworth Castle in Kent (1723) and Bearwood also in Berkshire (1865–70) in order to compare them within a common configurational framework. Several morphological changes can be shown to have taken place in the planning of these large country houses over the three-hundred year period. Over time, the houses have become shallower from the exterior and more ringy with their grounds, there is a shift in the dominant room arrangement from thoroughfare planning in the form of suites of apartments connected together into rings of bi-permeable rooms, to a strong preference for terminal rooms linked by intersection spaces. At the same time, the main circulation routes through the house no longer comprise a mixture of use-spaces and transitions but become devoted to circulation to the exclusion of all other household activities. The houses have also become much more integrated with the passage of time and the focus of integration has shifted from the rooms to the corridors and from deep to shallow in the plan. This points to a fundamental change in the spatial blueprint of the houses from a depth-maximising process to a depth-minimising process. All these changes can be interpreted in terms of shift in the form of social solidarity within the houses from a single, socially homogeneous 'great household' to a household divided into two differentiated and inimical social solidarities, the aristocracy and their servants, but this in turn entails that a more complex construction be put on the ethical meanings and values that can be attributed to integration.

The 'domestication' of the English house

The period stretching from the beginning of the seventeenth century up until the end of the nineteenth century has been described by economic and social historians as an era of power, prestige and prosperity. It was also an era of property and, some would say, a golden age for English domestic architecture. A buoyant economy spearheaded by improvements in agricultural production and the growth of domestic and colonial trade, generated ample resources within the English aristocracy which were expended in a widespread patronage of the arts and architecture. The gentry had always exhibited a fascination for large country houses to grace their great estates and a succession of architect-surveyors arose to cater to the tastes of these discerning aristocratic clients, who delighted in building 'prodigy houses' so named because of their prodigious size, architectural elaboration and the magnificence of their interior decoration. This was no passing fashion, but a form of conspicuous consumption that was to last until the opening decades of the twentieth century.

The houses which form the subject of this chapter span the period from 1590 to 1865. They share an architectural antecedent in the villas of Andrea Palladio. Insofar as each house embodied the needs and aspirations of a small segment of polite society, each can also be expected to reflect the economic, social, political and cultural inclinations of the succession of families who lived there. Yet for many architectural and social historians, houses like these seem to share a common way of life that originated in the ideal of the mediaeval hall house. In its ideal form, the mediaeval household lived together in a large, open and undifferentiated hall where its occupants shared meals, entertained one another and finally slept together as a community. The decay of that community and its division into the two distinct social classes of gentry and servants, is usually associated with an increase in the spatial differentiation of the interior of large country houses and a greater social elaboration in both public and private life.

The conclusion is therefore drawn that the gentleman's country house ought to become increasingly closed and impermeable to outside influences, more spatially sub-divided internally and more segregated as the process of social stratification proceeds. As the houses ceased to serve predominantly public and political ends and became more orientated towards private, domestic life they are assumed to have become functionally more differentiated, spatially larger and internally more complex and labyrinthine, and socially more hierarchical and separationist. The initial aim of this chapter is therefore to test these assumptions about the spatial consequences of domesticity.

The layout and life of four great houses

Hardwick Hall, built between 1590 and 1596 by Robert Smythson, Master Mason to Queen Elizabeth I, for Bess of Hardwick, Dowager Countess of Shrewsbury, on her family estates in Derbyshire, is best-known for its fenestration, interior decoration and fine tapestries. Some of the detailing of Hardwick has been traced to Serlio and the house is the first example in England of a plan based on a Palladian villa, showing the influence of the Villa Valmarana at Lisiera.

Hardwick is small, compared with other country houses of the period, for Bess retained the old hall nearby as overspill accommodation for both servants and guests and so she could afford to build a compact but magnificent house in which to entertain in state. The accommodation is compressed onto a small footprint and so, unusually for houses of the period, the high great chamber, state rooms, gallery and best lodgings are elevated to the second floor (see figure 6.1). The lesser chambers, including Bess's own lodgings when she was not receiving guests, and those of her favourite son William Cavendish and of her granddaughter Arabella Stuart, are on the first floor. The great hall, kitchens, service rooms and the nursery are on the ground floor. The ascending hierarchy of floors thus mirrors the prevailing social hierarchy of household, family, and state.

The symmetrical ground plan is in the form of a rectangle contained by six towers. The entrance is placed centrally in the main facade, and leads to a central 'cross-hall' which lies at right angles to the main frontage of the house, the earliest known example of its type. The main stairs are unusual in that they begin in the centre of the plan at ground level adjacent to the hall, but they gradually work their way out to the perimeter as they ascend to the second floor, thus allowing the lavish state apartments and long gallery to be accommodated without interruption. As a result, Hardwick's circulation is elaborated into a long processional route that winds up from the ground floor to the state rooms through the centre of the house.

Symmetrical house plans are rare before the Tudors, and the planning

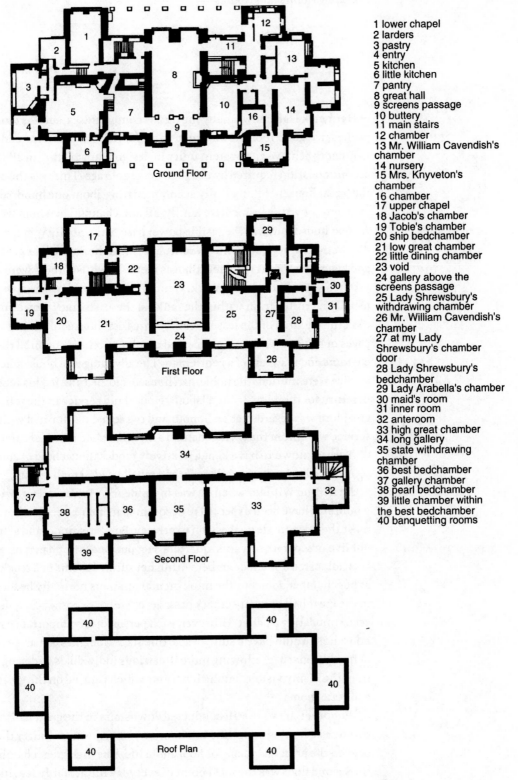

1 lower chapel
2 larders
3 pastry
4 entry
5 kitchen
6 little kitchen
7 pantry
8 great hall
9 screens passage
10 buttery
11 main stairs
12 chamber
13 Mr. William Cavendish's chamber
14 nursery
15 Mrs. Knyveton's chamber
16 chamber
17 upper chapel
18 Jacob's chamber
19 Tobie's chamber
20 ship bedchamber
21 low great chamber
22 little dining chamber
23 void
24 gallery above the screens passage
25 Lady Shrewsbury's withdrawing chamber
26 Mr. William Cavendish's chamber
27 at my Lady Shrewsbury's chamber door
28 Lady Shrewsbury's bedchamber
29 Lady Arabella's chamber
30 maid's room
31 inner room
32 anteroom
33 high great chamber
34 long gallery
35 state withdrawing chamber
36 best bedchamber
37 gallery chamber
38 pearl bedchamber
39 little chamber within the best bedchamber
40 banquetting rooms

Ground Floor

First Floor

Second Floor

Roof Plan

Figure 6.1
Plans of Hardwick Hall, 1590–6

of Hardwick Hall shows many ingenious compromises, such as close-packed, irregular room arrangements, blind windows and false-ceilings, in order to achieve an apparent unity in design whilst fitting in all the accommodation required by Bess and her entourage. This was the era of the 'great household', typically accommodating about one hundred people over and above the immediate family, all but a handful of whom were men. A great household was the visible power base of the nobility, in which the distinctions among servants were crucial, for some counted as gentlemen and behaved more as courtiers than as menials, whilst others were merely yeomen who did the heavy work. Gentlemen and gentlewomen were usually recruited from within the ranks of the aristocracy. Powerful lords took the children of the lesser nobility into their household to be raised as pages or squires. There, they received an education and acquired the customs and manners of a gentleman. The advantages of household service were mutual: the nobleman housed, clothed and fed his retainers in return for their loyalty and labour. Household service in the retinue of a great lord was regarded as an honour and the social ties formed whilst in service were often the springboard to a distinguished political career.

Bess is known to have kept a relatively modest household of about thirty. In addition her granddaughter Arabella had a small staff of servants, as did her son William when he was in residence. However, Hardwick would still have been expected to accommodate many people, though for most there was little concession to privacy. Bess's retainers and squires did not live in separate servants' quarters. Her personal attendants may have been allocated a small chamber within her suite of rooms or a truckle bed at her chamber door, but the more menial retainers normally bedded-down in the great hall or in any empty passage, chamber or corner capable of accommodating a pallet. However, each person of any importance in the household would have a suite of apartments or 'lodgings' set aside for his or her personal use, allowing more illustrious individuals to disengage from the highly visible, public functions which centred on the great hall and state rooms.

Public affairs were still conducted downstairs in the great hall, though this was beginning to decline in importance and it was no longer the only or even the principal focus for household life. The high great chamber on the second floor was the focal point of everyday life at Hardwick. Its importance was confirmed by the ceremonial serving of dinner and supper, which involved a public procession of the food from the kitchens, through the great hall and up the main stairs to the table. The social context was therefore one where the gentry was gradually retreating from the communal life of the hall and abandoning it to the servants, clients and hangers-on. However, all visitors to Hardwick Hall still needed to enter by way of the great hall, and so it retained its importance as the public interface with the outside world.

This meant that there was an inbuilt paradox in the design of great houses like Hardwick Hall. To the extent that the owner's personal power, status and categoric importance were bound up in the physical fabric of the house, this tended to be expressed in their depth and relative segregation within the domestic interior. At the same time, this effectively distanced him, or more rarely her, from the principal inhabitant–visitor interface space of the great hall and also prevented surveillance and control of many of the important circulation routes within the domestic interior. A solution to this paradox was to emerge in the design of the next generation of large country houses.

Hardwick Hall is perhaps the ultimate expression of a way of life which had its roots in mediaeval concepts of family and household. However architectural tastes as well as social habits were undergoing a dramatic transformation. Entourages were shrinking and households were becoming more streamlined. The 'grand tour' was gradually replacing service in a great house as an essential part of the education of an English gentleman. A sharp change of mood was brought about by the Civil War and its aftermath. People's homes were generally regarded as an outward manifestation of their political inclinations and so the Puritans ushered in a more modest style of living and the large country houses of the period tended to eschew ostentation and show. Domestic architecture was characterised by an austerity and a severity which were deemed to be more in keeping with egalitarian, god-fearing and republican social attitudes. This was the context in which Coleshill was commissioned by Sir George Pratt, a Puritan sympathiser, round about 1650.

The authorship of Coleshill is a matter of considerable controversy. Until the 1920s, the house was generally believed to have been the last great work of Inigo Jones, 1573–1652, who died aged almost eighty just two years after the shell of Coleshill was completed. However, in 1928 its design and execution were attributed to Sir George's cousin Sir Roger Pratt, 1620–84.[1] This view was accepted by subsequent scholars until the recent publication of a detailed account by Mowl and Earnshaw of the rise of Puritan classicism under Cromwell,[2] which repudiates the thesis in favour of Pratt and reclaims the house for Inigo Jones. Whatever its origins, at the time of its building in 1650, Coleshill was widely regarded as the most remarkable building of its period, well-suited to the lifestyle of an English country gentleman.

The exterior of Coleshill, which was destroyed by fire in the 1950s, was executed in the Italian manner, and was well-proportioned with a minimum of decoration. The house was rectangular in plan and was organised horizontally into a partially excavated basement, principal and chamber floors, and an attic storey which did not form part of the principal accommodation but was occupied by the servants and used for storage. The long, principal facades were divided into three groups of three windows, with the spacing of the central group wider than those on either side, so as to emphasise the main entrance and the principal living rooms. Well-proportioned chimneys, and a cupola giving access to the balustraded roof, completed the design.

Like Hardwick, Coleshill had a symmetrical ground plan rather than the rambling ranges of buildings which were characteristic of many English houses of the period (see figure 6.2). However, unlike at Hardwick, the principal reception floor of the house was raised-up over a basement so that the entrance was approached formally by an external flight of steps. The basement housed only the servants' quarters, including a house-keeper's room and a servants' hall as well as the usual domestic offices of kitchen, pantry, buttery, larder, dairy, cellars, still room and store room. This was a momentous break with the earlier tradition in which servants lived cheek-by-jowl with their masters and dined in the great hall, in company with the household. The development of a service basement emptied the principal, shallow interface spaces of the house of servants and allowed for a novel reconfiguration of the main reception spaces.

Above the basement lay a double-height hall of the new type, for circulation not for meals and containing a grand staircase. Thus the hall became a formal entrance and vestibule, a place for unimportant visitors to wait and a means of ascent to the gallery and principal rooms above. The arrival of the vestibule hall marked the departure of tenants, hangers-on and clients and their business from the public reception rooms of the house. Everyday hospitality ceased to be manifested to the entire house-hold. Company was entertained with more fastidiousness and in private. The house was gradually being 'domesticated'.

Figure 6.2
Plans of Coleshill House, c.1650

Attics, reconstruction

Chamber floor

Principal floor

Basement

1 great dining room
2 Sir Geo's bedchamber
3 Lady P's bedchamber
4 Sir T Dolanian's bedchamber
5 Sir H Forster's bedchamber
6 hall
7 saloon
8 living parlour
9 drawing room / nursery
10 state bedchambers
11 Sir G's gent's chamber
12 Lady P's withdrawing room
13 kitchen
14 pantry
15 larder
16 store room
17 servants' hall
18 housekeeper's room
19 cellars
20 dairy
21 still room
22 attics

However, the most important and lasting contribution that Coleshill made to the evolution of the English country house is that it established a 'double-pile' room arrangement as the most convenient layout for a house of substance. The defining feature of the plan is its central corridor giving independent access to separate and equivalent rooms on either side, as distinct from a 'single-pile' house where an enfilade of principal rooms orientated the house to the main front whilst the secondary accommodation was grouped along the back. This had hitherto been the more usual layout, and the one that had been adopted at Hardwick even though it was based on a regular plan. At the same time, the accommodation at Coleshill was reorganised to run from centre to periphery, so as to place the more public reception rooms in the geometric centre of the plan and the more private functions, such as parlours, withdrawing rooms, bedchambers and closets to the sides.

The formal reception room or saloon was located on the raised principal floor, with the great dining chamber above. These rooms were in a traditional relationship to one another and occupied the centre of the plan, beyond the double-height vestibule-hall. To the right of the hall on entry was a living parlour, a new household function which expressed the more intimate social relations which were emerging within even quite large households, in that it served as a family sitting and eating room. The equivalent position on the garden front was occupied by a room which could be used either as a withdrawing room or a nursery. To the left were two suites of state bedchambers. On the chamber floor, either side of the central hall and state dining room were four almost (but not quite) identical suites of rooms. Each suite had a large bedchamber and two smaller, linked inner rooms or closets. This was intended to provide flexibility, in which the large room could serve as a private parlour, withdrawing room or bedroom and the smaller closets as a study, servant's room or wardrobe. These rooms were allocated to Sir George and his wife, and to other important members of the household.

On all floors, access was by means of a central corridor running the length of the plan. English houses had lobbies and passages before this date, but the economy of the circulation was new. All rooms of any importance were entered from the corridor and could be reached without going through another. At each end of the corridor lay the back-stairs. This concept was also revolutionary, the first unambiguous example of a house where complete separation was achieved between the main staircase and the back-stairs. Effectively this meant that at Coleshill the servants had their own circulation so that the householder, his family and their guests did not meet the servants face-to-face on the grand stairs. Anything undesirable or offensive, from stale food to chamber pots, went up and down the back-stairs to the domestic offices in the basement. Whilst they generally conform closely to these constraints however, the local rules for connect-

ing each suite of rooms together by an arrangement of openings and doors
is slightly different, so that the configuration of the plan is not as regular as
the geometry and shapes of rooms suggest.

These configurational changes signalled both an increase in convenience for the family and a revolution in the structure of the household.
Servants were no longer regarded as gentlemen retainers who guarded their
master's bedchamber door whilst he slept. Instead a personal servant
shared a room with his master's commode, whilst the household servants
were banished to the basement and the attics. Servants were now recruited
from the middle classes, the sons and daughters of merchants, the clergy or
of army officers. They were fewer in number, their status was lower, and
there were more women among them. The housekeeper was replacing the
steward in supervising the running of the establishment. All servants were
much less visible at Coleshill than they had been at Hardwick, and the
daily routines of masters and servants were spatially insulated from one
another within the house. Although houses generally were becoming
smaller and more compact, the social distance between members of the
same household was increasing. In this respect at least, Coleshill and
Hardwick seem to have been characteristic of the country houses of
the day.

As the political climate stabilised after the upheavals of the parliamentary revolution, great houses were no longer seen as the principal
setting for the public display of mutual ties between the lord and his
entourage. The social apparatus of hereditary rights and obligations
which sustained the previous pattern of loyalty and service was becoming
increasingly obsolete. As the mutual ties slackened between the gentry
and the aristocracy and between both and the tenantry, it was seen as
demeaning to conduct business in public. The house was becoming a
private domain.

Yet there were still some houses built almost entirely for pleasure and
show, particularly in the opening years of the eighteenth century when the
shadow cast by the political turmoil of the previous century had lifted and
the aristocracy were once more proud to be known as dilettante. Culture
became an essential attribute of the powerful ruling elite, and architecture
once more served as one of the principal means of demonstrating wealth,
sociability, exclusivity and good taste. To begin with, the new dilettanti
formed a small social set, grouped around Lord Burlington and his protégé
Colen Campbell, whose design for Mereworth Castle in Kent is a copy of

Palladio's Villa Capra at Vicenza, also known as the Villa Rotunda. The house was built in 1723 for Colonel John Fane later to become Earl of Westmoreland.

Unlike Coleshill, Mereworth was conceived of primarily as a setting for the reception and entertainment of guests and only secondarily as a place of residence. Like Hardwick, the main house was supplemented by two flanking buildings, one containing additional bedroom accommodation and the other the stables, and so the main house could be designed as the exquisite centrepiece of a balanced architectural composition. The house has three storeys, cellars, principal and attic, topped by a domed roof. As before, vertical layering reflects the social order of servants in the cellars, state apartments on the principal floor and private apartments in the attic.

The plan of the main house is square, with a large portico on each side, and is based on a three by three square planning grid or 'triple-pile' (see figure 6.3). The principal axis runs north-south, and is approached from each direction by an imposing flight of external steps. The apartments are organised around a circular, double-height saloon which is located under the dome and has a gallery at the upper level. Unlike the double-height hall at Coleshill, the saloon at Mereworth is intended to be used as part of a complex of spaces for entertainment, including the long gallery which runs the width of the south front of the house and the reception rooms on the north front which are separated by a small vestibule. The east and west fronts each have an anteroom and state bedchamber, with a balcony beyond. All the adjacent rooms on the principal floor are permeable to one another and to the saloon, so that route choice is maximised within a plan which is designed to celebrate spatial exploration, parade, sociability and mingling.

Additional suites of private apartments and some smaller bedrooms are accommodated in the attic storey, which is approached by twin spiral stairs set within the thickness of the saloon wall. The kitchen and servants quarters are in the cellar, where the servants' hall is located directly under the saloon and the steward's room is set into the thickness of the wall. As at Coleshill, the geometry gives an appearance of unity in the design of the house which is not fully carried through into the pattern of internal permeability as subtle asymmetries are produced by the positioning of the servants' stairs leading to the cellars and by the incorporation of a more extensive guest suite in the attic storey overlooking the main entrance.

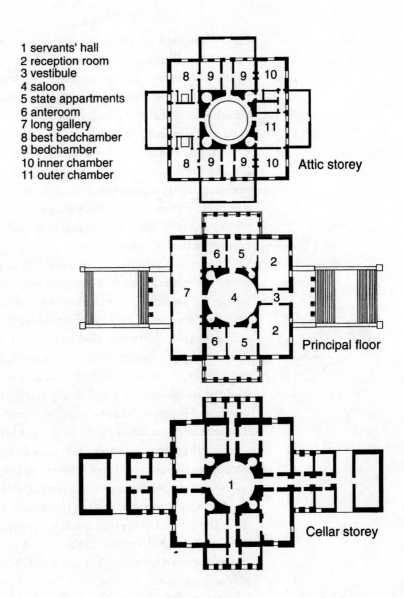

Figure 6.3
Plans of Mereworth Castle, 1723

1 servants' hall
2 reception room
3 vestibule
4 saloon
5 state appartments
6 anteroom
7 long gallery
8 best bedchamber
9 bedchamber
10 inner chamber
11 outer chamber

Attic storey

Principal floor

Cellar storey

Mereworth is a celebration of a polite world whose claim to power
was dependent on owning property, exercising patronage and engineering
representation through the parliamentary system, which became increasingly important as a counterweight to the power of the monarch during the
eighteenth century. The role of the state apartments as the private territories of important members of the household had declined and the need for
a public and ceremonial enactment of the principles which governed a

highly stratified, pyramidal society within the interior of great houses had
been all but eliminated by wider social changes. The architecture of the
country house was now responding to the need for a set of communal
rooms for entertainment which could accommodate a variety of
simultaneous activities such as dancing, cards, music, conversation and,
of course, admiring the architecture of the house and its magnificent
collections. The balance between the public and private functions of the
house had changed yet again, so that more space was devoted to communal
activities and less to maintaining individual statuses. This apparent
democratisation of the country house did not, however, extend to the servants, who now inhabited a separate, complex and internally partitioned
domain in the basement.

Country house building continued throughout the nineteenth century,
but now the wealth of the nation was becoming more diversified, and
homes were financed by speculation in land, mineral exploitation, property development in the new urban housing estates and investment in a
wide range of industries including factories, as well as from the older
source of agricultural production. Yet again, a new generation of houses
was built to accommodate these changing social practices. The segregation and specialisation which had begun to show itself in the servants'
quarters of eighteenth century houses became increasingly manifested
during the nineteenth century, so that the servants lived completely separate from the gentry, and served them by an elaborate system of back-stairs,
corridors and passages. To all intents and purposes, the family and the servants were separate communities living within the same household.
Furthermore, instead of sharing space, each group of servants and each
domestic activity was now allocated a separate territory. Related functions
were then grouped together in the plan. A separate circulation system
linked the territories together and made them accessible to the gentry's
part of the house.

Bearwood, Berkshire, designed by the architect Robert Kerr, is the
exemplar of this social hierarchisation. The house features prominently
in his book, *The Gentleman's House*[3] which is an attempt to codify the
accepted rules of domestic conduct of the day and to show how these
might best be supported in the space and form of the house. Franklin[4]
describes the house as an asymmetric variant on the classical Palladian
villa on three floors, though the elevational treatment is in the
Elizabethan manner. The ground floor is dominated by a top-lit picture

gallery, which is surrounded on three sides by the principal reception
rooms of the house. The fourth side is taken up by the principal staircase
and a wide transverse corridor which divides the villa-proper from the
irregular extensions to the plan. The first and second floors of the main
villa contain the principal bedrooms set around a central open court above
the skylight of the picture gallery (see figure 6.4).

Three aggregates of rooms sprawl to the left of the main house, the first
centres on the butler's corridor on the ground floor, the second on the
men's corridor and the third is an almost completely detached, single-
storey kitchen court, which is linked to the main house by the L-shaped
circulation system formed where the luggage entrance and housekeeper's
corridor meet with the kitchen entrance and cook's corridor. At the first
floor above the butler's corridor is a family corridor which controls access
to the family bedroom and schoolroom. At the second floor, this position
is occupied by the young ladies of the house. Above the men's ground floor
corridor is the first floor nursery corridor. The men's stairs rising up from
the ground floor do not have a landing on the intermediate floor but rise
straight up to the second floor where visiting menservants are accommodated, along with the luggage. The first-floor rooms above the housekeeper's corridor and beyond the nursery corridor are reserved for the
womenservants. The main staircase, back-stairs, menservants' stairs and
womenservants' stairs are located at the hinges between the major subdivisions of the house. In addition, a discreet bachelors' stair is placed next
to the principal staircase so that the young men of the house can come and
go more or less as they please.

The most striking feature of Bearwood is the size and complexity of the
accommodation, particularly given the advances which had occurred in
domestic technology. The size of the main household of a large country
house had remained stable for some time, at about fifty staff. The increase
in the size of the floor plan is produced by the increase in the number of
separate functions which the house is expected to accommodate and by
the way in which these more numerous domestic activities are disposed
within the layout. The main entrance at Bearwood has expanded into a
sequence of spaces which now includes a porch, waiting area, entrance
hall, lobbies and cloakrooms, picture gallery and stair-well. The activities
associated with daily living and the reception of guests are now dispersed
across six rooms where previously they would have been synchronised in
space and time. Even private, 'backstage' activities such as sleeping,

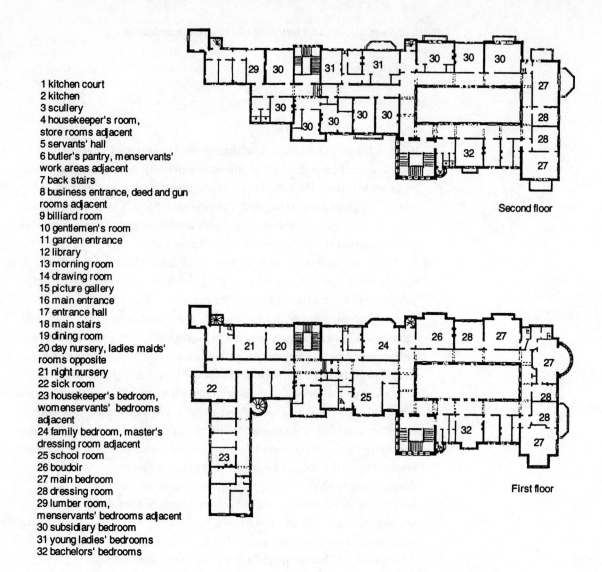

1 kitchen court
2 kitchen
3 scullery
4 housekeeper's room,
store rooms adjacent
5 servants' hall
6 butler's pantry, menservants'
work areas adjacent
7 back stairs
8 business entrance, deed and gun
rooms adjacent
9 billiard room
10 gentlemen's room
11 garden entrance
12 library
13 morning room
14 drawing room
15 picture gallery
16 main entrance
17 entrance hall
18 main stairs
19 dining room
20 day nursery, ladies maids'
rooms opposite
21 night nursery
22 sick room
23 housekeeper's bedroom,
womenservants' bedrooms
adjacent
24 family bedroom, master's
dressing room adjacent
25 school room
26 boudoir
27 main bedroom
28 dressing room
29 lumber room,
menservants' bedrooms adjacent
30 subsidiary bedroom
31 young ladies' bedrooms
32 bachelors' bedrooms

Second floor

First floor

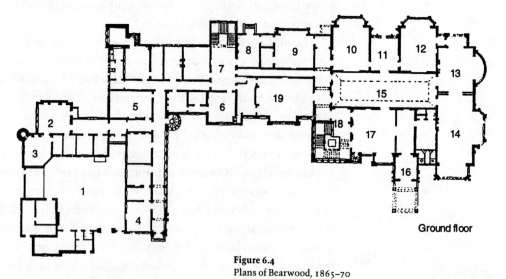

Ground floor

Figure 6.4
Plans of Bearwood, 1865–70

bathing and dressing take place in a suite of rooms as opposed to a single space.

The social history of the English country house can therefore be told as a story of increasing compartmentalisation of the domestic interior, accompanied by a greater tendency towards the social 'closure' of the household and family to outside influences. Spatially, it is possible to point to a shift in domestic room arrangements, from an emphasis on thoroughfare planning to an overwhelming preponderance of terminal spaces. A related line of argument might contrast the tendency to group rooms in enfilades or circuits with that of separating spaces for circulation from those devoted to use. Important changes seem also to have taken place in the 'choreography' of the country house, so that in some houses activities and people are concentrated in key function spaces like the hall and main reception rooms, whereas in others, activities are dispersed, groups separated from one another and spaces emptied of social content. All these changes seem to reflect key architectural distinctions such as those of route and destination, trajectory and position, mobility and stasis or anticipation and arrival. These ideas can be clarified by a more detailed comparison of the layouts.

Configurational analysis of the plans

If we look first at the four houses as pure space configurations, then a comparison of the justified permeability graphs of the spatial layouts is already instructive (see figure 6.5). The main spaces are keyed into the graphs, which also differentiate the transitions that are shown in black from the function spaces which are indicated by a circle. The relevant numerical data for each house are shown in figure 6.6. The graph representation and the numerical data suggest that Coleshill and Mereworth can be considered as small houses from the point of view of the number of rooms in the plan, whilst Hardwick is considerably larger and Bearwood is extensive. However, the numbers of function spaces in each case suggests that all three of the earlier houses are simply less elaborate than Bearwood, which has over double the amount of accommodation. This functional diversification within the country house seems to have taken place in the quite recent past.

Coleshill and Mereworth have a similar, relatively small number of transitions, that is corridors, passageways and stairs, giving rise to a low

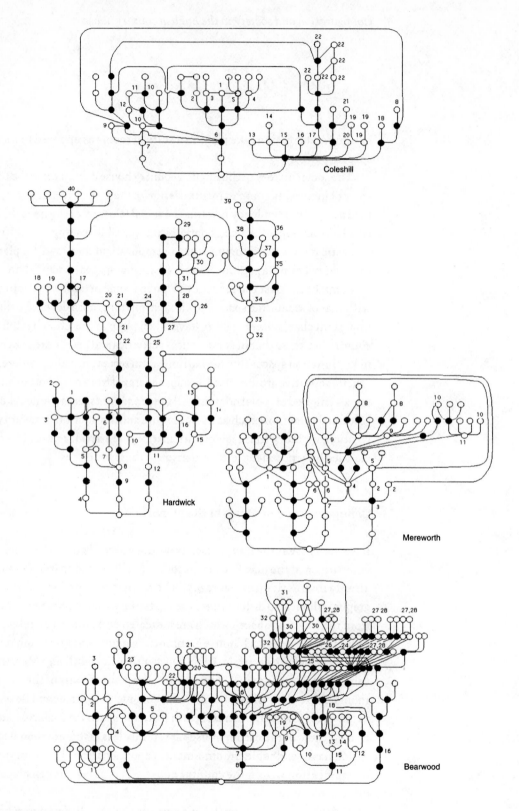

Figure 6.5
Justified graphs of the four country houses

Figure 6.6
Basic syntactic measures for the four houses

	rings	glob.int	loc.int.	ext	functions	transitions	total	t::s ratio
Hardwick	13	10	1	2	62	68	130	1.097
Coleshill	18	4	12	2	44	23	67	0.523
Mereworth	11	0	6	3	61	24	85	0.393
Bearwood	45	24	14	7	134	100	234	0.746

	a space	b space	c space	d space	dist.	asymmetry
Hardwick	33(25%)	10(8%)	71(55%)	16(12%)	0.4943	0.6049
Coleshill	21(31%)	5(7%)	22(33%)	19(28%)	0.6341	1.4815
Mereworth	39(46%)	7(8%)	31(37%)	8(9%)	1.1795	4.6676
Bearwood	102(44%)	26(11%)	73(31%)	33(14%)	1.2075	2.9661

	depth	max int.	min int.	mean int.	different factor	date
Hardwick	20	3.0512	1.6178	2.1947	.9186	1590
Coleshill	8	1.5241	0.6628	1.1215	.8699	1650
Mereworth	10	1.7703	0.6890	1.2345	.8357	1723
Bearwood	12	1.9833	0.6894	1.1880	.7876	1865

transition:space ratio in each case. Hardwick has a surprisingly high number of transitions for a plan which, in view of its early date, might be expected to lack lobbies and passages as these are generally considered to be a modern invention. It is the only example in which the layout has more transitions than spaces. The importance of the corridor circulation system at Bearwood is demonstrated by its high number of transitions but as these mediate an even larger number of spaces it is not as fragmented a plan as Hardwick. Moreover, despite its size and internal complexity, Bearwood is still a relatively shallow house, with just twelve levels of depth in its justified graph, whereas Hardwick is extraordinarily deep, with twenty levels of depth. This suggests that the impression that early houses are internally undifferentiated and highly permeable to the exterior is somewhat of an illusion.

The three earlier houses relate to their grounds in a rather similar way, with just two or three entrances which intersect within the interior and so create ringy circulation routes that pass through the house. Bearwood has eight entrances of which five are for different categories of domestic servants as well as a main entrance, garden entrance and an entrance for tenants visiting the house on estate business. One important distinction between Coleshill and the other three houses is that no function space participates in any of the global, ringy routes which pass through the exterior, whereas in the other three cases important function spaces such as the great hall at Hardwick, the saloon at Mereworth and the picture gallery at Bearwood feature as key intersections between external and internal rings of space.

Even more striking is the difference in the number and type of purely internal rings which are found in the four plans. Hardwick's internal circulation is dominated by extensive global rings which link spaces together into major processional sequences. There is only one local ring in the house which links the high great chamber and state withdrawing chamber to the picture gallery on the second floor. Here, it is impossible to move around the interior of the house without passing through important occupation spaces where the household gathers together and for the reception and entertainment of guests.

Coleshill has four substantial chains of directly-linked spaces which form major, global rings within the domestic interior that link together physically remote parts of the house. These global internal rings are also composed entirely of transitions so that it is possible to move throughout the house without ever entering a room. Coleshill also has a substantial number of local rings of space which directly link together physically adjacent rooms so that it is possible to enter by one door and leave by another. These local rings are found throughout the house but they are a particular feature of the private apartments.

Mereworth does not have any global rings in the plan other than those which have already been noted that pass through the exterior and link the outside to important destinations within the interior, the saloon on the principal floor and the servants' hall in the cellars. On the other hand, Mereworth has eight local rings, five of which are concentrated in the principal rooms of the main reception floor. The remainder are upstairs in the private apartments. The servants' quarters does not have any local rings at all.

Bearwood is an extremely ringy plan, with very many global internal rings which pervade the domestic interior but also a large number of relatively trivial, local rings which link suites of two or three spaces together locally. As at Coleshill, all the global internal rings at Bearwood are composed almost entirely of transitions. Local rings link the corridors either with pairs of reception rooms on the ground floor or with a bedroom and its adjacent dressing room at the upper levels.

Hardwick Hall is a building where very little of the space configuration is invested in tree-like sub-complexes, and most of these are only one or two steps away from the extensive ringy circulation system. The exception is Bess's' private quarters, which take the form of a seven-step deep, almost completely separate, locally ringy but globally tree-like sub-complex that is linked to the rest of the building by just one key transition, known to Bess and her contemporaries as 'at my lady's withdrawing chamber door'. Unsurprisingly in view of its pivotal position in the configuration and its dependency on a single point of access, this passage which kept the gate to the inner rooms where Bess was able to emancipate herself from her role as a figurehead, was the most heavily guarded space in the premises. Not much space is invested in elaborate limit sequences at Coleshill but at Mereworth the ringy sub-system is quite small as compared to the branching, tree-like parts of the justified graph. A substantial amount of the depth in the graph is invested in local tree-like sub-complexes, some of which extend several steps deeper away from the nearest major ring. Bearwood is more like Coleshill in that, in every part of the plan, little bushes of rooms can be found that spring up and away from the main circulation routes.

Space-types in the four houses

It may therefore be useful to describe the different characteristics of the individual spaces which make up the layout of each house. Locally, configurations can be made up of four broad topological space-types. First, there are terminal spaces, which are end points in the justified graph and are linked to the rest of the complex by only one entrance. Such spaces can only accommodate movement to and from themselves, and so it is in their nature that they are intended mainly for static occupation, either by people or things. The influence of these spaces is local, and eliminating any one space from the complex by unlinking it would make very little difference to the rest of the layout. Second, there are spaces which are themselves thoroughfares, but which are part of a larger tree-like complex. Such spaces cannot be dead ends, but they are on the way to or from a dead end so, by implication, any movement through the space is still highly directed. Third, there are spaces which have more than one link and so can be traversed, but which also lie on a single ring so that it is possible to enter at one point on the ring and leave at another. Finally, there are spaces with more than two links and which form the intersection of more than one ring. Movement through these spaces generates choice as to where to go within whole sub-complexes of spaces within the overall configuration. Hillier[5] has termed these four space-types, type a, b, c and d spaces.

Hardwick's dominant space-type is 'c' space, that is, spaces which are linked together into a single deep ring. There are seventy-one of this dominant type, 55% of the total number of spaces. The next most important space-type is 'a' space, or terminal spaces, of which there are thirty-three altogether scattered through the house, amounting to 25% of the total spaces. Sixteen spaces, or 12%, are type 'd' at the intersection of the deep circulation rings. Only ten spaces, 8%, are the 'b' type spaces which feature on unilinear sequences.

Most 'd' type spaces contain important functions, including the screens passage, great hall, kitchen and pantry on the ground floor, the low great chamber on the first floor, and the high great chamber, state withdrawing chamber and long gallery on the second floor. The rest are all passages where routes intersect, the most important of which is 'at my lady's withdrawing chamber door' on the first floor, as well as the main and secondary halls, passageways and landings connecting the levels through the house. Suites of apartments are found grouped into rings of 'c' type spaces, which permit the ebb and flow of reception and withdrawal to take place around the ring. Storage rooms, closets and privy chambers are 'a' type spaces, as are the chapel and the banqueting rooms on the roof.

A broadly similar distribution of space-types is found at Coleshill, though the proportion of both 'a' and 'd' type spaces increases slightly whilst the number of 'c' spaces falls dramatically to just 33% of the total. The slight increase in 'a' to 31% of the spaces can be attributed to the fact that, in addition to closets and stores, several of the household activities which are associated with food preparation and storage such as the pantry, dairy, still room and cellars are now located in terminal spaces in the cellars. The drop in 'c' spaces seems to be a by-product of the more economical planning of the house, though the state and private suites of rooms still retain the local ring which permits the subtleties of ceremony and intimacy to ebb and flow within the apartment. Despite its small size, Coleshill has the highest proportion of 'd' spaces of all the houses, 28%, though, unlike at Hardwick, these are invariably corridors, not function spaces. The proportion of 'b' spaces is a relatively small percentage of the total, 7%, as it is for all the houses.

Rather surprisingly in view of the permeable and highly connected appearance of its plan, the proportion of 'a' spaces at Mereworth at 46% of the total spaces in the house, is the highest among the four houses whilst the proportion of 'd' spaces, only 9% of the total, is the lowest. Although the principal floor is made up almost entirely of 'c' and 'd' spaces, the cellars and attic storey comprise mainly 'a' spaces. Mereworth has a greater proportion of terminal rooms but, on the other hand, all but two of the 'd' spaces are for occupation and use, the exceptions being the vestibule hall and upper-level gallery. Only 8% are 'b' spaces and 37% are 'c' spaces.

Bearwood also has a high proportion of terminal spaces forming 44% of the total. Here, 'a' spaces are found everywhere, not just in the servants' quarters. They are often placed in sequence with a 'b' transition lobby space so that, of the four examples, Bearwood has the greatest number of 'b' spaces, 11% of the total. Of the total, 14% are 'd' spaces and these are mainly transitions. Only 31% of spaces are 'c' spaces, including many of the reception spaces on the ground floor, the school rooms and nurseries and many of the principal bedrooms.

It seems that, although the proportion of each type of space varies from case to case, the numerical occurrence of each space-type shifts over time from the proposition that $(c > a > d > b)$ to $(a < c < d < b)$. This shows that during the mediaeval and early modern period the strongly dominant space-type numerically is 'c' space, that is thoroughfare space which participates in a single large ring, followed by 'a' space or terminal space. Some 'c' spaces are designed for occupation but the rings are elaborated by the insertion of lobbies and passages between the rooms. Hardwick Hall has this characteristic spatial pattern. However, during the second half of the seventeenth century and early on in the eighteenth century, terminal rooms with a single entrance gradually came to dominate the plan.

This confirms that there has indeed been a general and pronounced shift in domestic room arrangements away from thoroughfare planning and towards terminal spaces. But it adds the important clarification that the change is a quite specific one, from a clear preference for constructing deep rings of space linked together by a common system of access comprising a mixture of use spaces and transitions, to that of making bushes of terminal rooms one or two steps deeper from global circulation routes which are made up almost exclusively of transitions.

Despite the architectural interest in 'd' space or intersection space with several ways through, this seems never to have played a major role in the space planning of the large country house, though at Hardwick Hall and

Mereworth Castle important functions which interface members of the household with their guests occur in powerful 'd' spaces which also control the intersection between the exterior and the interior global rings of circulation. Throughout the period, 'b' space or bi-permeable space which is part of a larger spatial sequence, has only a small part to play in constructing the overall space configuration and its deployment remains quite stable over time.

Integration analysis of the plans

However, it is in a comparison of the maximum, minimum and mean integration values for the four houses, given in figure 6.6, that the most significant difference between the four houses emerges, which suggests that Hardwick is a completely different kind of configuration altogether from the later houses. The most integrated space of all at Hardwick is over twice as segregated as those at Coleshill, Mereworth or Bearwood, all of which have rather similar values between 0.65 and 0.70, and it is also more segregated than the mean integration value for all spaces in the other three houses. The mean integration value for Hardwick at 2.1947, is more segregated than the most segregated spaces of all at Coleshill, Mereworth and Bearwood. The design of Hardwick seems to be one which is intrinsically segregating in the layout of its activities and spaces.

When the distribution of integration is given for each house, the differences between them come into even sharper focus. Integration at Hardwick centres on the private first-floor lodgings of Lady Shrewsbury (see figure 6.7). In fact all of Lady Shrewsbury's rooms, even those which serve her most intimate needs, are more integrated than the average value for the whole house. Her son William's chambers are also well integrated but, unlike Bess whose lodgings are on the first floor at least nine steps away from the exterior, he has one suite of rooms on the ground floor which is both well integrated and shallow to the exterior and another on the first floor, adjacent to Bess's own withdrawing chamber, which is deeper and relatively segregated.

Hardwick's great hall is well integrated, rather more so than the reception space of the great low chamber, but the core of most integrated spaces does not quite reach the exterior. The main entrance is more segregated than the informal, garden side of the house. As befits their relative formality

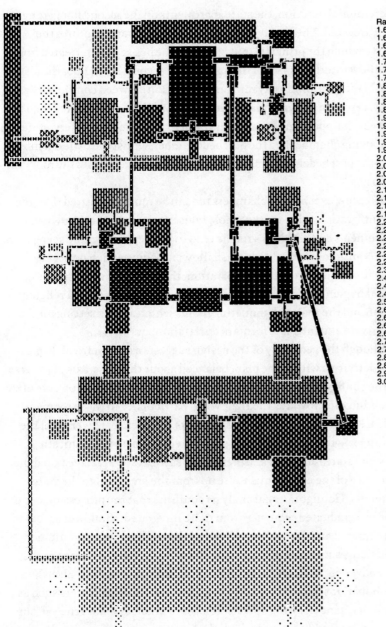

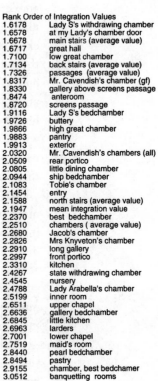

Rank Order of Integration Values

1.6178	Lady S's withdrawing chamber
1.6578	at my Lady's chamber door
1.6678	main stairs (average value)
1.6717	great hall
1.7100	low great chamber
1.7134	back stairs (average value)
1.7326	passages (average value)
1.8317	Mr. Cavendish's chamber (gf)
1.8330	gallery above screens passage
1.8474	anteroom
1.8720	screens passage
1.9116	Lady S's bedchamber
1.9726	buttery
1.9866	high great chamber
1.9883	pantry
1.9913	exterior
2.0320	Mr. Cavendish's chambers (all)
2.0509	rear portico
2.0805	little dining chamber
2.0944	ship bedchamber
2.1083	Tobie's chamber
2.1454	entry
2.1588	north stairs (average value)
2.1947	mean integration value
2.2370	best bedchamber
2.2510	chambers (average value)
2.2680	Jacob's chamber
2.2826	Mrs Knyveton's chamber
2.2910	long gallery
2.2997	front portico
2.3310	kitchen
2.4267	state withdrawing chamber
2.4545	nursery
2.4788	Lady Arabella's chamber
2.5199	inner room
2.6511	upper chapel
2.6636	gallery bedchamber
2.6845	little kitchen
2.6963	larders
2.7001	lower chapel
2.7519	maid's room
2.8440	pearl bedchamber
2.8494	pastry
2.9155	chamber, best bedchamer
3.0512	banquetting rooms

Figure 6.7
Distribution of integration at Hardwick Hall

and ceremonial function, the state apartments on the second floor are even more segregated. The relative segregation of these rooms captures the extent to which the principal inhabitants of the house have retreated from the shallow interface space of the hall. On the second, state, floor the distribution of integration closely mirrors the relation between community and privacy, ceremony and intimacy. The anteroom is more integrated than the high great chamber, which is more integrated than the long gallery, state withdrawing chamber and the best bedchamber, whilst the little chamber within the best bedchamber is amongst the most segregated of the rooms in the house.

With a few exceptions, chambers tend to be more segregated than the mean integration value for the whole house. Apart from Bess's own lodgings, women's and children's rooms tend to be deeper and more segregated, men's rooms more integrated and shallower. Rooms which perform a service function such as food preparation, the storage of comestibles or personal hygiene are segregated, as is the chapel which serves a religious function and the rooftop banqueting rooms which are the setting for the most private and intimate forms of entertainment.

Although the geometry of the design suggests a symmetrical disposition of activities within the plan, balanced about the cross-axis of the great hall, the configuration of space is uneven so that the integration core of the house is directed towards the right wing, particularly to those rooms which are clustered close to the main stairs. The vertical layering of the floors appears to mirror the broad social divisions between domestic, family and state functions and previous historical studies have noted the importance of the ceremonial route up from the great hall to the state apartments. Configurational analysis confirms that the processional route is indeed a graduated sequence from more integrated, shallower spaces to less integrated and deeper spaces, so that the configuration simultaneously affords a measure of increasing status and greater intimacy as the visitor advances towards the interior of the state apartments. Elsewhere in the house, integration reflects the importance of other factors such as personality, gender, age and status at least as much as it does the various public and private functions which the house needs to accommodate.

Overall, Hardwick seems analogous to a great hive in which both domestic and ritual activity is centred on Bess, its queen, in that the configuration of the house seems designed seamlessly to interface the formal and informal aspects of Lady Shrewsbury's domestic life. The integration focus on her private apartments celebrates her power and centrality to the instrumental running of the house, whereas the processional route from the shallow and integrated hall to the segregated state apartments expresses the categoric importance, ceremonial role and high status of Bess in relation to her guests. The controlling relationship between Bess and the members of her household is only weakly expressed in the layout of space, especially when it is born in mind that her retinue would have pervaded the interior and that the deep rings of circulation at Hardwick must have made the overt control and surveillance of servants particularly difficult to achieve. The halls, chambers, passages and corridors at Hardwick variously accommodate purposeful, programmed, ritual movement and casual, unprogrammed movement and loafing about. However, the layout is not conducive to over-familiarity, particularly when the extreme segregation of the house is taken into account.

Not only is Coleshill the most integrated of the four houses but the focus of integration has also shifted from function spaces to the circulation system and at the same time from spaces located deep in the interior to ones which are shallow, so that the exterior is drawn into the core of well integrated spaces (see figure 6.8). The novel architectural element of the vestibule hall together with the main stairs which rise up through the central volume of the house are the most integrated spaces of all. All the passages, porticoes, vestibules and stairs are more integrated than the mean value for all the spaces in the house, so although there are relatively few transitions at Coleshill when compared with the other three examples, these dominate the core of most integrated spaces in the house. Unlike the halls and passages at Hardwick Hall, these vestibules and corridors are intended to be empty for most of the time and so the integration core of the house no longer functions as an interface with the outside world, nor even as a place of association for members of the household.

Surprisingly in view of the centrality which is visually so self-evident in the plan, the more intimate drawing room/nursery is the most integrated function space, followed by the great dining room and only then by the room for formal entertainment, the saloon. The state bedrooms and private apartments of the principal inhabitants are quite well-integrated, but the living parlour is rather more segregated. The distinctions between more integrated and more segregated locations at Coleshill therefore seem to express how and where the different members of the family may choose to pass their time, either formally or more casually and intimately and

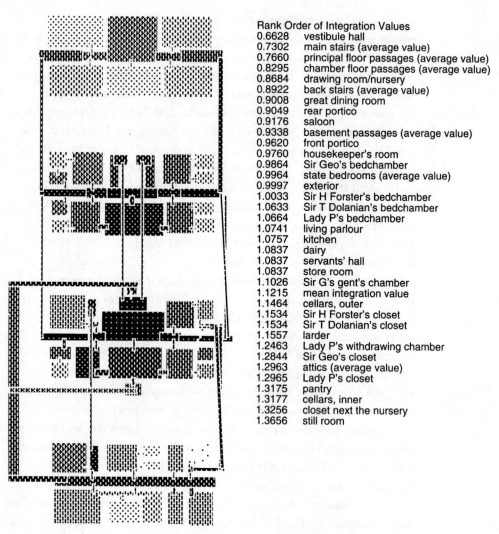

Rank Order of Integration Values

0.6628	vestibule hall
0.7302	main stairs (average value)
0.7660	principal floor passages (average value)
0.8295	chamber floor passages (average value)
0.8684	drawing room/nursery
0.8922	back stairs (average value)
0.9008	great dining room
0.9049	rear portico
0.9176	saloon
0.9338	basement passages (average value)
0.9620	front portico
0.9760	housekeeper's room
0.9864	Sir Geo's bedchamber
0.9964	state bedrooms (average value)
0.9997	exterior
1.0033	Sir H Forster's bedchamber
1.0633	Sir T Dolanian's bedchamber
1.0664	Lady P's bedchamber
1.0741	living parlour
1.0757	kitchen
1.0837	dairy
1.0837	servants' hall
1.0837	store room
1.1026	Sir G's gent's chamber
1.1215	mean integration value
1.1464	cellars, outer
1.1534	Sir H Forster's closet
1.1534	Sir T Dolanian's closet
1.1557	larder
1.2463	Lady P's withdrawing chamber
1.2844	Sir Geo's closet
1.2963	attics (average value)
1.2965	Lady P's closet
1.3175	pantry
1.3177	cellars, inner
1.3256	closet next the nursery
1.3656	still room

Figure 6.8
Distribution of integration at Coleshill

whether this be in company or alone, rather than to embed an over-arching conception of ceremony. In this sense, the domestic environment appears modern and perhaps this is the most subtle but the most significant shift of all in the planning of the house.

As at Hardwick, the pattern of permeability amongst the rooms and the location of the staircases introduces fundamental configurational asymmetries into the symmetrically composed plan, so that those rooms in the servants' quarters which connect directly to the basement passage, including the kitchen and the servants' hall, are relatively well-integrated. Active functions which entail movement such as those that are related to the processing of foodstuffs and the workings of the household economy tend to be directly linked to the passage which enhances their propensity to integration, whereas the storage functions such as the pantry, cellars and still room, are linked to the basement passage by way of intermediate spaces and tend to be much more segregated. Closets, attics and cellars, those spaces which are occupied exclusively by servants or household goods, are highly segregated.

The centralised geometry of Mereworth's layout is so dominant that the most integrated space in this house is a function space, the saloon, whilst the servants' hall in the cellars is the second most integrated function space (see figure 6.9). However, the stairs, galleries and vestibules which link and separate the various levels in the house are also within the core of most integrated spaces. As at Coleshill, the distribution of integration is unbalanced by the fact that there is only one flight of servants' stairs down into the cellars but, on the whole, integration mirrors the vertical layering in the plan and therefore captures the public–private interface within the house so that the state rooms are more integrated than the bedchambers, which in turn are more integrated than closets and inner chambers.

All the rooms on the principal reception floor are well-integrated and shallow to the exterior, but the centre of gravity of the house is drawn towards the less formal long gallery and garden front, whilst the more formal front entrance and reception rooms are set a little apart within the nexus of integrated spaces for assembly and entertainment. The upper-level gallery of the attic storey is also well-integrated but the lobbies to each of the apartments ensure that, although the house is quite shallow overall, spatial seclusion is afforded to the private suites of rooms of each of the principal occupants. With the exception of the servants' hall, the service rooms in the cellars tend to lie on the segregated side of the mean value for the whole house as well as being a set of terminal spaces accessed by passages and corridors. These intersect in the servants' hall, ensuring mutual surveillance of the servants by one another and from the immediately adjacent steward's room.

Integration at Mereworth reclaims a shallow and well-integrated core of interface spaces in the house where the gentry can gather and mingle.

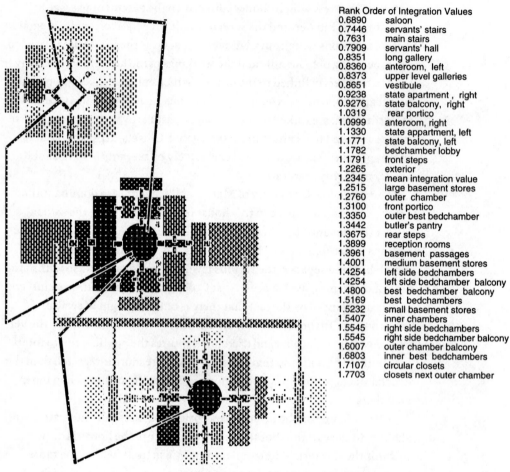

Rank Order of Integration Values

0.6890	saloon
0.7446	servants' stairs
0.7631	main stairs
0.7909	servants' hall
0.8351	long gallery
0.8360	anteroom, left
0.8373	upper level galleries
0.8651	vestibule
0.9238	state apartment , right
0.9276	state balcony, right
1.0319	rear portico
1.0999	anteroom, right
1.1330	state appartment, left
1.1771	state balcony, left
1.1782	bedchamber lobby
1.1791	front steps
1.2265	exterior
1.2345	mean integration value
1.2515	large basement stores
1.2760	outer chamber
1.3100	front portico
1.3350	outer best bedchamber
1.3442	butler's pantry
1.3675	rear steps
1.3899	reception rooms
1.3961	basement passages
1.4001	medium basement stores
1.4254	left side bedchambers
1.4254	left side bedchamber balcony
1.4800	best bedchamber balcony
1.5169	best bedchambers
1.5232	small basement stores
1.5407	inner chambers
1.5545	right side bedchambers
1.5545	right side bedchamber balcony
1.6007	outer chamber balcony
1.6803	inner best bedchambers
1.7107	circular closets
1.7703	closets next outer chamber

Figure 6.9
Distribution of integration at Mereworth Castle

Segregation is a spatial device which removes important formal functions such as the reception of guests from the intimacies of informal social intercourse. Domestic space arrangements separate the activities of servants from those of the assembled company and protect the privacy and status of important members of the household. Corridors and passages are largely confined to the servants' domain in the cellars. Here, the straight, intersecting and axially direct corridors ensure easy access among service functions but they also guarantee that the servants are subject to a strong, centralised visual control.

Bearwood is a strongly corridor-centred house, with an integration focus on a set of large, intersecting rings of circulation which pass through the main and servants' stairs and link together the extensive system of ground and first floor corridors (see figure 6.10). Integration is strongly focused on the first floor corridors which surround the open court that overlooks the skylight of the picture gallery but all of the corridors, including those at the second floor, are on the integrated side of the mean value for the whole house. Though integrated, these circulation spaces clearly are not intended to loiter in. Strict separation of the gentry's and servants' routes, high levels of mutual awareness and supervision and a strict sense of timing ensure that opportunities for unprogrammed interaction are minimised and that the corridors remain empty for most of the time.

The most integrated function spaces at Bearwood centre on women's intimate household activities including the boudoir, nursery suite, ladies' maids' rooms and family bedroom on the first floor and the housekeeper's room on the ground floor. However, women are located on the deeper levels in the plan whereas male spaces tend to be shallower. The garden entrance and grounds are more integrated than the main, formal route into the house but neither is as well-integrated as the business entrance, although this has a restricted access to the rather segregated, exclusively male sporting domain of the deed room, gun room and billiard room. The gentlemen's room is also rather segregated, but less so than the library which is the most segregated of all the principal ground-floor rooms. The picture gallery is the most integrated of the principal ground-floor rooms, though this space seems to be more an extension of the entrance hall than a reception space in its own right. The female reception rooms, the morning room and the drawing room, are rather more segregated than the equivalent male gender-specific spaces, though admittedly most of the important, named function spaces are to be found on the integrated side of the mean integration value for the whole house. The dining room is the most integrated of the main ground-floor rooms and it is also a neutral space from the point of view of gender in that it supports the only social activity which regularly draws all the genteel members of the household together.

Apart from the boudoir and family bedroom which rank amongst the most integrated of all the spaces in the house, the main guest bedroom suites which surround the first and second floor galleries are, on average, more integrated than the young ladies' bedrooms, which are in turn more integrated than the bachelors' bedrooms which are placed adjacent to the relatively segregated bachelors' stairs. Although the boudoir is the most

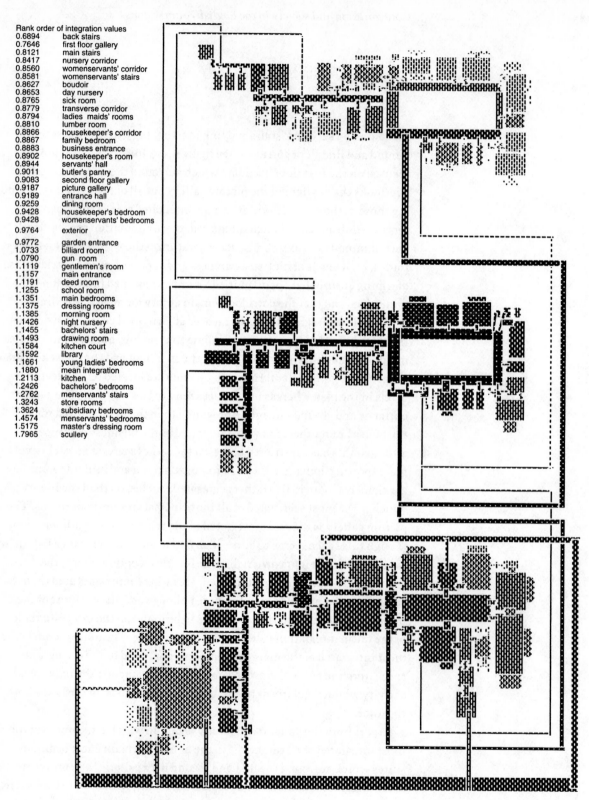

Rank order of integration values

0.6894	back stairs
0.7646	first floor gallery
0.8121	main stairs
0.8417	nursery corridor
0.8560	womenservants' corridor
0.8581	womenservants' stairs
0.8627	boudoir
0.8653	day nursery
0.8765	sick room
0.8779	transverse corridor
0.8794	ladies maids' rooms
0.8810	lumber room
0.8866	housekeeper's corridor
0.8867	family bedroom
0.8883	business entrance
0.8902	housekeeper's room
0.8944	servants' hall
0.9011	butler's pantry
0.9083	second floor gallery
0.9187	picture gallery
0.9189	entrance hall
0.9259	dining room
0.9428	housekeeper's bedroom
0.9428	womenservants' bedrooms
0.9764	exterior
0.9772	garden entrance
1.0733	billiard room
1.0790	gun room
1.1119	gentlemen's room
1.1157	main entrance
1.1191	deed room
1.1255	school room
1.1351	main bedrooms
1.1375	dressing rooms
1.1385	morning room
1.1426	night nursery
1.1455	bachelors' stairs
1.1493	drawing room
1.1584	kitchen court
1.1592	library
1.1661	young ladies' bedrooms
1.1880	mean integration
1.2113	kitchen
1.2426	bachelors' bedrooms
1.2762	menservants' stairs
1.3243	store rooms
1.3624	subsidiary bedrooms
1.4574	menservants' bedrooms
1.5175	master's dressing room
1.7965	scullery

Figure 6.10
Distribution of integration at Bearwood

integrated room in the house the equivalent male space, the master's dressing room, is only indirectly accessible by way of the family bedroom and is therefore one of the most segregated function spaces.

The servants' hall and butler's pantry are strategically located in well-integrated and highly visible locations, but the adjacent spaces where the menservants actually carry out their work are rather more segregated. Not only are womenservants' work areas at Bearwood more integrated than those of their male counterparts but their bedrooms are likewise more integrated than menservants' bedrooms. The kitchen court with its surrounding laundry, service and store rooms accounts for most of the segregation in the house, though pockets of segregation are found wherever work rooms and service areas, store rooms, bathrooms and toilets are concentrated.

It is a striking characteristic of Bearwood that, despite its great size and large number of separate spaces, the mean integration value of the house is comparable with those of the much smaller examples of Coleshill and Mereworth. Yet despite the fact that Bearwood is relatively shallow and spatially integrated for a building of its size, the rooms are separated from one another – even insulated from one another – by intervening layers of transitions and they are not strongly differentiated from one another spatially by the way in which they are differentially embedded within the overall space configuration. In a sense, to inhabit these rooms is to obey social conventions but not to exercise real spatial choices as to whether to be sociable or reclusive.

Integration analysis has highlighted the ways in which the four houses differ as a consequence of their social programmes. Yet in spite of the manifest variety of their plans, there is at least one morphological feature that all of the examples have in common which relates to the broad, generic functions which the houses serve and which might therefore be regarded as characteristic of the country house as a building type. Among the spaces for occupation the functional genotype: informal activities > formal activities > private activities > service activities seems to hold. Social activities and places which are assigned to important residents in order to perform their everyday, mundane roles tend to occupy the most integrated spaces whereas the more formal social interfaces between household members, such as the spaces where guests are received or where celebrations marking special occasions are held, tend to occur in rather more segregated locations, though these are still usually to be

found on the integrated side of the mean value for all the rooms in the
house. Private, intimate functions are normally located in segregated
spaces. So are service functions and storage rooms but both these activities, especially where they are associated with servants, also tend to be
located shallow in the building whereas rooms which are set aside for the
private use of important residents tend to be both segregated and deep
from the exterior.

Many of these changes in the morphology of the country house seem to
echo the developments in ordinary people's homes that have been traced
in previous chapters. In particular, the function of the hall appears to have
varied over time from that of drawing the members of the household
together informally in an everyday living space to that of creating a more
formal space for the reception and entertainment of guests, or even in providing an uninhabited buffer zone to separate people and activities from
one another. These social functions are similar to the distinctions which
have already been made between the *salles communes*, parlours and
vestibules of the smaller houses of the period.

At Mereworth, integration is focused on the saloon, a 'd' space at the
intersection of three global rings which pass through the exterior and also
the focus of localised, internal pattern of movement. Intuitively, this space
seems more like the informal, everyday living room or *salle commune* of
much smaller houses. At Coleshill and Bearwood, the equivalent 'd' spaces
are the vestibule hall, entrance hall and, at Bearwood, the picture gallery
but these spaces are largely or exclusively for movement, not for occupation. Functionally, they behave in a similar way to the *vestibule* type of
entrance hall in a small house in that they are shallow and well integrated
but empty for most of the time. The main reception rooms at Coleshill and
Bearwood are 'c' spaces that are on purely local rings which do not integrate the house. They therefore seem rather more formal, like the *grand
salle* in small houses.

However, Hardwick is quite unlike the other houses in the way in
which occupation is related to movement within the interior of the house.
Each of the thirteen circulation rings at Hardwick contains at least one and
up to two or more important 'd' type spaces where rings intersect, but
which are also function spaces in their own right. Invariably, these spaces
are at one and the same time the domain of a named occupant, a destination for processional movement towards and away from that occupant and
a setting for important inhabitant–visitor interactions with that occupant.

This type of space is not found to anything like the same extent in the later houses

Spatial patterning in the English country house

The set of plans will now be characterised in terms of just four key spatial measures which characterise the layouts of these complex buildings; namely the transition:space ratio which measures the economy or insulation of the layout, the ratio of rings to sequences that captures the extent to which the building frames activity, the property of symmetry/asymmetry which express the potential of space to classify activities or social roles and finally the mean integration value of the house which records the extent to which the layout draws people and things together or keeps them apart.

The first distinction which spatial analysis permits is that between size and complexity. Size, measured in terms of the total number of spaces in a house and which may be a reflection of the relative wealth of the occupants, seems in many ways less informative of the social programme of these houses than the number of use or function spaces, the number of rings in the plan, the number of transitions which link and separate the function spaces and the ratio between them, all of which seem relatively unaffected by economic constraints but to be more directly a product of social practices.

Most houses employ transitions to a greater or lesser extent, but we can conceive of plans which minimise the number of transitions with respect to function spaces and thus configure space efficiently to achieve social purposes, whereas others seem to have an excess of transitions which suggests that space has been deployed divisively, to separate and insulate activities and people from one another rather than to draw them together. This property is measured by the transition:space ratio, and it gives a rank order for the four houses of Mereworth < Coleshill < Bearwood < Hardwick, with Mereworth being the most efficient layout and Hardwick the most highly insulated.

These spatial effects can be further explored in that 'a' and 'b' space-types emphasise tree-like configurational properties whereas 'c' and 'd' space-types are conducive to ringiness. Sociologically speaking, tree-like plans offer no route choice to their occupants whereas ringy plans can be used to give people choice in how they navigate and explore the building interior, as in the case of museums and galleries, or to differentially embed the circulation patterns of different groups of occupants such as men and women, hosts and guests or gentry and servants. Put another way, in a tree-like or non-distributed layout the building strongly frames the activity of its occupants whereas a distributed building is more permissive.

The distributedness or non-distributedness of the layout (spaces on rings or spaces within trees) can be calculated by the formula $(a+b) / (c+d)$ = distributedness, where a low value is distributed and a high value is non-distributed. This gives a rank order for the four houses of Hardwick < Coleshill < Mereworth < Bearwood, suggesting that route choice at Hardwick is weakly-framed and elaborated in the interests of the shared world view which celebrates the persona of Lady Shrewsbury and which is framed also by the passage of time and by rules governing behaviour. In the remaining houses, routes become increasingly constrained over time functionally to separate out the circulation patterns of different categories of occupants, both gentry and servants, so that subtle spatial segregations are maintained between the two classes in the interests of the smooth and impersonal running of the household.

On the other hand, 'a' and 'd' space-types both add asymmetry to the plan, whereas 'b' and 'c' spaces are symmetrical, so $(a+d) / (c+b)$ = asymmetry, where a low value is asymmetric and a high value symmetric. This measure expresses the categoric and classificatory potential of the house to differentiate and express the various roles and statuses of its occupants in space. The asymmetry measure gives a rank order of Hardwick < Coleshill < Bearwood < Mereworth. According to this measure, Hardwick and Coleshill emerge as strongly categorised plans that have the potential to express wide social distinctions, whether these be among personalities as at Hardwick or social situations and settings as in the case of Coleshill.

Finally, the properties of depth from the outside and integration suggest that a subtle and profound change took place in the configuration of the country house during the early seventeenth century, well before the country house began to grow in functional complexity. These measures indicate that a major rupture took place at about this time in the layout of the country house. The rank order for the depth of the interior layout with respect to the exterior is Coleshill < Mereworth < Bearwood < Hardwick. Thus, Coleshill is a rather shallower layout than Mereworth and

Bearwood, but Hardwick is by far and away the deepest. Generalising this property in the form of integration, the mean integration values for the four cases gives the rank order Coleshill < Bearwood < Mereworth < Hardwick, where again Hardwick turns out to be markedly more segregated than the other three examples which are all strongly integrating.

Spatially speaking, Hardwick Hall is quite unlike the three later examples in that its justified graph is deeper than it is wide. Clearly, this is not just a function of the number of external entrances, though in the case of Bearwood the larger number of rings which pass through the exterior helps to overcome its greater size by drawing all parts of the house relatively shallow to the outside. Numerically speaking, Hardwick also stands at an extreme of the range for each and every variable which has been examined to date. It is maximally insulated in its separation of use spaces by transitions, distributed in its choice of routes, asymmetric in its classification of spaces, deep from the exterior and segregated.

Depth-maximising and depth-minimising processes

In his recent book, *Space is the Machine*, Bill Hillier[6] has identified two possible ways in which any small building can mutate into a large one which, he suggests, result from the morphological laws which govern growth in all types of building. This fundamental generic choice may go some way to explaining why larger houses seem to be rather like small houses in some respects and yet so radically different in others. The first mode of growth takes the form of a 'depth-maximising' process in which the configuration approximates an unilinear sequence at every stage. The alternative is a 'depth-minimising' process where the generic mode of expansion is through bush-like space arrangements built on a ring of circulation.

Put another way, depth-minimising processes tend to local groupings of 'a' spaces linked together globally by 'd' spaces. Depth-maximising processes comprise long, global sequences of 'b' spaces linked locally by small numbers of 'c' spaces. Depth-maximising forms based on deep tree-like room arrangements tend to be functionally inflexible. Depth-minimising forms tend to be flexible and suited to large numbers of potential activities and functions and so, as buildings grow larger, a greater proportion of the architectural record will tend to approximate this general form. The reason why this is so has to do with the relation between occupancy and movement in space which is organised for social purposes.

> 'b' and 'c' type spaces raise issues for the relationship between occupation and movement which are not raised either by one-connected or more than two-connected space, in that they require the resolution of the relation between occupation and through movement within each convex space. This has a powerful effect on the usability of space and space complexes of this kind. In general, it can only occur where the sequencing of spaces reflects a parallel functional sequencing of occupation zones and where movement is, as it were, internalised into the functional complex and made part of its operation.'[7]

Put simply, the proposal is that as buildings grow, 'a' and 'd' spaces tend to perform distinct morphological roles, in that the 'a' spaces are rooms and the 'd' spaces are transitions. Few 'd' spaces accommodate both circulation and occupation because these are fundamentally different kinds of activity. Where these two roles coincide, in 'b' and 'c' spaces, movement tends to dominate and the space is emptied of its use potential except in the special case where the use is to frame movement.

Hillier goes on to argue that ordinary people's houses are made up of functional inter-dependencies between fundamentally different kinds of local space arrangement which embed distinctive, culturally-ascribed patterns of occupation and use. The example he cites is that of La Bataille from the sample of farmhouses from the Normandy region of France, a house that has already been discussed in this book and which was illustrated in figure 3.5. Spatially speaking, La Bataille is made up of a small b-complex or unilinear sequence which is associated with male working activity, a small c-complex or ring which is associated with female working activity, a single a-space, the *grande salle*, which is associated with formal reception and an integrating d-space, the *salle commune*, in which all the everyday living functions of the house and the informal reception of guests are concentrated. Two *vestibules* mediate the relations among the d-space, the a, b and c complexes and the exterior. It is these differential spatial embeddings of household activities and functions in fundamentally different space-types which give rise to different distributions of integration and hence to the stable genotypical characteristics that can be retrieved from an analysis of samples of house plans.

As houses grow, Hillier suggests, less of the movement which is internal to the house will tend to be generated by the execution of functionally interdependent activities such as household tasks and work processes, and more will be between sub-complexes which are functionally much more independent of one another. The house will accommodate less necessary or programmed and more contingent or unprogrammed activity and so space will bring together what the occupational requirements of the complex divide. The more that this is so, the more movement will tend to follow the integration pattern of the building and, all other things being equal, the global social outcome will be a probabilistic encounter field of mutual awareness and co-presence.

Great country houses are much larger than La Bataille and so have had to adapt to take account of increased size and organisational complexity, and in so doing they have obeyed the laws of space as well as of society. As they grow, these houses increasingly have to accommodate movement among people, activities and functions and, unless this is an intrinsic aspect function, it is likely to produce a configurational shift in favour of an 'a+d' space-type of a kind which has been identified here. However, the social significance of 'c' and 'd' spaces also seems to have been completely inverted by these transformations. At Hardwick, 'd' space is for occupation and 'c' space for movement, whereas in the other three cases 'd' space is for movement and 'c' space for occupation. As 'd' spaces also tend to be strong local control spaces whereas 'c' spaces are usually weak local control spaces, the local properties of each space-type can also be mobilised in the interests of these very different generic functions.

Communities and differential solidarities

The dominant social fact which seems to lie behind all these changes is the separation of the household into two distinct and spatially differentiated social classes during the later part of the seventeenth century, namely the gentry and their servants. The former now constitutes the immediate family of the owners of these houses, the latter an unrelated group of permanent visitors to the space who are resident in the home and on whom its smooth running depends but who have little or no status or voice in relation to the organisation or operation of the household. In essence the household at Hardwick is a single community, that of the later houses is split into two differential solidarities. The houses therefore offer a clear illustration of the proposition that space acts in an inverse relation to society at least as often as space reflects social structure. In the highly segregated case of Hardwick Hall, space contrives differences within what is essentially a single social group; in the later, more integrated houses, space re-integrates what society has irrevocably set apart.

It would seem that the dominant form which social solidarity took in the 'great household' at Hardwick is analogous to Durkheim's concept of a mechanical solidarity[8] in that, whatever their status, the inhabitants were directly bound to one another by a complex web of shared sentiments and values. According to Durkheim, the social landscape of mechanical solidarity is sparse and dispersed. The deep and segregated layout of Hardwick may be the means to achieve these social ends within the scope of a single dwelling. Likewise, the form which the household took after Coleshill is analogous to Durkheim's concept of organic solidarity,[9] at least in the sense that the occupants are bound to together more by their economic and occupational differences than by a shared world view. The space of organic solidarity is usually dense and nucleated in order to facilitate exchange and interaction. This may begin to explain why the later houses become so much more integrated. At Mereworth even the layout itself is specialised so that the reception rooms assume a more grid-like, integrated character that is normally associated with urban space (and its potential for social encounter and exchange) whereas the servants' quarters are more tree-like and segregated. Integration at Coleshill and Bearwood is more obviously functional in that it supports the division of labour within the household but it does not encourage social exchange between the gentry and the servants.

Spatially, Hardwick has many generic features in common with the complex public buildings of the modern state such as museums and galleries, notably its deep ringy structure. The social programme of these buildings tends not to be about constructing inhabitant–visitor interfaces so much as about laying out knowledge in a systematic way. At Hardwick Hall, however, the knowledge which is celebrated in its programme is not scientific or aesthetic but knowledge of social structure and social relations. But, the consequence of deploying space primarily to index status through asymmetry – a spatial gesture which can be compared with the retreat of old people into the parlour in the small yeoman houses of the period – is that the shallow reception spaces of the house are stripped of their most prestigious occupants for most of the time. Meanwhile, the anterooms, lobbies and passages play a dual role. By increasing the insularity and asymmetry of the house they support people's roles and statuses but for the rest of the time they are the places where these differences in status are suspended and where informal, unprogrammed social interactions can take place so that the household can continuously re-constitute itself as a community. The deep, ringy structure which lies beyond Bess's private, separate and protected sub-complex is well nigh impossible to police but this may be unnecessary and even undesirable where the occupants have shared attitudes and values.

In the later houses, though, the occupants do not form a single community. Under these circumstances, it would seem that the potential of space to amplify roles and statuses is sacrificed to a more systematic spatial control of movement and unprogrammed activity. Spatially, Coleshill, shares morphological features with many modern group residential homes. Though well integrated, the lobbies, passages and corridors of Coleshill are designed to institutionalise avoidance. Movement within the interior, particularly the domestic routines of the servants, is programmed by rules governing conduct which ensure that the spaces designed for efficient movement remain empty for most of the time. Activities are assigned to rooms which, by means of their local and global configurational characteristics, rationally differentiate service functions from those which are served and common areas from private places. Those spaces occupied by the residents are no longer so powerfully embedded in the space configuration as they were at Hardwick but the daily life of family members is well-integrated, privacy is assured through relative depth and segregation and the reception functions are drawn back into the shallower levels of the house.

The nexus of integrated function spaces on the principal living floor at Mereworth reclaims the shallow interface with the exterior for the dominant social class. Mereworth's passages, on the other hand, use the axial potential of space to institutionalise surveillance, which is why this occurs only in the cellars in the domain of the servants. The sharp differentiations of configuration between sub-complexes suggests that Mereworth is closer to an 'overgrown' house than any of the other examples in that it retains many genotypical features that are associated with smaller houses of the period.

Bearwood employs a combination of institutionalised avoidance and axial surveillance to govern the way in which its different spatial sub-complexes come together into a single complex building. The programme at Bearwood is so strong and explicit that the non-residential building type with which it is most in common would seem to be a court house. Spatially, a court house comprises a set of differentiated, tree-like sequences which enter the building from different points of origin and converge on the court room where all the participants in the trial are brought together in a highly contrived and spatially controlled setting. Although the court room appears integrated it is spatially differentiated and each territory is physically separate and bounded – judge's bench, dock, witness box, clerk's desk, jury, public gallery. Movement within the well of the court is further hedged about by rules, so that the interface is an illusion and the relative roles and statuses of the social actors are guaranteed by inaccessibility. In this sense, the daily rituals of the dining room at Bearwood, the most integrated reception room of the house, can be viewed as the formal counterpart of the courtroom drama and as with the court house it is the back stairs and passages which integrate the building.

This sobering analogy may serve to highlight the fact that integration does not always serve benign social purposes. The property of pronounced inter-accessibility among spaces, activities, functions or things should not always be taken as indicative of a gregarious and communitarian way of life. Integration is only a virtue to the extent that it can give rise to useful multiplier effects upon social solidarity by generating a dense, probabilistic and unprogrammed space of human co-presence and encounter, over and above that which is already enshrined in the programme of the building. If the locus of integration is itself strongly programmed so as to inhibit global movement, the related local property that well-connected spaces strongly control movement amongst their immediate neighbours may come to the fore.

Houses may appear to offer a retreat from society into a domain where individuals and families are free to exercise personal choices but this is just an illusion. A house is the primary space where society is continuously constituted in the shape and pattern of everyday living. This is as much the case in the great country houses as it is in ordinary people's homes. At the same time houses, like other buildings, obey the laws of space. Because society is continuously constituted in the patterns of movement and interaction that take place in space, social purposes take hold of space and shape it through generic function. All of which goes to show that, in understanding the way people relate to buildings, it is necessary to take account not only of social rules but also of the law-fulness of space.

Notes

1 R.T. Gunter, *The Architecture of Sir Roger Pratt* (Oxford University Press, 1928).

2 Timothy Mowl and Brian Earnshaw, *Architecture Without Kings* (Manchester University Press, 1995), pp. 48–59.

3 Robert Kerr, *The Gentleman's House: or How to Plan Residences from the Parsonage to the Palace* (London: John Murray 1871), pp. 456–7.

4 Jill Franklin, *The Gentleman's Country House and its Plan, 1835–1914* (London, Routledge & Kegan Paul, 1981), p.146.

5 Bill Hillier, *Space is the Machine: a Configurational Theory of Architecture* (Cambridge University Press, 1996), pp. 318–20

6 Ibid., p. 321.

7 Ibid., p.324.

8 Emile Durkheim, *The Division of Labour in Society* (New York: The Free Press, 1964), pp.70–110.

9 Ibid., pp.111–32.

Visibility and permeability in the Rietveld Schröder house

(with David Rosenberg)

Summary

The remaining chapters of this book turn to an examination of contemporary architects' houses, beginning with a detailed exploration of the relation between space planning and furniture design in the configuration of what is now widely regarded as one of the most influential icons of modern architecture, the Rietveld Schröder house. The Rietveld Schröder house, built in 1924, was greeted at the time with reactions which varied from cautious approval to scornful dismissal. However, its influence upon subsequent generations of architects has been considerable. Its initial renown was, in some measure, due to its adoption as an exemplar of 'the new architecture' by the De Stijl group of artists and architects under the leadership of Theo van Doesburg. Later, Mrs Schröder, who commissioned the house and continued to live there until her death in 1985, was careful to ensure that its unique contribution to the development of twentieth-century architecture was widely recognised. Before her death, Mrs Schröder donated the house to the city of Utrecht and it has now been restored to its original condition and functions as a museum and study centre. In his recent appraisal of the debt which modern architecture owes to the house, Paul Overy[1] suggests that it has been more widely published than any other domestic building of the early modern period, including the villas of Le Corbusier. However, the significance of the Rietveld Schröder house is not so much in the simplicity and modernity of its appearance as in the fact that it is claimed by many critics to be the original open and flexible plan and, as such, it is seen to propose a new, informal way of living which is deemed appropriate to the modern, nuclear family. The argument is advanced here that the unique contribution of the Rietveld Schröder house resides not so much in the flexibility which is inherent in the plan, as in a novel relation between permeability and visibility which is submerged and disguised by the open appearance of the interior.

A blueprint for modern living

From the very outset, Mrs Schröder saw her home as a living example of how twentieth-century family life should take on a material form. Even before she entered into a collaboration with Rietveld for the design of the Rietveld Schröder house, she had remodelled her existing family apartment in Biltstraat, Utrecht, to express her deep dissatisfaction with the popular tastes and values of the day. The simplicity of the apartment was in sharp contrast with the opulence which would normally be associated with the home of a well-off family from the bourgeois social stratum to which Mrs Schröder belonged. This conspicuous lack of ornament and ostentation was to become a feature of the Rietveld Schröder house:

> The house was a statement of intent, a stance taken; a declaration of how an independent modern woman intended to live her life. It would be wrong, however, to see the Schröder house as in any way a prototype for working-class, mass housing – despite its economic specification. It is far too individualistic. Rather it was a prototype for the 'reduced' circumstances of a middle class living in the later part of the twentieth century, when servants can no longer be afforded and space is at a premium.[2]

Integral to the 'prototype' for this more intellectual and aesthetic lifestyle were two features which have since become synonymous not only with the house, but with the whole of modern architecture – the 'open plan' and 'flexible living'. The openness and flexibility of the interior, with its sliding screens and built-in furniture, appears to have resulted from Mrs Schröder's influence upon the design, whilst the spatial structure of the house is due to Rietveld.

The Rietveld Schröder house broke new ground in two fundamental aspects of its interior design. First, it was designed to operate in two modes, with either an open-plan first floor or with a partitioned room arrangement at the first-floor level (see figure 7.1a).

> Not only in the exterior, but also in the whole interior planning of the house, new ideas have been pursued . . . by rejecting the normal method of dividing space with fixed walls, and choosing a system of sliding partitions, an extremely flexible arrangement of the interior is achieved. The whole upstairs can be used as one large space, with the stairs

coming up in the middle. However, it is also possible to divide it up into a separate entrance hall and a number of smaller or larger rooms.[3]

The form of the house, which results in its open and closed states, has been interpreted by architectural critics as a fundamental expression of modern attitudes to domestic privacy. Specifically, the potential for an open, light and airy upper floor is contrasted with the closed, separated and darker rooms of the ground floor, and is interpreted as a choice between communal openness and enclosed domestic privacy.[4]

Ida van Zijl gives the following description of the feeling of transparency which was achieved in Mrs Schröder's ground-floor studio, but it might equally well apply to any part of the interior of the upper floor, for 'we are virtually sitting in the same space. The distinction between inside and outside disappears as a result of the detailed articulation, and we experience with our senses a spatial quality that extends far beyond the physical surface of the house'.[5]

Large areas of glazing blur the visual distinction between inside and out, and the overhanging balconies extend the house volumetrically to some extent, if not quite to 'the totality of infinite space' to which Rietveld aspired.[6] Within the interior, long views extend through flowing space to reveal the inner relationships amongst its constituent volumes. Van Doesburg included open planning in his agenda for 'the new architecture', suggesting that living might take place in a general area which could be subdivided by separating planes, which might even be furniture.[7] This description might almost be a specification for the Rietveld Schröder house, and the house does seem to embody the concepts of transparency and de-materialisation which underpin the architectural philosophy of De Stijl.

Second, the Rietveld Schröder house contained items of built-in furniture which were conceived of as an integral part of the design and which could operate in concert with either the open-plan or the partitioned versions of the upper level (see figure 7.1b). Rietveld was, of course, a furniture-maker and not an architect by profession. Mrs Schröder's initial idea was that her house should offer 'all sorts of possibilities'.[8] Yet in its realisation, particularly in the experiments Rietveld has made in saving space by incorporating built-in furniture and fittings, the house generated unforeseen difficulties. Built-in furniture gives a clear indication about the way rooms are intended to be used, and how the residual spaces are to be occupied and related together visually and permeably. As Mrs Schröder herself

Figure 7.1
Plans of the Rietveld Schröder house

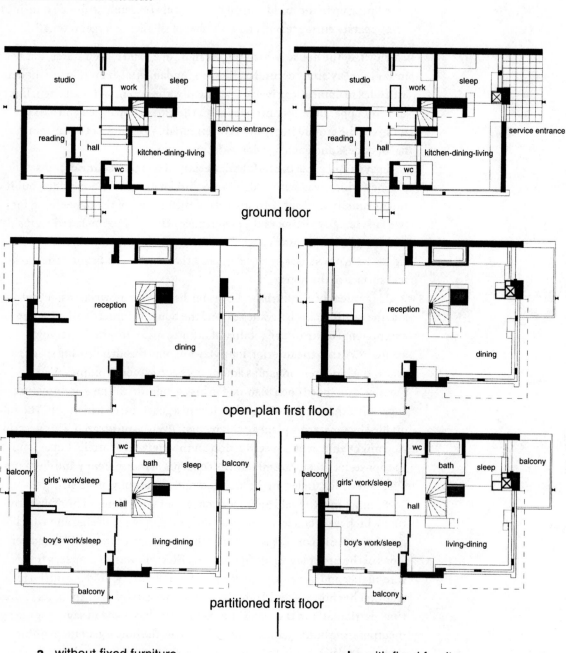

ground floor

open-plan first floor

partitioned first floor

a. without fixed furniture

b. with fixed furniture

Figure 7.2
Convex break-up of the four modes of the
Rietveld Schröder house

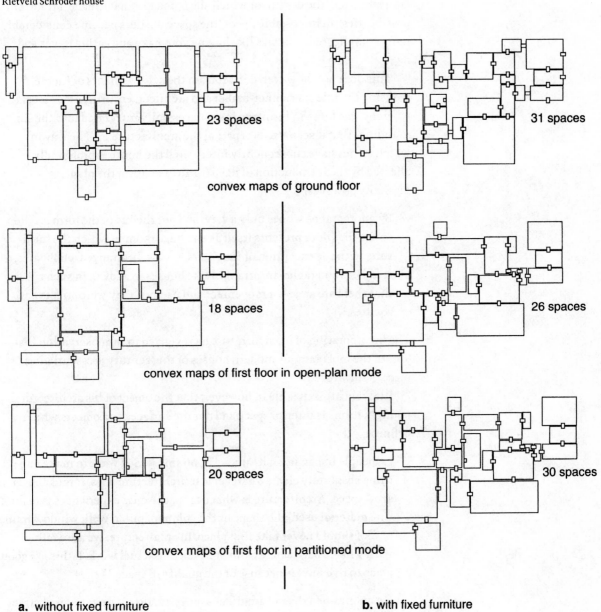

23 spaces

31 spaces

convex maps of ground floor

18 spaces

26 spaces

convex maps of first floor in open-plan mode

20 spaces

30 spaces

convex maps of first floor in partitioned mode

a. without fixed furniture

b. with fixed furniture

later admitted, the design for which she opted may have made 'all sorts of possibilities' an impossibility, for 'the space upstairs became considerably more complicated . . . it was like having your cake and eating it; yes and no'.[9]

This does not, however, detract from the achievements of Rietveld in fusing the roles of cabinet-maker and architect, ensuring a symbiosis whereby 'the built-in furniture is so successfully integrated into the surroundings that it seems to be a part of the architecture'.[10] The way in which critics have subsequently interpreted the house is profoundly affected by the introduction of fixed furniture within the plan. As Lissitzky observes,

> By photographs we see only a view and not the life of the form . . . the entire first floor presents itself as one huge room in which the furniture, with the exception of the chairs, is closely arranged: cupboards, sofa-beds and tables are arranged like houses in a town, in such a way that there are areas for movement and use as if they were streets and squares.[11]

The incorporation of fixed furniture has even led to the observation that 'one of the most famous modern houses of this century is essentially a piece of furniture'.[12]

Rietveld himself is clear, however, that the object of his architectural manipulations is interior space and not the surfaces and objects which define it:

> . . . people live in it, on it, among it, around it. So I want to make one thing absolutely clear: whatever else architecture does, it must never spoil space. Architecture is what our space-sense experiences is reality. The material used, the shape or the colour of pillar, wall, window frame or roof should never take first place. In architecture, we are dealing with what is between, within or beside the actual work. If this is a good place to live in, it is because of the quality of space.[13]

He maintained that an architect's most important material is abstract space and that the purpose of giving form to a building and shaping space is one of 'revealing reality' in that it is the life of the occupant which is inscribed within the form of the house. For Rietveld, architecture is primarily an act of space creation which is at the same time a celebration of a new way of life.

The house which has resulted from this unique collaboration between architect and client combines the concept of 'openness' – the apparent abandoning of traditional ways of partitioning space with walls, with 'flexibility' – the inbuilt potential for creating more than one space configuration within a space shell by moving internal partitions. But if openness and flexibility are the defining features of space in the Rietveld Schröder house, the way in which these properties are manifested is through the incorporation of moving screens and fixed furniture, thus reversing the more normal domestic condition in which the walls are fixed and the furniture is mobile.

This has led to a significant innovation in the spatial structure of the Rietveld Schröder house in that it is potentially four separate buildings, with and without furniture, and with the first-floor partitions closed or open. The house is able completely to transform itself by the opening or closing of screens, and by disregarding or taking full account of the way the interior is furnished. These changes inevitably affect the space of which they are a part and, to the extent that this is so, it is not possible to talk of one 'revealing reality' to be apprehended by the space-sense but of several. These are not normally available simultaneously to the occupant for direct comparison, but appear as choices in how the house may be inhabited and used.

However, analysis is able to achieve what reality finds impossible in that it can synchronise the various descriptions of the interior of the Rietveld Schröder house and present them together for comparison and interpretation. A detailed examination of the way the space configuration of the Rietveld Schröder house is fine-tuned by screens and furniture begins to clarify precisely what measure of choice is available to the user in its different states. It even sheds new light on the configurational and social significance of the less tangible architectural phenomena of 'openness' and 'flexibility' as a blueprint for a modern way of life.

Monument in miniature

The Rietveld Schröder house is small, but surprisingly complex internally. The inter-relationships in plan and volume derive from Rietveld's architectural grammar, which:

consists of a number of space-dividing elements, that determine
unambiguously what is inside and what outside. In addition to these,
are transitional elements such as eaves, balconies, pillars, railings,
door-frames and window-frames which relate both to inside and
outside. These elements structure the transition between inside and
outside in a different way in each situation, depending on the position
and function of the space, and on the light.[14]

However, these are not mere formal architectural devices, but bear a close
relationship to how Mrs Schröder wanted to live, both intimately with
her children and in entertaining her extensive circle of clients and
friends.

The main entrance leads into a hall, from which a curving flight of stairs
ascends to the upper level. To the left is a reading room, and to the right a
kitchen-dining-living area which has a separate tradesmen's entrance. At
the rear of the house is a studio where Mrs Schröder exhibited paintings by
friends for sale to the public, a work room and a sleeping area for the household help. In practice, Mrs Schröder did not employ a live-in maid, so the
room became an extension of the downstairs living rooms. Upstairs, the
house can be used as one large living area to take full advantage of the view,
or sub-divided into an upper landing, three rooms and a small bathroom and
toilet. The boy's room is at the front of the house over the reading room, and
the girls' room is over the studio. The main upper-level living-dining area is
located over the kitchen-dining-living room below, with Mrs Schröder's
tiny bedroom tucked in behind. Every small detail of the plan is designed to
support the family life of Mrs Schröder and her children. Space-sense and
space-use are intimately, almost tenderly, related.

From a configurational point of view, the domestic interior articulates
four propositions for a way of life: open and unfurnished, open and furnished, closed and unfurnished and closed and furnished. The first point
which this reveals is the additional complexity which the furniture introduces into both the open-plan and partitioned versions of the whole house
(see figure 7.2). The ground floor is sub-divided by load-bearing walls rather
than flexible screening, but the number of convex spaces increases by eight,
from twenty-three to thirty-one when the fixed furniture is added to the
room arrangements. On the first floor, the plan can be modified both by the
addition of furniture and by the closing of screens. In the open-plan mode,
the addition of the fixed furniture increases the convex break-up of the first

floor by eight spaces, from eighteen to twenty-six. This is a larger increase in convex complexity than when the unfurnished first-floor plan is partitioned. This produces a further two spaces over and above the open room arrangement. However, partitioning and furnishing the upper floor renders its convex articulation complex to about the same degree as found in the furnished ground floor. This mode adds ten spaces to the partitioned but unfurnished version of the first floor. Thus, the aggregate effect of adding the furniture appears to have a greater effect on the domestic interior than does the opening and closing of partitions. The unfurnished shell of the entire house has a mere forty-one spaces, the partitioned but unfurnished version has forty-three, the open and furnished arrangement has fifty-seven, whilst the furnished and partitioned mode has sixty-one spaces.

The most integrated view of the home is the unfurnished open-plan version, followed by the unfurnished and partitioned plan, the open and furnished case and finally the partitioned and furnished variant. The mean integration rises from 1.534 for the open-plan and unfurnished version of the whole house, through 1.725 and 1.731, to 1.883 in the case of the partitioned and furnished home. Thus, furniture segregates the whole house where open-planning integrates, but the effect of the furniture is stronger than that of the partitions.

In practice, the furniture is integral to the design of the house and so, having noted its overall segregating effect on the interior, it is the precise distribution of integration within the open and closed versions of the whole which gives a more true-to-life account of how the space structure of the house makes itself available for use (see figure 7.3). Convex integration in the unfurnished open-plan version shown in figure 7.3a centres on the ground-floor entrance hall, stairs and upper-level landing, and spills out into the large open-plan living area at the head of the stairs. The vertical axis of the stair transition is not only detailed with great precision as a series of small, articulated and functionally discrete areas to contain a half-landing, telephone shelf and bench, but is also illuminated by a stream of light pouring down from a skylight. It would seem that the concentration of integration on the vertical stair transition, which acts as 'a central area of stability, a core around which the transformable spaces are grouped'[15] is quite deliberate.

The core gradually reaches out from this central vertically-integrating shaft, at the ground-floor level towards the kitchen-dining-living area and the studio, and at the first floor to the set of flexible interior reception

Figure 7.3
Integration values for the four modes
of space configuration in the Rietveld
Schröder house

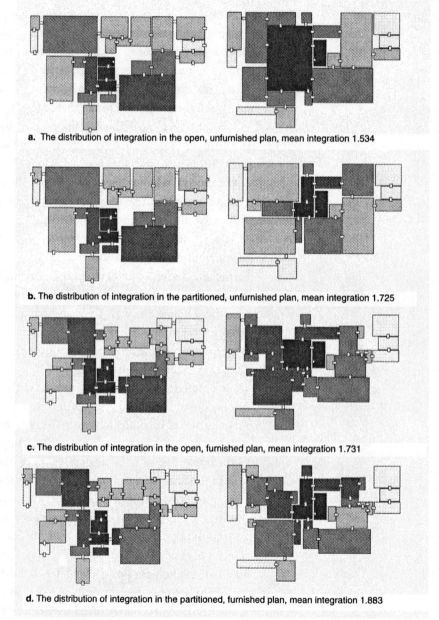

a. The distribution of integration in the open, unfurnished plan, mean integration 1.534

b. The distribution of integration in the partitioned, unfurnished plan, mean integration 1.725

c. The distribution of integration in the open, furnished plan, mean integration 1.731

d. The distribution of integration in the partitioned, furnished plan, mean integration 1.883

spaces which lie immediately adjacent to the point of arrival. Mrs
Schröder's small sleeping area is more segregated, as are the first floor balconies. The introduction of partitions redistributes integration as shown
in figure 7.3b. The effects are confined to the first floor, where the integra-

tion core shrinks back into the upper-level hall at the head of the stairs. Mrs Schröder's study-bedroom occupies a strategic, well-integrated location on a small ring of circulation which passes through the living areas, around the head of the stairs and through her private rear corridor off the common hallway. Among the remaining function spaces, the children's study-bedrooms overlooking the street at the first floor level are more segregated than the upper-level family living-dining area, despite their visual continuity through the glazed hallway with the reception spaces. The external balconies, though visually continuous with the interior, are more segregated still. Downstairs, the most segregated areas are the work room, maid's room and service entrance at the back and the reading room which is close to the front door but visually screened to provide the seclusion and quiet which are appropriate to this more contemplative activity.

The open, furnished plan shown in figure 7.3c is the most lifelike version of how the house was laid out when Mrs Schröder entertained guests within the home. It is known that Mrs Schröder drew back the screens when she entertained, 'to see if, on coming upstairs, they (visitors) were struck by the space and light'.[16] In this version of the plan, integration is still strongly concentrated on the vertical circulation through the hall and stair-well. Among the function spaces, integration links the front upper-level spaces where guests are received with a more secluded dining area where guests are entertained and with Mrs Schröder's more intimate bedroom space which, in this version of the plan, becomes an extension of the living-dining area. The integration core draws these upper-level spaces close to the downstairs studio and living room, whilst more strongly segregating the service spaces and the reading room.

When the Schröders were living in the house 'en famille', however, the partitions tended to remain closed, and the distribution of integration through the house is as shown in figure 7.3d. Mrs Schröder did not believe in handing over her children to the care of a nursemaid, but she does appear to have believed in their right to a private space. In the closed version of the plan, integration still centres on the stairs and hallways, but it moves inwards and upwards to emphasise Mrs Schröder's pivotal position in the home. Her downstairs studio and upstairs bedroom are strongly drawn together by the space pattern, whilst the upstairs work and sleep areas of her two children are held apart from one another by the convex articulation of the threshold spaces to their respective rooms. The girls' room is more integrated than the boy's room. The living-dining areas on both

Figure 7.4
Isovists from key spaces in the Rietveld Schröder house

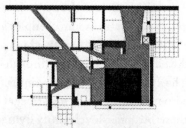

Isovist, furnished ground floor kitchen-living-dining area

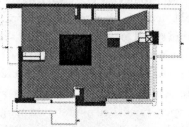

Isovist, furnished first floor open-plan reception area

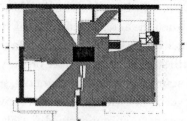

Isovist, furnished first floor hall

floors are relatively segregated for an activity which normally functions as a focus for family life. The integration order of the rest of the plan is largely unchanged by the act of shutting the screens.

Shutting the screens, therefore, seems to affect the balance of sociability and privacy within the heart of the house. This is not just a matter of erecting a boundary between mother and children and among children of different genders (Mrs Schröder was widowed by the time she commissioned her house). Indeed, the transparency of the staircase prevents complete visual privacy even when the screens are in place, as figure 7.4 shows. At the upper level, furniture does not impede the perception of the whole of the open-plan living floor, and closing the partitions makes only minor differences to the transparency of visual fields throughout the upper level, largely due to the decision by Rietveld and Mrs Schröder to use glazed partitions around the stair-well. With the partitions open, almost all of the upper floor is revealed at a glance but, when the screens are in place, the built-in beds are not visible from the upper hallway, a sensitive modulation of the interior which is not at all obvious from plans and photographs of the house. The ground floor produces a more conventional arrangement whereby visual fields reveal partial views through the interior living rooms, but these include penetrating views which link a series of convexly-articulated spaces together 'like beads on a string'.[17] This is a property of external space, and it may contribute to the feel that the house with its fixed furniture is town-like. At the same time, the ground-floor studio and reading area are almost entirely visually shielded from casual surveillance from within the downstairs kitchen-living-dining room.

By these spatial means, the house seems to generate a degree of social distance between its occupants by the precise way in which its space is articulated, so that it is possible to achieve a measure of personal identity without being isolated. This is all the more remarkable when the diminutive size of the house is considered. It seems that one of the most important effects is to prevent enforced intimacy where space is at a premium by a series of more or less secluded spaces, which are insulated from one another by a series of transitions and linked together by the central staircase.

However, these effects on the whole house mask a more subtle series of changes which take place if the two storeys of the plan are considered separately. This is a valid approach, since the inclusion or exclusion of built-in furniture and fittings affects both floors whilst the open-closed transformation applies only to the upper, living floor of the house (see figure 7.5). Perhaps not surprisingly, the six most integrated systems of the ten analysed are those of the individual floors. As before, the inclusion of built-in furniture and partitioning, both tend to increase segregation. However, opening the partitions on the first floor has a far greater effect in enhancing the mean integration of the plan than does the addition of furniture in increasing overall segregation, with or without partitions. Closing partitions does not greatly increase the convex complexity, but it increases the relative segregation amongst the constituent rooms of the home. Adding the built-in furniture greatly increases the convex complexity of the upper floor. Where the built-in furniture adds eight to the total number of convex spaces at first-floor level in the open system and ten to the closed

Figure 7.5
Convex integration distributions of each
floor considered separately

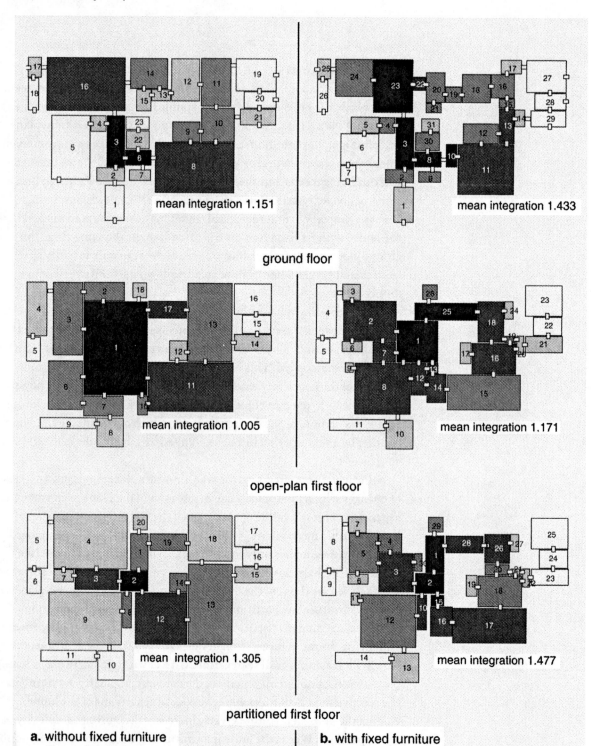

mean integration 1.151

mean integration 1.433

ground floor

mean integration 1.005

mean integration 1.171

open-plan first floor

mean integration 1.305

mean integration 1.477

partitioned first floor

a. without fixed furniture   **b.** with fixed furniture

Figure 7.6
Justified access graphs of the four versions of the first floor plan

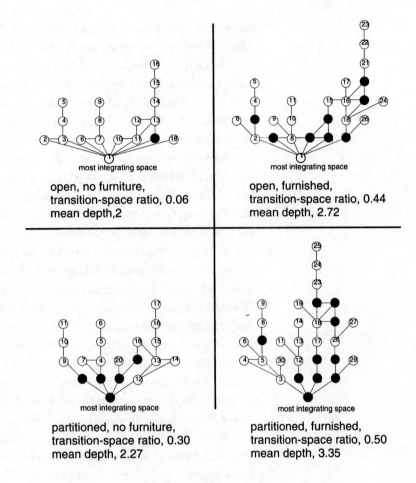

open, no furniture,
transition-space ratio, 0.06
mean depth,2

open, furnished,
transition-space ratio, 0.44
mean depth, 2.72

partitioned, no furniture,
transition-space ratio, 0.30
mean depth, 2.27

partitioned, furnished,
transition-space ratio, 0.50
mean depth, 3.35

system, closing the partitions only adds two to the unfurnished and four to
the furnished versions respectively. Adding furniture to the rooms on the
ground floor increases the convex articulation there by eight spaces, and
considerably increases its overall segregation.

Justified graphs of the four versions of the first floor from their most
integrating space, clearly display their individual properties of depth and
ringiness (see figure 7.6). The mean depth of the open, furnished floor is
comparatively high, exceeding that of the partitioned, unfurnished floor.
Similarly, the closed, furnished version is very deep as a result of the
combined effect of the partitions and furniture in articulating the plan.

However, despite the apparent depth of the open-plan, furnished
arrangement it is well-integrated, much more so than the shallower,

closed but unfurnished version of the home. The ringiness that openness affords appears to offset the depth which furniture imposes.

The ratio of transitions to spaces is minimal in the open, unfurnished plan, suggesting that a by-product of the innovative removal of boundaries is that it reduces the number of transitions required to negotiate the interior. The open unfurnished plan is an unitary, flowing space. The closed, unfurnished house separates into just two areas for frontstage reception and backstage sleeping. The ratio rises considerably when the built-in furniture is added to the plan, showing how the furniture modifies the interior subtly to distance one space from another. The result is increased articulation of the function spaces, and the break-up of the domestic interior into a set of independently perceived spatial domains, insulated from one another by transitions. This confirms the tendency, noted earlier, for the articulation of space by furniture to reproduce something of the character and complexity of urban space. This may be a product of Mrs Schröder's expressed dislike of large, open and rectilinear rooms, but it may equally well have to do with reconciling her apparently contradictory needs for a space to withdraw, in order to be herself, and her desire to do away with all the interior walls of the upper living area.

Despite the fact that the ground floor is highly compartmentalised whilst the first is a more fluid space arrangement, a striking feature of the house in both its unfurnished and furnished partitioned states is that the first floor is consistently more segregating than the ground floor. In both instances of the closed first-floor plan, the spaces allocated to the girls' and boy's rooms and to a lesser degree to Mrs Schröder herself, are more segregated than in the open plan, where the same spaces are used for entertaining. Thus the partitioning allows for a more traditional domestic layout, separating sleeping areas from living areas and relating them in a more segregated way. The main first-floor living spaces are well integrated because they are located shallow in the overall configuration, and they also feature on the important ring which takes in Mrs Schröder's bedroom and the bathroom.

These tendencies are confirmed by examining in more detail the distributions of integration in the furnished versions of the ground, open first floor and closed first floor respectively. The importance of the ring of ground-floor circulation through the work room, maid's room and kitchen is clearly revealed, and the centrality of the hall, studio and kitchen to the integration of the ground-floor room arrangement is confirmed. Mrs

Schröder's work room is more separated, expressing her need to withdraw, whilst the reading room is the most segregated part of the downstairs interior. Connections to the space outside are all relatively segregated, especially that which leads to the tradesmen's entrance, which is very segregated and strongly controlled. A locking window and shelf is even provided in this area, linked to the upstairs by a speaking tube, so that tradesmen may leave deliveries without Mrs Schröder's having to go downstairs to receive them.

In all the versions of the first floor, the landing space adjacent to the stair-well is the most integrated space of all, which may be a reflection of the 'centrifugal concept of planning' which Theo van Doesburg advocated in his manifestos. However, in the open-plan version of the home, the bedrooms cease to be distinct spaces and 'de-materialise' in shape, thus tending to integrate more strongly than in the closed version. Integration centres on the reception area at the head of the stairs, and illustrates the subtle privacy gradient which is contained in the articulated set of living spaces even more clearly than was revealed in the analysis of the whole house. The dining area, used under these circumstances for formal eating, is rather more segregated. Relative separation, in this instance, enshrines the increased status of the room as a formal eating space.

When the partitions are closed, however, the living-dining room features amongst the most integrated of the spaces on the first floor, as befits its informal function in providing a focus for family life. Mrs Schröder's centrality in orchestrating the life of the home is marked by the relative integration of the spaces within her personal domain, including the large ring of circulation which passes through her bedroom. As before, the children's domains are held apart and insulated from one another by their location in the configuration. This is particularly so of the boy's room, which is one of the most segregated function spaces in the interior at the upper level, and which therefore affords him considerable privacy.

Revealing reality

The open first floor has been described as a 'richly articulated space, even when the panels are fully drawn back'.[18] Articulation, it appears,

produces segregation. At a more mundane level, Brown has noted that
equipping the first floor with sliding partitions has resulted in those elements which house them when open constraining the use of space.[19]
But what a consideration of the relative significance of screens and furniture does reveal is that the idea of the open plan seems to allow for
the architectural manipulation of the distinction between permeability
and visibility within the configuration. Traditional housing layouts
keep this difference to a minimum, as walls, when opaque, serve to
hinder both movement and sight. The introduction of furnishings
within a conventional domestic setting further reduces the scope for
permeability and increases spatial articulation within each room,
regardless of where the furniture is put. Open planning increases both
permeability and visibility, but its effects upon the layout of this particular house are more visual than functional. The built-in furniture seriously reduces the potential for throwing back the walls to unify the
plan. It does not affect visibility to the same extent, and the result is
that one can see far beyond where one can immediately go. This is the
fundamental feature of the perception of space in the Rietveld Schröder
house. It looks more open than it feels when moving about in the
domestic interior.

The addition of furniture decreases the potential flexibility of this
new way of living, particularly in a home so tiny that every inch of space
becomes a premium. Flexibility exists for the most part in the abstract, not
in the mode of living it affords, and 'although it was the first truly flexible
dwelling which took into account the increasing informality and freedom
of social living arrangements in the twentieth century, yet at the same
time . . . it clearly placed enormous demands on its occupants'.[20] Indeed,
Rietveld himself has speculated that only Mrs Schröder could live in the
house which resulted from their unique collaboration.

The function of each item of fixed furniture in the Rietveld Schröder
house seems therefore to establish the relative status of the space it occupies, or of the person for whose use it is intended. Furniture is more than
just a decorative and useful household artefact. By virtue of its presence,
it exercises a subtle form of spatial control within the interior: the dinner
party furniture is not for moving, the table and chairs are clearly arranged,
and the way the places are allocated form an arrangement with which one
does not tamper. Indeed it is the dining area which is most affected by the
fine-tuning of the home in its whole and in its parts, and it seems no

accident that people 'naturally gravitate to this spot . . . this is the most magical area of the house'.[21]

This is not the first time that this less-than-obvious relationship between room arrangements and their furnishings has been noted. The historian, Robin Evans, has also described the close relation between the planning and furnishing of eighteenth- and nineteenth-century houses as a situation where, 'the furniture occupies the room, and then the figures inhabit the furniture',[22] and this observation seems equally pertinent to the analysis of the Rietveld Schröder house. Evans argues that developments in the planning of domestic interiors and placing of furniture, such as the change in fashion which took place in the closing years of the 1700s from placing furniture at the periphery of the room to locating it at the centre of the plan, also signalled a shift in the way in which the space of the interior was used in social gatherings. Thus furniture may be seen both to encode and to elaborate the space of which it is an integral part.

In the case of the Rietveld Schröder house, it may be that despite the supposed potential for introducing changes in the way in which space supports social function within modernism, Rietveld has elected to recreate within the liberated, newly available space of the open plan something of the compartmentalisation which was previously enshrined by walls and partitions. Whilst walls and boundaries are not structurally necessary to the flexible, open plan, the construction of the spatial separations between occupants seems to have been preserved as a social imperative.

However, the architectural result of building-in fixed furniture is entirely different from that of building walls. Movement is restricted, but visibility is not impaired. The occupant retains an impression of openness and freedom of movement, even when this exists only virtually and visually. The practical consequence of open planning in the Rietveld Schröder house is to restrict movement and to reinforce the discreteness of its constituent spatial domains, whilst at the same time integrating the domestic interior visually, through the transparency and completeness of its visual fields. This dominance of visual over permeable relations is indeed a new way of 'revealing reality' through space configuration. But where the potential for transparency in volume to overcome spatial discreteness by purely visual means becomes such a conscious and manipulated aspect of architectural technique, it can be argued that what 'the new architecture' expresses is not so much a new 'way of living' as a new 'way of seeing'.

Notes

1 Paul Overy, Lenneke Büller, Frank den Oudsten and Bertus Mulder, *The Rietveld Schröder House* (London: Butterworth Architecture, 1988), p. 13.

2 Ibid., p. 22.

3 Theodore M. Brown, *The Work of G. Rietveld, Architect* (Cambridge, Massachusetts: MIT Press, 1958), p. 57.

4 Gavin Stamp,'How to Live in a Piece of Furniture', *The Times Saturday Review*, 15 Dec. 1990, pp. 16–17.

5 A. Buffinga, *Gerrit Thomas Rietveld, the Schröder House Utrecht* (Amsterdam: Meulenhoff, 1971), p. 18.

6 Ibid. p. 8.

7 Daniele Baroni, *The Furniture of Gerrit Thomas Rietveld* (London: Academy Editions, 1978), p. 90.

8 Overy, Büller, den Oudsten and Mulder, *The Rietveld Schröder House*, p. 60.

9 Ibid., p. 56

10 M. Friedman, *De Stijl 1917–1931: Visions of Utopia* (Oxford: Phaidon, 1982), pp. 137–8.

11 Brown, *The Work of G. Rietveld, Architect,* p. 58.

12 Stamp, 'How to Live in a Piece of Furniture', p. 16

13 Paul Overy, Büller, den Oudsten and Mulder, *The Rietveld Schröder House*, p. 81.

14 Ibid., p. 120.

15 Ibid., p. 28.

16 Ibid., p. 106.

17 Bill Hillier and Julienne Hanson, *The Social Logic of Space* (Cambridge University Press: 1984), pp. 10–11.

18 Friedman, *De Stijl 1917–1931*, p. 137.

19 Brown, *The Work of G. Rietveld, Architect,* p. 54.

20 Overy, Büller, den Oudsten and Mulder, *The Rietveld Schröder House*, p. 38.

21 Paul Overy, *Rietveld Furniture and the Schröder House* (London: South Bank Centre, 1990), p. 28.

22 Robin Evans, *Translation from Drawing to Building* (London: Architectural Association, 1997), pp. 195–228.

Chapter eight

The anatomy of privacy in architects' London houses

Summary

A sample of eighteen post-war family houses designed by architects living in London for their own occupation is examined to see the extent to which they exhibit similar characteristics to the houses constructed by speculative builders to serve the private housing market. Although the houses are very much individuals, key continuities are identified with the domestic space configurations of modern speculative homes. The most important of these is the way in which the transitional zones in architects' houses tend to be elaborated into a richly articulated 'privacy gradient' from the more accessible to the more secluded parts of the home. However, the way in which architects manipulate space to achieve this spatial insulation is shown to be quite different from the way in which it is provided by the speculative house building sector. In the speculative sector, spatial insulation is achieved only through the use of transition-spaces such as lobbies and hallways whereas architects also directly shape the use-spaces which are provided for occupation and use in order to modulate spatial relations among domestic activities. This principle is linked to the balance between movement and occupation in the domestic interior and its relation to the perceived values of family life and individual privacy in giving a physical form to contemporary family structures.

The architecture of architecture

The samples of houses which have formed the basis for previous chapters originate, for the most part, in traditional and vernacular roots. They are representative of what Rapoport has elsewhere referred to variously as 'the folk tradition', 'unself-conscious design', 'the culture of the majority' or 'life as it is lived' as opposed to 'the grand design tradition', 'self-conscious design' or 'the culture of the elite'.[1] Whether or not these distinctions are accepted in whole or in part, they serve to remind us that these mundane dwellings tend to crystallize in their built form and space organization a record of ordinary people's lives, and hence their configurations tend both to resemble one another quite closely and systematically to relate spaces to functions in what has become known in space syntax as a 'genotype'.

Rapoport has very little to say about architect-designed homes, but the few references he does make are always by contrast with popular traditions. Of modern American speculative houses he argues that:

> These roadside and tract buildings represent certain values which are lacking in architect-designed buildings, and which tell us something about life-styles, thus explaining their acceptance and commercial success. Even though people no longer build their own houses, the houses they do buy reflect popular values and goals more closely than do those of the design sub-culture, and these houses constitute the bulk of the built environment. This difference between the popular and the architect-designed house can still help us gain an insight into the needs, values and desires of people.[2]

By implication, architects' houses celebrate a different and incompatible set of values, including the search for uniqueness and a preoccupation with formal design considerations and aesthetics.

However, architects are also socially situated, and the question therefore arises as to whether any assumed difference between speculative and architect-designed houses is one of degree, or one of substance. This chapter sets out to explore this question by examining the houses which architects build to live in themselves. In designing for owner-occupation, the architect is also the client. He (or more rarely she) is free to generate the brief, and so the product is more likely to be an authentic expression of the architect's design philosophy and system of beliefs, specifically those beliefs about the nature of contemporary family life and household organization insofar as these are capable of translation into a physical form. At the same time, the ideal is likely to defer to the real in the balance between ideology and pragmatism. Because the architect will literally 'live with the consequences', unconstrained freedom of expression is likely to be moderated by the practical considerations of decision making. This leads to circumstances under which the greatest progress is likely to be made in understanding the extent to which architects' conceptions of 'the good life' are similar to or different from the majority of householders.

The eighteen houses which form the basis of this study have been selected from Miranda Newton's recent book, *Architects' London Houses*.[3] Newton's book features 30 houses built over a fifty-year period between 1939 and 1989. By restricting her selection of homes to London, Newton hoped to highlight the values and choices made by modern architects who shared a common context of working in a vibrant, international and architecturally-speaking influential, capital city. It was intended that the constraints of land and construction costs, density, privacy and planning restrictions would be comparable and that this would allow the individuality of the homes to reveal itself. For our purposes, Newton's self-imposed limitation means that cultural factors may also be assumed as a constant, rather than a variable. Culture may influence design both through the frameworks of ideas and social practices which architects acquire by socialization and in the more restricted concepts and values which have been acquired during their architectural education. If there is such an entity as an architectural 'sub-culture' it may become apparent in the way these houses have been designed. The analysis of space configuration may, in this case, uncover the architecture of architecture.

Apart from this unity of urban context, Newton's examples have all been chosen to demonstrate high quality in design, but beyond this she deliberately set out to embrace the widest possible variety of architects' homes. Some are examples of 'outstanding originality': others are 'typical' products of their time, place and genre. Newton has included examples of newly constructed homes and conversions from other premises, of self-build homes and houses built by a contractor, of low-budget and more opulent houses and of houses which are highly constrained by their context and examples which are relatively independent of their site and local context. A consequence of this diversity may be that these houses have no invariant characteristics and no space genotype. To the extent that this is so, this would lend support to Rapoport's suggestion that it is in the nature of architecture to seek for novelty, perhaps even for its own sake and at the expense of the transmission of cultural values.

However, as Newton observes, 'Architects are, on the whole, idealistic people. Many of them believe that better buildings will make better lives for the people who live and work in them. Architects' own homes embody their real passions, on a scale which is comprehensible. Interesting value systems and priorities come to light when the architect becomes the client.'[4] One plausible source of architectural innovation might be a desire to transform cultural values. For some, the definition of architecture includes showing people possibilities they have never dreamed of, as well as giving shape to the ideas they have already. The question arises as to whether the houses have anything in common, or are they simply a collective manifestation of the idiosyncratic lifestyles of their occupants? Through their widespread publication, these houses may become influential housing prototypes, in which case it is of interest to see whether they embody ideas about family life which are capable of generalization.

The eighteen examples which are presented here represent the individual choices of a group of postgraduate students who worked collectively to assemble the configurational database of analyzed plans during the Autumn of 1992. All the houses they selected were originally designed and built after the Second World War for the architect's own use, and were conceived of as 'family houses'. Most of the designers are male, though the sample contains four houses designed jointly by a married couple and one designed by a woman architect. All but two of the architects are of British nationality. All were educated within a Western European architectural tradition, and eight of the designers undertook some or all of their architectural studies at the Architectural Association, though this may be indicative more of Newton's circle of acquaintance (she too was AA trained) than of the existence of a monopoly in designing fine houses amongst AA graduates. Nine houses are from the 1960s and 1970s, and nine from the 1980s. The sample contains two single-storey homes, eight two-storey houses, six with three storeys and two four-storey examples. The majority, fourteen out of the eighteen cases, are located in London's 'urban villages', traditional, inner-city residential areas. The remaining four are in suburban areas on London's outer fringe.

The plans of the eighteen houses are shown in figures 8.1 to 8.3 inclusive. It is immediately apparent from the plans that these architects'

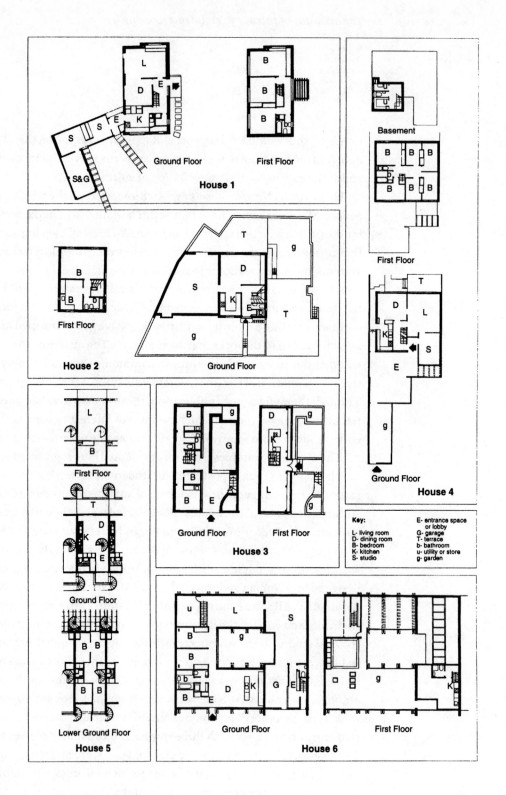

Figure 8.1
Plans of architects' London houses

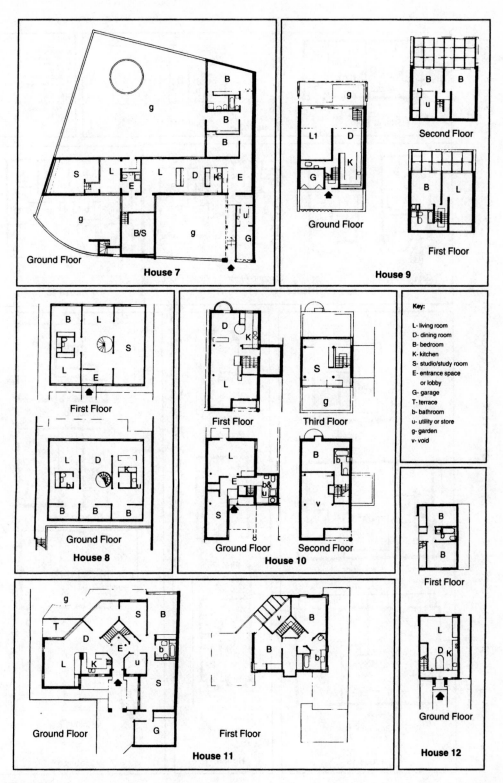

Figure 8.2
Plans of architects' London houses (continued)

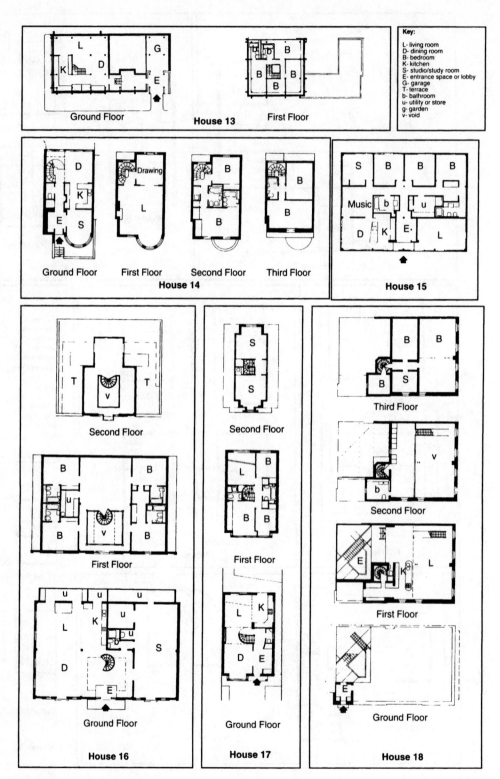

Key:
L - living room
D - dining room
B - bedroom
K - kitchen
S - studio/study room
E - entrance space or lobby
G - garage
T - terrace
b - bathroom
u - utility or store
g - garden
v - void

House 13
Ground Floor — First Floor

House 14
Ground Floor — First Floor — Second Floor — Third Floor

House 15

House 16
Second Floor — First Floor — Ground Floor

House 17
Second Floor — First Floor — Ground Floor

House 18
Third Floor — Second Floor — First Floor — Ground Floor

Figure 8.3
Plans of architects' London houses (continued)

houses come in all shapes and sizes. The two single-storey houses are quite unlike one another in their geometry and 'parti'. House 7 is an extensive layout and has four wings which define three courtyards, whilst House 15 has simple, regular rectangular proportions and its geometry is based on a very compact room arrangement around a central T-shaped circulation core. This group of two-storey dwellings includes several regular two storey houses which are augmented by a single-storey extension (Houses 1,2, 3 and 13), a courtyard house (House 6), two simple, well-proportioned rectangular plans (Houses 8 and 12) and a rather irregular, eroded plan (House 11). The three-storey houses include an example with a small basement (House 4), a modern interpretation of a traditional London terraced house with a lower ground floor which is fully exposed on the garden side and has a small basement 'area' at the front (House 5), and three examples with a conventional ground, first and second-floor plan but which are nonetheless compositionally very different from one another in terms of geometry, proportions and layout (Houses 9, 16 and 17). Of the four storey houses, House 10 is also a modern interpretation of a London terraced house with strongly modelled front and rear facades and a small side extension, House 14 is a new house but its appearance is conventional in that its modelling and detail is reminiscent of London's town houses of the Regency period. House 18 inhabits the remodelled shell of a Georgian terraced house but the interior has been completely gutted to form separate, self-contained apartments on the lower levels and a four-storey main house which leaves only a residual 'footprint' on the ground floor entrance level. Clearly, all the houses have been thoughtfully planned and some of the house plans are recognizably modern. At a purely visual level, the most striking feature of the set of layouts is not their architectural elaboration but their restraint. Compared with the extravagant, rambling plans of contemporary high-income houses by speculative house builders, these houses appear at first sight to be rather unpretentious, elegant and efficient in their space planning. This inverts the popular mythology that architects' houses are replete with unnecessary detail whilst speculative houses are simple and efficient and so represent 'better value for money'.

The respective integration distributions of the houses are summarized in figures 8.4 to 8.6 inclusive. Integration values for the houses have been calculated both with and without the exterior, but the representation shown in figures 8.4 to 8.6 is a standardized view which includes the

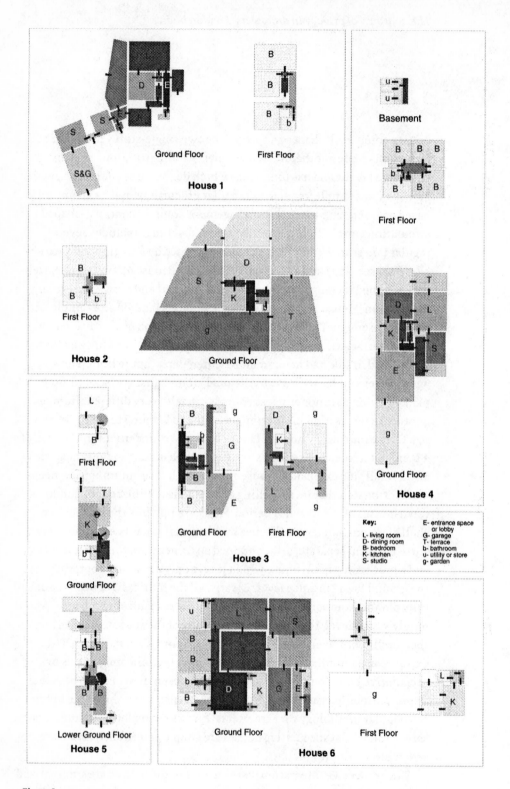

Figure 8.4
Distribution of integration in plans of
architects' London houses

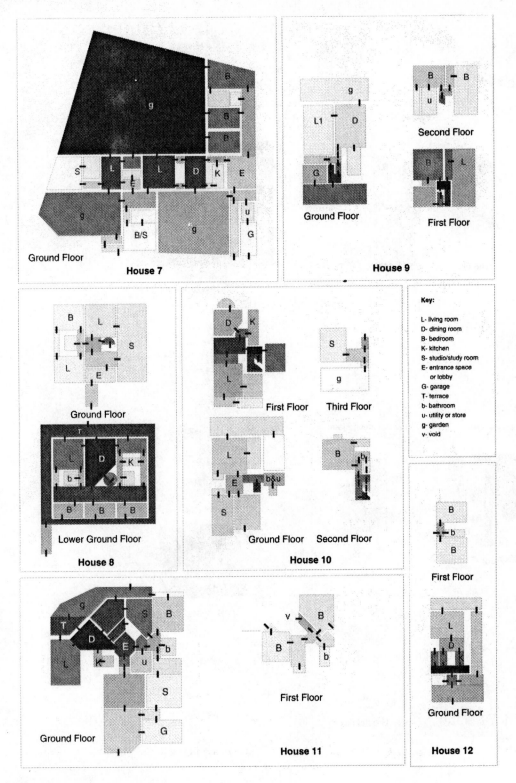

Figure 8.5
Distribution of integration in plans of architects' London houses (continued)

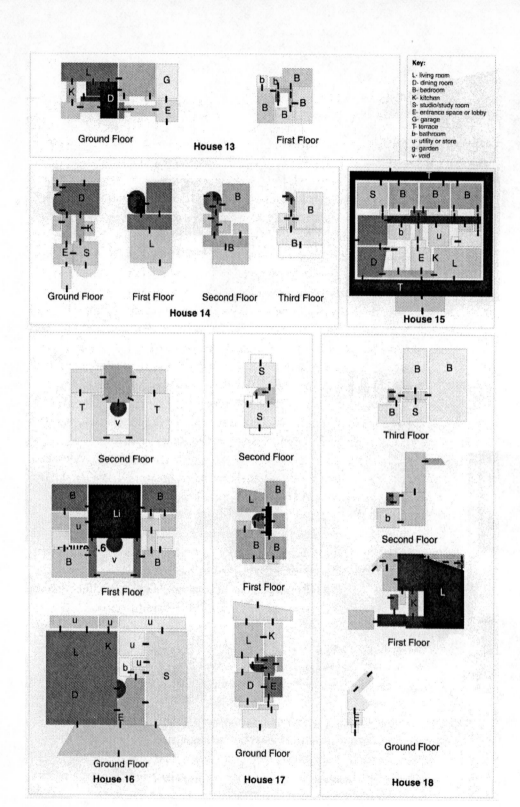

Figure 8.6
Distribution of integration in plans of
architects' London houses (continued)

exterior spaces in all cases. All other things being equal, integration tends to gravitate to the geometric centre of a compact configuration, whether this be a room arrangement in a house plan or a network of streets in a city. Thus, in a regular single-storey plan with three structural bays the most integrated space would naturally be the centre bay, in a three-storey house one room deep it would be the middle floor and in a 'triple-pile' house the most integrated space would be the central room on the *piano nobile*. As we have seen in previous chapters, much of the social 'effort' which can be detected in design is aimed at overcoming the 'inertia' of space to arrive at a space configuration whose structure is principally orientated to fulfilling social purposes. What is immediately striking in this sample of houses is the manifest visual variety in the way in which the tone representing bands of integration is distributed from dark to light in relation to the underlying geometry of the plans. No visual consistency can be detected in the gradation of integration cores according to such factors as orientation, the number of storeys in the house, rectilinearity, geometry or proportion. The most integrated space may be in the geometric centre of the plan or it may be located at the front, rear, side or corner of the house or even in the surrounding house plot. All the dark, well-integrated areas may be concentrated on one floor or they may be spread through the entire house. More often than not, the tones are distributed in an irregular array even where the underlying geometry seems regular, thus indicating that the pattern of access and permeability is weighted towards certain parts of the house and away from others, distorting the balance of the architectural composition and privileging some rooms over others in terms of their relative accessibility or seclusion. As with the country houses which were examined in chapter six, these houses appear to be so different from one another that it is difficult to imagine what they might have in common, even though they are set within a shared cultural context and were constructed within a relatively compressed time-frame. In what follows, a quantitative approach will therefore be adopted in order to search below the 'surface structure' of appearances for configurational regularities by which the 'deep structure' of architectural thought can be recognized. Whilst admittedly this approach is less accessible to intuition and designerly thinking, a numerical and statistical exploration of the data can often reveal spatial patterns which are invisible to the naked eye and may point to trends which are difficult to establish from a purely qualitative account.

Anatomy of dwelling

Basic quantitative data are presented for the London architects' houses in figure 8.7. Configurational variables are unaffected by such factors as the year in which the house was built, or its location in the inner city or the suburbs of London.

The first variables to be compared are those of metric area and the total numbers of interior and exterior convex spaces into which the house is broken up. The average floor area of the houses in this sample is two hundred and twenty square metres. The smallest house in the sample, with a total floor area of seventy square metres, is much more compact than the remainder of the sample of architects' houses but it approximates closely to the average floor area of speculative houses which is about seventy-five square metres. The architects' sample has a large number of smallish houses, and a small number of very large houses. At the top of the range, four houses are over three hundred and fifty square metres in area, and the largest of these has an approximate floor area of four hundred and fifty square metres. Comparable, large 'executive' speculative houses at the top of the range that is available within the private housing market, which have floor areas of between one hundred and fifty and one hundred and seventy square metres, are still quite a lot smaller than the average floor area for the architects' sample. Architects' houses are simply more spacious than those inhabited by even quite wealthy members of the general population.

The interiors of the architect-designed homes are also convexly quite elaborate, with between ten and thirty-four convex spaces, and an average of twenty-four spaces. Here too, the average number of spaces in the architects' sample is comparable with those for the very largest and most elaborate of speculative homes. For example, the average house built by speculative builders in the Milton Keynes area, a growing city where most of the major UK house builders are active in laying out new estates based on their 'own-brand' standard house types, has only thirteen convex spaces and the figures for the most spacious examples fall within the low twenties. What is more, the exteriors of speculative homes – courtyards, gardens, pathways, balconies, patios and the like – tend to be relatively simple with only one or two distinct outdoor spaces. By contrast, the architects' houses that have been analyzed in this sample have between three and ten such spaces, with an average of between six and seven. This

house number	year built	location	integration focus	area, square metres	convex total	exterior spaces	interior spaces	bounded spaces	boundary : convex ratio	integration with exterior	integration interior only	external rings	internal rings	function spaces	transitions	space : transitition ratio
1	1960	suburb	trans	163	27	4	23	12	0.522	1.342	1.690	5	1	9	14	0.643
2	1961	city	trans	146	20	6	14	7	0.500	1.434	1.579	1	0	5	9	0.556
3	1964	city	trans	144	26	9	17	6	0.353	1.297	1.391	1	1	6	11	0.545
4	1964	city	trans	183	32	8	24	16	0.667	1.313	1.484	3	1	11	13	0.846
5	1964	city	trans	117	30	9	21	8	0.381	1.379	1.598	4	1	10	11	0.909
6	1966	suburb	space	370	40	9	31	16	0.516	1.292	1.771	1	2	14	17	0.824
7	1976	city	space	350	35	10	25	10	0.400	1.038	1.859	12	1	11	14	0.786
8	1976	suburb	space	220	31	6	26	4	0.154	1.197	1.377	7	9	11	15	0.733
9	1977	city	trans	184	27	4	23	7	0.304	1.842	1.933	0	0	9	14	0.643
10	1983	city	trans	225	42	8	34	8	0.255	1.912	1.952	0	0	18	16	1.125
11	1984	city	space	252	37	9	28	13	0.464	1.449	1.708	5	1	14	14	1.000
12	1985	city	trans	70	17	7	10	4	0.400	1.294	1.491	1	1	6	4	1.500
13	1986	city	trans	150	25	6	19	10	0.526	1.490	1.412	0	1	10	9	1.100
14	1987	city	trans	225	35	4	31	14	0.452	1.667	1.662	0	2	16	15	1.067
15	1989	city	trans	180	29	3	26	8	0.308	0.815	1.056	7	1	11	15	0.733
16	1989	suburb	space	448	40	8	32	17	0.531	1.280	1.287	2	4	9	23	0.391
17	1989	city	trans	156	34	5	29	12	0.414	1.646	1.597	2	1	14	15	0.933
18	1989	city	trans	369	30	3	27	9	0.333	1.880	1.771	0	1	9	18	0.500

Figure 8.7
Data for eighteen architects' London houses

is despite their being located in London, where land is at a premium and plot sizes tend to be small.

Unsurprisingly, the metric area of the house has a positive statistical correlation with the total number of convex spaces within the interior, 0.668, but this bears almost no relationship to the number of exterior spaces which are associated with the home. The correlation between the metric area of the house and the total number of exterior spaces is 0.173, whilst that between the total number of interior spaces and the number of exterior spaces is negligible.

However, just like the large country houses that formed the basis for chapter six, the sheer size and complexity of these architects' houses is less informative than the number and proportions of the different types of spaces which make up the domestic configuration. Spaces in these houses can be classified in three ways according to their topological extension and edge condition: the numbers of spaces designed primarily for static occupation, the use-spaces in the home which are extended convexly in two dimensions and are large enough to contain domestic activities, the number of transitions within the interior which tend to be small, narrow and to function as a part of the circulation system or to define the threshold between use-spaces and the total number of rooms; that is, the bounded compartments within the home which can be completely separated and sealed off from one another at the perimeter by walls and doors.

In traditional, vernacular and modern speculative houses we have already seen that the first two types of space – use-spaces and transitions – tend to be synonymous with the separate rooms in the house. Use-spaces are normally simple square or rectangular rooms which are aggregated together and linked by a circulation system of long, thin rectangular transitions that are defined by the exterior wall surfaces of the rooms. Counting the separate, bounded compartments therefore proves to be otiose. The only widespread example of a more complex use-space is where a projecting bay or oriel window adds a degree of articulation to the exterior wall surface of a room.

However, the case of the Rietveld Schröder house which was examined in chapter seven has already pointed to the possibility that 'architectural space' may take the form of a more fluid, articulated but 'open-plan' shape made up of several convex spaces, which differentiate activities and occupations from areas intended for circulation and movement but without delineating these by walls. Where rooms do exist, they tend not to be square or rectangular in shape but to have more irregular and articulated shapes which fit together like the pieces of a jigsaw.

The houses in this architects' sample have between five and eighteen convex use-spaces and an average of eleven for the sample as a whole, whereas the Milton Keynes speculative sample that was presented in chapter five had comparable figures of between three and fifteen use-spaces with an average of eight use-spaces. Architects' London houses contain between four and twenty-three transitions, with an average of fourteen per home. In the speculative houses, these figures were one, nine and four respectively. Over half the architects' sample has between nine and eleven convexly defined use-spaces, with the balance made up from three less elaborate homes with only a few spaces, and five houses which are much more spatially elaborate than the norm. So far as convex use-spaces are concerned, architects' houses contain only a few more spaces which are intended to contain domestic activities, functions and occupations than do the speculative houses.

Values for the number of transitions in the architects' houses cluster close to the mean. Nearly half the examples have either fourteen or fifteen transitions. The average space: transition ratio of these houses is 0.786, which can be compared with that of 1.462:1 for the speculative homes looked at earlier in chapter five. This shows just how much more elaborate the use of transitions has become within the design of architects' homes. In these houses, it cannot simply be a matter of making the interior appear larger and more complex than its actual size warrants, for architects' homes already have an inbuilt spaciousness to which speculative homes can only have pretensions. But over and above their sheer size, architects' houses are characterized by a generosity in the spatial modelling of the system of access and circulation, and by the relative insulation of use-spaces from one another through subtle articulations of the thresholds between rooms.

The number of rooms in the architects' London houses, defined as the separate, bounded spatially identifiable compartments within the plan, varies between six and seventeen, with an average of ten. This is also the norm in speculative homes. This suggests that the functional programme of the modern British home is interpreted in a rather similar way in these architects' houses to that found in ordinary people's houses. If houses are an expression of family membership and domestic practices, and to the extent that key dimensions of shared and personal space are at all marked in the compartmentalization of the home, then it seems that architects may not have a radically different view of which people and activities should be accorded the physical protection of walls and doors. The domestic circumstances of these architects, whilst varied, are not so different from those which obtain among the population at large and, at least in terms of allocating activities to spaces is concerned, these houses adopt similar broadly middle class conventions about how family life should be spatialised within the home.

However, the average boundary:convex ratio of architects' homes, a measure which sets the number of separate rooms against the total number of convex spaces in the plan, is very different from that of the speculative houses. Amongst the former group this is 0.42:1 whilst for the latter group it is 0.77:1. This tells us that in speculative houses most compartments are simple square or rectangular rooms, and that the only part of the interior which is convexly elaborated is the common halls, stairs and landings. In architects' homes, most rooms are more complex spatial domains made up of a mixture of use-spaces and transitions, and it is this which gives the architects' houses a degree of uniqueness which is in such marked contrast to the rather stereotyped and box-like configurations of many modern speculative homes.

In some architects' houses, rooms are made up of several convexly defined use-spaces which flow directly into one another without walls or doors. Here the smallest bounded compartment is a set of activities and occupations that are visually, aurally and permeably synchronized, which is, in effect, what is meant architecturally and sociologically by the term 'open-plan'. In other cases, a significant compartment is the circulation core of halls and landings on different floors. In architects' houses this is usually not restricted to just providing access to a series of rooms as it was in the speculative homes, it also contains significant use-spaces which are clearly intended for occupation, either as a deliberate pause in the movement structure of the house or as a place where people engaged in static domestic activities can interact informally with passers-by. In yet other cases, a mixture of transitions and use-spaces is assembled into a discrete but elaborately shaped room which is devoted to a single or related household activities and functions. The spatial extent, articulation and modelling of the boundary of the 'room' is occasionally so subtle that it is difficult to appreciate either from the plans or experientially, that the space is actually a separate compartment which can be shut off if complete separation is required.

Although space standards in these architects' houses are generally high, there is no correlation between increasing floor area and more sub-division of the plan into use-spaces (0.266). Again, this contrasts sharply with speculative houses, where higher space standards tend to be utilized in the provision of additional daytime living rooms. The correlations between the number of use-spaces and the number of boundaries (0.421), and of use-spaces to transitions (0.445), are both poor. The relation between the number of separate bounded compartments and the metric area of the house is positive but weak (0.550), as is the relation between the number of transitions and the number of boundaries (0.571). However, the relation between increasing metric area and increasing numbers of transitions is strong (0.825). This confirms numerically what has already been suggested in principle, that as architects' houses become larger more and more emphasis is given to designing an elaborate system of 'buffer zones' which links and separates the constituent use-spaces of the dwelling.

Yet this does not lead to the uniformity in layout which we have already seen in speculative houses because, unlike their counterparts in the general housing market, the homes architects build for themselves permutate the possibilities for combining different kinds of space into a domestic layout. Houses 2, 3, 5 and 12 are small, simple and directly related homes. Houses 1 and 13 are small, compartmentalized plans, with few use-spaces and transitions. House 4 is also small, with a comparatively elaborate system of use-spaces and compartments and rather fewer transitions. House 15, also small, elaborates a system of use-spaces and transitions but does not support these in the form of boundaries. House 17 is small and elaborate with many compartments, use-spaces and transitions. The remaining houses are all larger than average. House 9 is a large open plan, with relatively few use-spaces, transitions or compartments. Houses 8 and 10 are large, with many use-spaces and transitions but few compartments. Houses 16 and 18 are amongst the largest of all and have few use-spaces but many transitions. Houses 7 and 11 are large with relatively few transitions but many compartments and use-spaces. Houses 6 and 14 are large fragmented cases, with many transitions, use-spaces and compartments. Unlike the speculative housing sector, very few of these homes are compartmentalized plans, and the sample manifests much more invention in the way in which space is manipulated than is found in comparable examples of modern houses which are built for sale.

At the same time, the almost complete absence of 'open-plan' dwellings in the sample is surprising when set against the attention which they have received in architectural discourse. Rather like the influence which the concept of the 'panopticon' has exercised upon the design and appraisal of modern institutional buildings, the idea of 'open-plan living' may have been more influential in shaping people's attitudes and perceptions of modern homes than in dictating how they were actually built, if the evidence provided by these architects' houses is anything to go by.

The mean integration value for the sample of architects' houses is 1.590 for just the interior spaces, and 1.419 when all links to the exterior are taken into account. This compares with values of 1.684 and 1.423 for speculative houses. The houses which architects design for themselves to live in are not noticeably more integrated than their more traditional middle-class peer group. If integration is considered to be a crude measure of gregariousness, a rather simplistic generalisation but one which is not completely outrageous, architects do not seem to opt spatially for a closer-knit, more communal lifestyle than their contemporaries in the suburbs. However, the houses architects build for themselves do exhibit a greater range of values than in the speculative sector, where homes tend to resemble one another more closely on this variable as they do on most others.

Because most of the spaces are common between house configurations with and without the exterior, the correlation between the mean integration value of the interior spaces of the architects' sample and of the houses including their exterior spaces, is also quite strong (0.650) but, as before, it disguises individual differences among the homes which are produced by the fact that the pattern of linkages between spaces can be either marginally affected or radically modified by how the house is made permeable to its surroundings. House 15, is by far and away the most integrated in both versions of the plan, whilst House 10 is the most segregated. Houses, 3, 4, 8, 12 and 16 are well-integrated both internally and with their grounds, unlike houses 2, 13 and 17 which are more integrated internally than average but where connectivity to the exterior leads to the houses becoming amongst the more segregated in the sample. Houses 5, 9, 11, 14 and 18 tend to greater segregation than the norm with and without their exterior, but Houses 1, 6 and 7 are relatively segregated interior space complexes which are nonetheless better integrated than average with their exteriors. Speculative house builders have a shared view as to how the house should relate to its plot but architects adopt personal strategies in relating the house to its grounds and to whether the exterior should function as a series of exteral rooms or as a convenient place to park the car.

So far as internal rings are concerned, three houses (2, 9 and 10) are tree-like, following the suburban model for a domestic interior. Over half the sample, 11 cases, have one internal ring linking downstairs living areas – usually the dining room and living room – with the hall. Only four cases have more than one internal ring to create the kind of significant route choices within the home which were used to such great effect by the 'new middle-class' householders whose lifestyles were described in chapter four. In this respect, therefore, architects' houses are very similar to modern speculative homes, and seem set within a domestic space tradition which can be traced back at least as far as the mid-nineteenth century. Half the sample has either no rings at all or only one ring with the exterior, normally through the kitchen, but there is considerably more variation in the numbers and types of rooms in these architects' houses which form rings with the exterior than is found in contemporary speculative housing.

The configuration of eight examples is markedly tree-like, both inside and out. A further seven cases are internally tree-like but exploit two or more rings through the house plot. House 14 is very much an exception to the rule, in that it has a ringy interior but a tree-like relationship to its plot. House 16 has four internal and two external rings, whilst House 8 is exceptionally ringy, with 9 internal and 12 external rings. The configurational differences among architects' own houses are therefore quite pronounced.

This tendency towards individuation is further demonstrated if the relationship between the pattern of domestic activities and the unlabelled space pattern is examined. Six houses, Houses 6, 7, 8, 11, 16 and 18 are space-centred, in the specific sense that the most integrated place in the interior is a use-space. By contrast, modern speculative houses are invariably transition-centred and extensive inspection of these mass-market homes has yet to unearth a space-centred example. Of those cases where a major use acts as a focus for an architect's home, in three cases this is the living area, in two it is the dining area, and in one case, House 18 which is shared by an architect and a sculptress, it is the studio. Whether the home is centred upon a major living function or held together by its circulation is a powerful experiential factor in shaping everyday living, which may or may not be affected by whether links to the exterior are included or omitted. In three of the five examples, the precise nature of the integrating use is not sensitive to the inclusion or exclusion of the exterior, but in two of the living-centred cases the focus shifts to the dining area when links to the garden are taken into account.

The remaining houses in the achitects' sample are transition-centred, in the precise sense that parts of the circulation system – stairs and corridors – are the most integrated areas of all. Among transition-centred homes, it is also the case that the integrating function may vary according to whether the internal relations of the house are looked at in isolation or where the house is connected to its surroundings. In the sample as a whole, a most integrating kitchen occurs only twice, and this is unaffected by whether the house is linked to or separated from its grounds. A most integrating main bedroom occurs three times, twice in equal rank order with a living space. In two of the three cases its most integrating position is supplanted by the living area when links to the outside are included. In the remaining cases, either the living area or the dining area integrates the home, with roughly equal numbers of cases.

So far, only the most integrating function has been considered and, for the most part, this has tended to be either a living or dining area, with kitchens, main bedrooms and studios rarely providing a physical focus for the configuration. The next step is to see if it is possible to detect consistent relations among these five domestic activities – relaxing, eating, cooking, sleeping and working – which might amount to a domestic space genotype of the kind which is frequently found in samples of traditional and vernacular homes. Six of these architects' houses do not have a separate studio, but most members of the profession habitually work at home and so these homes are unusual in the extent to which work is incorporated into the domestic setting. Two examples compress two or more activities into a single convex space but, for the most part, each function is allotted its own region of the plan even where these are not contained in rooms and divided from one another by walls and doorways.

Unlike the opposition between space-centred and transition-centred, the rank order of the integration of living functions of the eighteen houses exhibits almost no duplication. This is not the case with traditional and vernacular samples of plans which, as we have seen in earlier chapters, tend to be consistent in their configurational features to the point that this becomes the primary means to detect the imprint of culture on house form. Here, the only close match that can be detected in the rank order of integration among labels is between Houses 13 and 14, where the rank order dining > living > main bedroom > kitchen occurs. In House 14 the studio is shallow in the home but it is in the most segregated position and in House 13, where this use is amalgamated with the garage, the studio is also shallow and highly segregated. The rank order is invariant, with or without links to the outside. Both are transition-centred homes. In the other sixteen cases, the labels are permutated in the label string so that they occur as if at random. Architects' houses do not have a clear functional genotype.

The ranking of activities and functions on the integration/segregation dimension even for an individual house tends to be highly sensitive to links to the outside. In these architects' houses, generalizations are extremely difficult to make even about a single case let alone for the entire sample. If the stability of the rank order with and without the exterior is compared for each example, the rank order is stable in only two cases, House 11 and House 18. In two more cases, Houses 3 and 9, the rank order is preserved as a result of the fact that two functions in separate parts of the home happen to have the same integration values when just the interior spaces are considered, and in two more, Houses 12 and 16, because several of the major living functions take place in one space. For the rest, the most that can be said with confidence is that bedrooms and studios tend to occupy segregated locations, living and dining rooms are nearly always amongst the most integrated functions, whilst kitchens tend to occupy the middle of the range, but there are exceptions to even these rules.

Just for the three daytime living functions of living, dining and cooking, of the thirteen possible combinations of function, all but two permutations are found within the eighteen examples looked at with and without external links. The integration order D > L > K is the most popular with twelve citations, the interior configuration of House 4, the exterior configuration of Houses 6, 7 and 15, and as a stable relation in Houses 8, 11, 13 and 14. However, the order L > D > K is almost as popular with 10 citations, the interior configuration of Houses 6 and 7, the exterior configuration of Houses 3 and 10, and as a stable relation in Houses 9, 17 and 18. Other orderings occur, and all these are unstable with and without the exterior except for Houses 12 and 16 where the stability is achieved because functions are amalgamated. Just as in ordinary people's houses, it seems to be a matter of personal preference whether the main living spaces are drawn together by the eating/entertaining function or whether everyday living is perceived as the spatial hub of the family home.

Community and privacy

We are now in a position to begin to answer the question which was posed at the beginning of the chapter as to whether configurational differences exist between speculative and architect-designed houses and, if they do, the extent to which these are differences of degree or of substance. It would seem that in this sample of architects' London houses design decisions do seem to bear the stamp of contemporary popular values and, although the differences between speculative and architect-designed dwellings are many, they are not so great as to give substance to the accusation that architects form a separate sub-culture whose aspirations and values are completely at variance with those of ordinary people of a comparable social standing.

However, the space standards of architects' houses are more generous than the generality of British homes, and the added investment tends to be in elaborating the transitional zones rather than in adding more rooms to contain proliferating household functions. 'Open-plan living' is rather little in evidence, and for the most part spaces which flow into one another are confined to the everyday living areas. Even here, the plan tends to be functionally zoned and articulated by 'buffer zones' rather than free-flowing and flexible. Moreover, walls and openings maintain separations between the major household functions, albeit in a more discreet way than in speculative houses.

Whether integration centres on the living area or the dining area seems to be a matter of personal preference, as indeed it is in speculative plans. However, the architects' houses display a much richer array of configurational possibilities than their speculative counterparts, and this is achieved both by the way in which spaces are linked and separated by the system of transitions, and by the relative ringiness of the domestic interior looked at in isolation or when the house is considered within its setting. Space in these homes is fine-tuned both by the way it is convexly articulated, and by the enhanced possibility which ringiness brings to manipulate the pattern of permeability through the opening and shutting of doors.

All these factors point to a greater spatial investment in articulating the relationship between the inhabitants of the dwelling. These houses propose a more subtle articulation of the relation between home and workplace, parents and children, and family and guests than is found in speculative houses, the spatial domains which are afforded to shared household practices and to individual family members are more expansive and the relations among them are more carefully modulated and controlled. Even so, configurational analysis suggests that the aspirations and lifestyles of architects are not dissimilar from those of contemporaries in other walks of life and that, far from articulating a radically different view of modern family life, the shaping of space is mobilized to support a relatively conventional way of living which seems to find a common origin in the Victorian family home.

But there are differences, which speak of other influences which may be attributed to the wider architectural context. The convex elaboration of the houses, whilst not amounting to an open, flexible way of generating space, is suggestive of the richly articulated interiors which we have come to associate with 'international style' of 'modern movement' houses. But these British homes are clearly not the intellectual heirs of the *'plan libre'* and the *'promenade architecturale'*, and their designers manipulate space to support a rather different programme from that encapsulated in the Corbusian idea of a house. The space patterns which are found in contemporary London have little in common either with the open and flexible arrangements of partitions and furniture which were the subject of the previous chapter.

There may be a good reason why this is so, for as Muthesius remarked over a century ago:

Perhaps the most striking difference [from the continental] is the lack in England of communicating doors between the rooms, which means that the only access to a room is from a passage or hall. Thus the

English room is a sort of cage, in which the inmate is entirely cut off
from the next room. Englishmen usually shake their heads at the sight
of a continental ground-plan with its communicating doors, and in a
continental house they might feel as though they were perpetually
sitting out in the street. They would see this as an interference with
one of their most conspicuous needs, their desire for privacy, for
seclusion.[5]

And he goes on to add that:

The rule known to every Englishman says that the door must open
towards the main sitting area in the room, which usually means
towards the fire place: in a study it opens towards the desk, in a
bedroom towards the bed. The idea behind this is that the person entering shall not be able to take in the whole room at a glance as he opens
the first crack in the door, but must walk round it to enter the room, by
which time the person seated in the room will have been able to prepare
himself suitably for his entry. . . . In fact it is not at all unpleasant to
enter a room in this way. *It is only like passing through a kind of
porch or small vestibule.*[6] (my emphasis)

Muthesius seems to be alluding here to a different balance historically
between community and privacy in the layout of English houses from
those of continental Europe, which extends even to such minor matters
as the position and opening of doors.

Seen in this light, the concept of 'open-plan living' may even be interpreted as giving a modern shape to a way of living which had its historical
counterpart in the inter-connected, space-centred apartments found in
many European cities. English houses seem not to have evolved in this
way. Rather, the historical record suggests that from at least the seventeenth century onwards English homes have exhibited a tendency to be
transition-centred, tree-like and rather segregated. The exceptions merely
draw attention to the prevalence of the rule.

However, it should be borne in mind that the modern formulation of
the tendency for transition-centred homes also has its champions within
Anglo-American architectural discourse. The arguments in favour of a
carefully controlled re-integration of family members in the home are at
least as well-rehearsed in architectural circles as are those which urge families to live an open, gregarious lifestyle. Perhaps the most influential of

these, Chermayeff and Alexander's *'Community and Privacy'*,[7] sets out the social agenda for a well-designed home as follows:

> Irrespective of their function and size, the diverse domains of the modern world are multiplying and are susceptible to rapid change and to a variety of conflicts between them. These domains can not only be abstractly explained in terms of function or need, but can be precisely described in terms of physical properties which can be directly perceived. The conflicts between these properties can be very real and sharply drawn. The integrity of each space, the preservation of its special, carefully specified environmental characteristics, depends on the physical elements that provide separation, insulation, access and controlled transfer between domains. We have discussed the hierarchy of domains. Once one realizes that the joints between domains are themselves physical elements of no less importance, one can see that it is these elements that give the plan its hierarchical structure.[8]

Here, the idea of 'buffers, zones and locks' between household activities and to protect the spatial domains assigned to parents and to children, is proposed as the measure of social refinement, and is quite a different concept from that of a circulation system comprising hall, stairs and landing, and which is simply designed to give mutual access to a set of homogenized and spatially undifferentiated rooms. There is no doubt that this text was influential in schools of architecture in the United Kingdom throughout the 1960s and 1970s. It seemed to articulate principles in keeping with a view based on mutual esteem among family members rather than on the unmediated force of parental authority. This alternative and more muted tradition to that of the open plan, one which tips the balance in favour of the individual rather than the group, may therefore provide a social interpretation of these modern architects' London houses.

There is, it seems a middle, peculiarly English approach to the design of the domestic interior which is half way between a completely compartmentalised plan made up of separate rooms and a fully open plan where all walls are abolished and activities and spaces flow directly into one another. The shared architectural proposition of the houses that have been presented here is that, by articulating the perimeter boundary of the major rooms or compartments in the house, a series of smaller and larger convex spaces results within the overall shape of the room which can be utilised to zone compatible activities, insulate them experientally from one another by transitional 'buffer zones' and yet conserve visual and aural synchrony among them. Activities which unite household members tend to be located closer to the global circulation routes which run into or across these major spatial compartments, and this gives rise to a 'privacy gradient' in each compartment from the more integrated locations to the more locally secluded, globally segregated parts of the space, so that individuals and activities best pursued in isolation can withdraw at will from the centre of the social arena to the sidelines.

Moving around such a house is therefore rather like passing through a series of spatial beads, or even a sequence of 'streets and squares' where transitional buffer zones are orientated more to movement and are everywhere interspersed with convex spaces that support the different activities which take place in the house. These spatial gestures seem to originate in a new, more sociological way of articulating the relation between community and family privacy which became popular in the schools of architecture in post-war Britain. The emphasis on individual privacy and the care with which family life was perceived to be best-supported in space seems to owe a great deal to emerging concepts of dignity, mutual esteem and equality within the family. This is the spatial signature which identifies these houses as a group. It is also a set of ideas which – more contentiously – shaped the design of entire housing estates in post-war Britain.

The concept of a 'privacy gradient' to modulate relative states of accessibility and seclusion among a set of spaces seems qualitatively to specify the property which is measured in a pattern of spatial integration. Applied simply, this might tend to monotony and rigidity, as it seems to have done in speculative houses. But this is not the case in these architects' London houses. Chameleon-like, some homes completely change their complexion when opened up to the garden. Others re-configure themselves by the opening and closing of routes through the interior. Few are ringless trees, and even in these rooms tend not to be 'cages' but convexly articulated domains. Explanation in configuration tends to begin with morphology, extend to sociology and finish with psychology. In the final analysis what is so striking about the houses architects build for themselves is not so much that they give a variety of spatial interpretations for a complex social principle, but that so many give a very personal, intimate and flexible response which enriches our understanding of family life.

Notes

1 Amos Rapoport, *House Form and Culture* (New Jersey: Prentice Hall, 1969), p. 2.
2 Ibid., p. 127
3 Miranda Newton, *Architects' London Houses* (Oxford: Butterworth, 1992).
4 Ibid., p. viii
5 Herman Muthesius, *The English House* (London: Crosby Lockwood Staples, 1979), p. 79.
6 Ibid.
7 Serge Chermayeff and Christopher Alexander, *Community and Privacy* (Harmondsworth: Penguin, 1963), p. 213.
8 Ibid.

Chapter nine

'Deconstructing' architects' houses

Summary

In this final case study, space syntax analysis has been used by architecture students to investigate the relation between composition and configuration in the houses of four influential modern architects whose work betrays a pre-occupation with the formal decomposition of the cube. Analysis revealed that the houses permutated the morphological properties of depth and rings, differentially to embed domestic functions within the home and to interface household members. Two of the houses were judged to be well-composed but configurationally banal: two appeared more inventive in relating compositional principles to space configuration, to create a measure of subtlety and richness in lifestyle which was lacking in the examples where form was manipulated in the abstract. The students discovered that knowledge of both the internal laws of form and the social logic of space are required to generate the practical conjunction of formal rigour with functional ease which we recognise in the houses of great architects.

Composition and configuration

Normally, space syntax analysis is used to explore the cultural patterning which is found in large samples of plans, particularly of vernacular and traditional houses where examples appear visually to be unique and it is not obvious whether there are any configurational consistencies beneath the surface variety which is presented to the eye. Under these conditions, configurational analysis of the plans can be conceived of as an 'archaeology of space'. If the houses display morphological regularities then the buildings speak directly of culturally significant household practices which have been crystallised in the form of the dwelling.

What follows is an account of a recent experiment in which the techniques of the archaeology of space were imported into the design studio, in order to investigate the form-function relation in the houses of influential modern architects. The aim of the project was to reach beyond the discourse, to extract directly from the configuration of the houses the 'design pre-structures'[1] which the architects appeared to be using to get from an idea for a building to the form of a building. The two-week project involved a group of architecture students in a collaborative study of houses by four 'star' architects, using configurational analysis to make comparisons between the dwellings and the stated aims of the architects. The four architects shared a common interest in exploring simple cubic forms, and the volumes of the examples were roughly comparable. All were single family houses. These broad dimensions of comparability enabled the spotlight to shine directly on the relation between basic compositional design concepts and the configuration of architectural space within the domestic interior. The exercise set out to bring together the students' intuitive experiences of architectural design and criticism with forms of rigorous analysis which stood outside them, and enabled them to see their ideas and evaluations in a shared, comparative context.

Architects compose a building along axes, differentiate its parts by articulating larger and smaller spaces, and render its overall form more or less comprehensible by the strength of visual fields. People move along axial lines, form groups in two-dimensional convex elements, and see three-dimensional non-convex visual fields or isovists. We therefore have a convenient homology between formal, compositional architectural principles and the configurational tools we use in space syntax analysis. The two sides of architectural appreciation – form and function – can be brought within the scope of a common analytic framework.

The four houses were therefore broken down into their convex and axial organisation, and the integration value was calculated for each convex space or axial line with respect to the dwelling as a whole. Permeability graphs were drawn for each house from the point of view of the house plot, the main living room, the kitchen and the main bedroom, to see how these living functions were differentially embedded within the configuration. The graphs revealed a second configurational property – ringiness – which described the extent to which each house offered its residents route choice. Ringiness is frequently exploited by architects to achieve a dramatic *'promenade architecturale'* but perhaps its most significant contribution to domestic space organisation is that route choice enables the same configuration to modulate different, often radically different, kinds of spatial experience for household members, and to articulate formal and informal relations within the home.

Depth and rings are the basic dimensions of space configuration, and convex and axial organisation are its architectural dimensions. Convex organisation relates to the house experienced in repose, and axial organisation to the house experienced through movement. Isovists were also drawn to reveal the shifting visual fields experienced from different parts of the house, and as people move about within it. Visual fields may vary from exposing a panoramic vista of the house to offering penetrating directed glimpses through the domestic interior, or they may conform closely to the room arrangement. Isovists were drawn from rooms and halls, to see how these related to the strength or weakness of the static visual fields within the interior.

One way of exploring this volumetrically and in movement is through the construction of a model which aligns isovists vertically in a stack that simulates the shift in visual fields as an individual moves along a route. The route selected for comparison was the shortest path from the formal entrance (most public space) to the main bedroom (most private space) of each dwelling. This technique gave rise to a visually most integrating three-dimensional isovist for each house. Equipped with this space-analytic toolbox, the students set to work to unlock the relation between what each architect seemed to be doing compositionally, visually and volumetrically and how this related to the experiential dimension of each house as configured space, and to the differential embedding of functions within the home.

Mario Botta, house at Pregassona, 1979–80

Mario Botta has gained a reputation for a domestic architecture which engages in a search for formal archetypes, but not at the expense of its context. His house at Pregassona is a simple brick and glass box which occupies a suburban site on the outskirts of Lugano, Switzerland and is widely regarded as a summation of Botta's early work.

The visitor first sees the principal facade from a path which curves slightly to the left on approach, to give the appearance that house meets the earth with a clean line. The house on three levels is an essay in the exploration of cubic form. The main elevation is cleft in two by a vertical glazed shaft, which widens towards the base in apparent defiance of gravity. The rear elevation is also symmetrical about a central stair drum which is flanked by glazing at the upper levels. The sides are centrally pierced at the base, glazed at the *piano nobile* and balconied at the upper level.

At the ground floor, the house is entirely devoted to a portico for sheltered outdoor living, entry and utilities, while the *piano nobile* is devoted to the main living functions. From the head of the stairs, a living room lies to the left and a kitchen-dining room to the right, with a study beyond. The living room fireplace conceals a shower room. The second floor contains two principal bedrooms, each of which has a private external balcony, a bathroom and dressing area on the left and a further small bedroom on the right. The planning of the house is classic (see figure 9.1a). Vertical layering expresses arrival, daytime and night-time activities respectively, whilst the front-back dimension differentiates major and subsidiary functions on each floor. Vertical circulation at the heart of the house delivers the visitor to the geometric centre of each floor.

But the house is not a modern interpretation of a neo-classical plan, which is a ringy nexus of inter-related, well-integrated but discrete rooms. True, the convex organisation closely follows the compartmentalisation of the house into rooms (see figure 9.1b). The compositional privileging of the *piano nobile* in the section, and front relations over back, are reflected in the configuration, but the convex distribution of integration shows that rooms are not integrated directly, but rather are held

Figure 9.1
Mario Botta's house at Pregassona,
plans and convex break-up

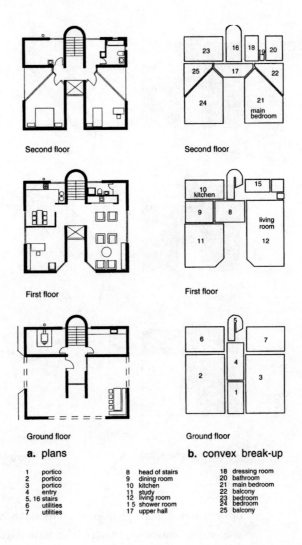

Second floor   Second floor

First floor   First floor

Ground floor   Ground floor

a. plans   **b. convex break-up**

1	portico	8	head of stairs	18	dressing room
2	portico	9	dining room	20	bathroom
3	portico	10	kitchen	21	main bedroom
4	entry	11	study	22	balcony
5, 16	stairs	12	living room	23	bedroom
6	utilities	15	shower room	24	bedroom
7	utilities	17	upper hall	25	balcony

apart by the circulation core (see figure 9.2a). The axial organisation of
the plan (see figure 9.2b), is simple and symmetrical about the stair-well.
Axial integration confirms what the convex organisation indicates: that
movement organises a simple, vertical and frontal experience of the
house.

Justified graphs (see figure 9.3), reveal the tree-like configuration of the
interior. Different functions occupy separate branches, and the house does
not allow for subtle differences to be introduced by the closing off or opening

Figure 9.2
Mario Botta's house at Pregassona,
convex and axial integration maps

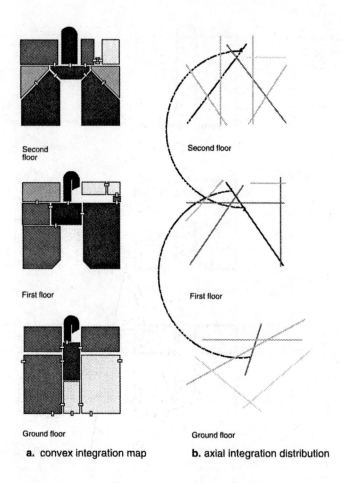

Second
floor

Second floor

First floor

First floor

Ground floor

Ground floor

a. convex integration map   **b.** axial integration distribution

up of routes. The graph from the outside shows that the construction of a
single, attenuated approach to the main living floor heightens anticipation
for guests, but distances the occupants of the house from immediate contact
with the site, with the result that it is the most segregated place of all. The
living room draws more of the functions of the house towards it, but the relative separation of the kitchen hints at a gender division within the home
which is, if anything, more significant than the public-private dimension
displayed in space unfolded from the main bedroom.

Isovists from halls and rooms, shown in figure 9.4, reveal just how
dominant is the construction of strong visual fields in relation to vertical
circulation and arrival, by contrast with the relatively restricted visual
fields from the main living spaces, which systematically, partially reveal

Figure 9.3
Justified permeability graphs from the
principal rooms of Mario Botta's house
at Pregassona

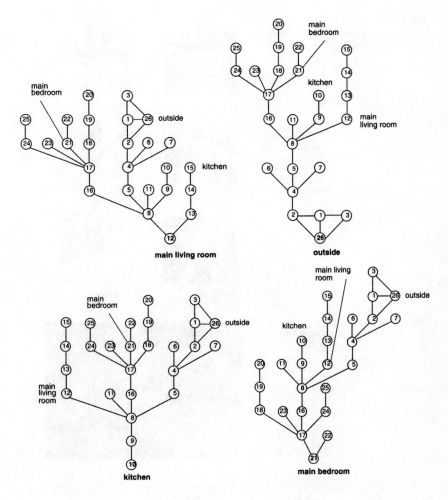

adjacent rooms. The visually most integrating three-dimensional isovist
(see figure 9.5), shows the volumetric importance of the stair-well which
traces the route from the entry up to the main bedroom, yielding glimpses
into the adjacent horizontal layers of space at each level *en passant*.

The students concluded that the configuration of space in the Botta
house can be interpreted as an essay in 'dramatic space' constructing a
simple social theatre which modulates backstage and frontstage activities.
Centre stage is on the main living floor where strong visual fields, particularly in the public circulation areas of the house, contrast with partial
seclusions in each room where it is possible to wait in the wings, or

Figure 9.4
Isovists from halls and rooms in Mario
Botta's house at Pregassona

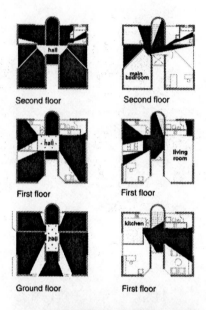

Figure 9.5
The visually most integrating three-
dimensional isovist in Mario Botta's
house at Pregassona

modulate front stage activities. However, the house does not generate either significant cultural-functional differences or route choices. Its tree-like, separationist space configuration is typical of the speculative houses we encountered earlier, in contemporary housing in the new town of Milton Keynes. By comparison with these homes, Botta's house at Pregassona may be well composed but it is configurationally boring.

Richard Meier, Giovannitti House, 1967–9

Meier's Giovannitti House is situated on a gently sloping, suburban site in Pittsburgh, Pennsylvania. The house takes the form of an eroded double

Figure 9.6
Richard Meier's Giovannitti House plans
and convex break-up

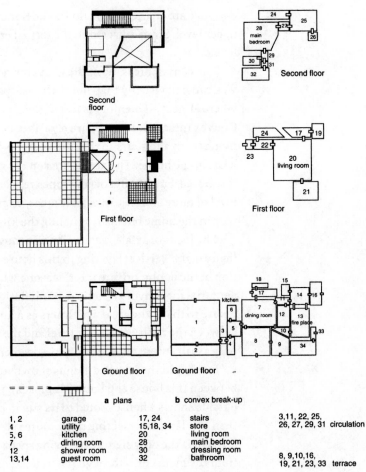

Second
floor

Second floor

First floor

First floor

Ground floor   Ground floor

a plans   **b** convex break-up

1, 2	garage	17, 24	stairs	3,11, 22, 25,
4	utility	15,18, 34	store	26, 27, 29, 31 circulation
5, 6	kitchen	20	living room	
7	dining room	28	main bedroom	
12	shower room	30	dressing room	8, 9,10,16,
13,14	guest room	32	bathroom	19, 21, 23, 33 terrace

square, with one square expressed as a three storey cubic volume and the other implied by an entry-level terrace delineated at its furthest extremity by an open screen. The main approach through the screen partially reveals the interior living areas of the house but completely conceals the sleeping areas above. The garage elevation is almost entirely solid, save for one corner, which is eroded at the base and glazed and balconied at the main living level. The remaining facades are more transparent, particularly to the south which reveals most of the interior to the site. The whole is a sophisticated, balanced composition of solids and voids.

The lower ground level contains service functions, garage and kitchen, dining room and guest room (see figure 9.6a). The living room and main entrance are on the middle floor. The library and main bedroom are at the upper level. Stairs adjacent to the formal entry directly connect all three levels.

The convex break-up of the Giovannitti House (see figure 9.6b), is less well ordered visually than Botta's house, particularly at the upper levels, where almost all memory is lost of the regulating shape of the cube. Convex integration (see figure 9.7a) is concentrated on the formal entry, living room and stairs so that the visitor is brought immediately into the heart of the house. The dining area on the ground floor is relatively well integrated, but the mix of grey tones reflects a subtle modulation at this level of more and less accessible areas, to give guests a degree of seclusion within the home but also including the kitchen.

The focus of axial organisation and movement is at the lower level (see figure 9.7b). Vertical layering in this house organises a subtle interpretation of the public-private interface: one which assigns the maximum potential for active, dynamic perambulation to the lower ground floor and repose to the living area, which acts as a hinge for vertical circulation between the multiplex lower level and the secluded upper floor. This is not only axially more remote but also a dead-end.

But it is in the justified graphs shown in figure 9.8, that the difference between this house and Botta's is most apparent. The graph from the outside shows a house rooted to its site in permeability, with no fewer than five large intersecting ringy routes passing through the garden. The kitchen is the only significant living space which is not on a ring. The ring from the main entry through the living room to the dining area and guest room permits a degree of fine-tuning of the host-guest relation in the house, which is unavailable in Botta's design. The day-night split here is not just a compositional device in the vertical layering of space. It is built into the very configuration of the dwelling in a more thoroughgoing way, as the deep bedroom tree shows clearly. The most telling graph is that taken from the living room, which shows how the shallow, ringy set of living spaces and the deep, tree-like bedroom and study areas are articulated through a ring which links the main living space with both formal and informal modes of entry to the house.

Isovists (see figure 9.9) illustrate the utter transparency of the upper halls and living areas. Only the study beyond the main bedroom is visually shielded. The dining area also has a powerful isovist, but one which is discrete with respect to the kitchen and rooms used by guests. The kitchen

Figure 9.7
Richard Meier's Giovannitti House,
convex and axial integration maps

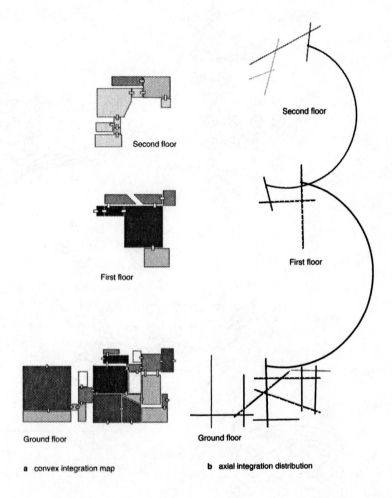

Second floor

First floor

Ground floor

a convex integration map

Second floor

First floor

Ground floor

b axial integration distribution

has a very poor isovist indeed. The route from the formal entry to the main bedroom is characterised by a rapid succession of rich, contrasting visual fields. At the entry level, visual fields are generous and omni-directional, each space affording the eye a contrast between panoramic views through the main volume to the surrounding landscape and glimpses into other parts of the house. Between levels, visual fields are first constricted dramatically and then partially opened, on arrival, in an expansive gesture to the main volume.

The three-dimensional isovist of the visually most integrating volume is, by contrast, a simple cube which rises from the dining area through the main, double-height living space to hint at the private domain above

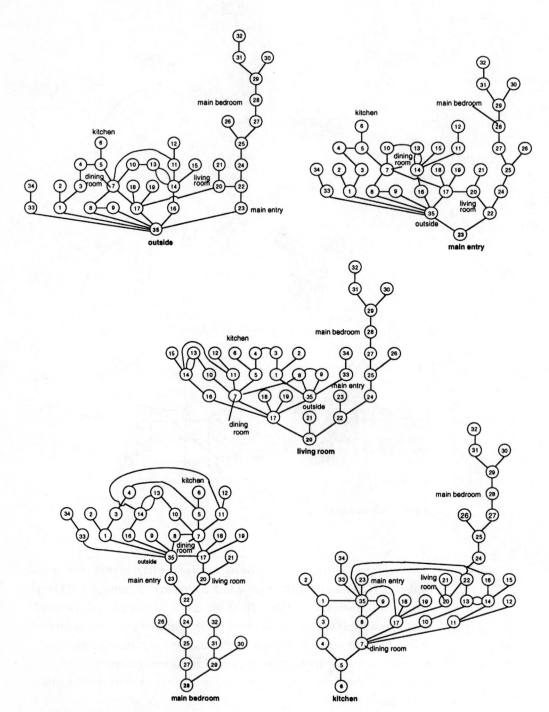

Figure 9.8
Justified permeability graphs from the
principal rooms of Richard Meier's
Giovannitti House

Figure 9.9
Isovists from halls and rooms in Richard
Meier's Giovannitti House

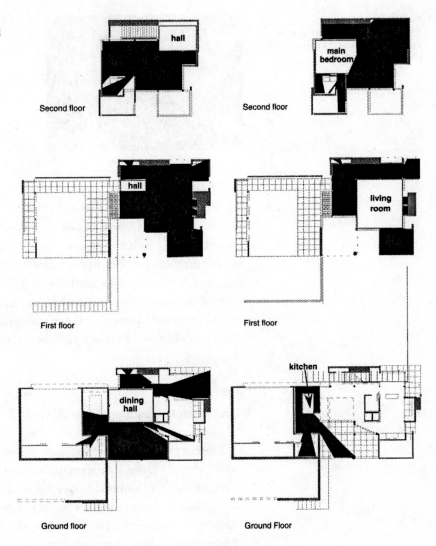

without exposing it to direct view (see figure 9.10). The asymmetry of
height ensures that residents looking down command an unimpeded view
over all the principal living areas of the house, but without intruding on
the privacy of their guests.

Critics make much of Meier's inspiration by Synthetic Cubism, suggesting that his houses are an exploration of transparency revealed in
movement.[2] The students concluded that in this house, composition is
more than just a geometric device but that the architecture supports

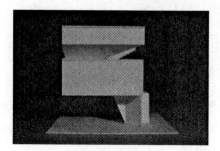

significant aspects of the lifestyle of its occupants. It has resulted, they conclude, in a house for guests to explore and which will provide divertissement for its owners. Plasticity in route choice within the interior and through the site allows for fine-tuning to accommodate formal and informal occasions, and a subtle depth gradient in permeability shields areas of contemplation from action spaces. Transparency and sculptural volume are used to intensify the experiential dimension of social action. The students have interpreted this house as the creation of 'sensuous space'.

John Hejduk, Diamond House A, 1962–6

Unlike the previous examples, we turn now to a purely hypothetical house, one of a series also generated out of the formal exploration of Cubist space.[3] Hejduk's Diamond House A stands on a transparent, columned base in which resides the glass box of the ground floor entrance level. The elevations of the centre two floors propose the fragmentation of light through angled bars, in an irregular arrangement which makes little concession to function. The fourth level is open and encloses free-standing curvilinear sculptural forms under a sheltering roof. The external observer is aware of the vertical stratification of the house and of the interplay between edge and interior, but not of the identity of individual facades.

As one might expect from Hejduk's theoretical interests, the house is approached at the corner (see figure 9.11a). The visitor enters directly into a sitting area which is sub-divided at low level by fixed seating. An enclosed stair shaft on the right leads straight up to the first-floor circulation corridor, off which are three hierarchically sized bedrooms, each of which has a

Figure 9.11
John Hejduk's Diamond House A,
plans and convex break-up

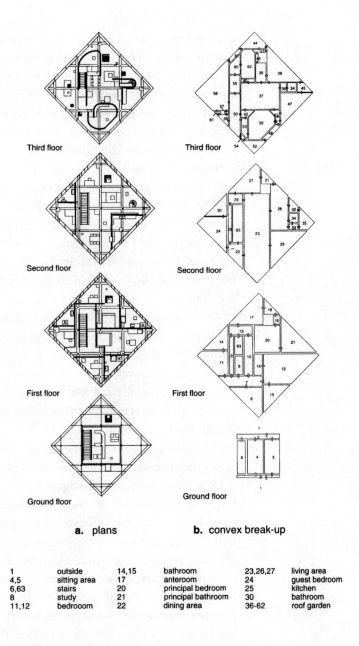

Third floor   Third floor

Second floor   Second floor

First floor   First floor

Ground floor   Ground floor

a. plans   b. convex break-up

1	outside	14,15	bathroom	23,26,27	living area
4,5	sitting area	17	anteroom	24	guest bedroom
6,63	stairs	20	principal bedroom	25	kitchen
8	study	21	principal bathroom	30	bathroom
11,12	bedrooom	22	dining area	36-62	roof garden

separate bathroom beyond. The principal bedroom sequence also contains
an anteroom and a study. The second floor is more open and contains the
main living functions. The visitor enters directly into the smaller dining
area, to the right of which is a guest bedroom and bathroom. The kitchen is

enclosed on the left. The act of turning reveals the larger, open living area containing the rectangular lift shaft and a stair drum which leads up to the roof garden. The outdoor living areas are separate curved spaces which enclose a central entry space, and which are surrounded by an irregular perimeter promenade. The shapes are positioned in such a way that it is difficult to see directly across the terrace. The plan organises household activities as a series of horizontal layers. There is little effort to relate these in volume, and the only novelty lies in the reversal of the everyday convention that sleeping is upstairs and living downstairs.

The convex map (see figure 9.11b) reveals Hejduk at play with the geometry of the diamond on a square grid, with different compositional principles invoked on each level. Parallel zones are sandwiched between narrow threshold strips at ground level. The house is centrifugally organised on the first floor, vertically stratified on the second and centripetal on the third.

Convex integration (see figure 9.12a) is concentrated on the second, living floor and roof terraces. This association of integration with everyday living areas is found in most ordinary houses, and it seems that social knowledge has played a tacit role in generating the space configuration. However, the degree to which the focus of the house withdraws from the site and entrance is remarkable. The privacy gradient of the main bedroom is also striking.

The axial organisation of Diamond House A is more disordered than either the appearance of the plans or Hejduk's source of formal inspiration in De Stijl might predict (see figure 9.12b). Axial integration is also concentrated on the second floor, in the main living area. The segregated relation of the house to its site, which is belied by its visual transparency, recalls Botta's house but here it is exaggerated to an unusual degree, so that even the main vertical circulation integrates levels weakly.

The permeability graphs shown in figure 9.13 describe a house that is locally ringy but globally tree-like. The levels differentiate themselves clearly as separate groups of spaces, which grow in complexity as they ascend from the entry to the roof terrace. Each level has at least one ring, but these provide exercise for the occupant of each floor rather than offering some alternative place to go. The graph from the main living area shows how the spaces on each floor are separated and homogenised. The kitchen is a dead-end, only marginally deeper than the living space. The main bedroom, by contrast, is remote from most other rooms in the house.

Figure 9.12
John Hejduk's Diamond House A,
convex and axial integration maps

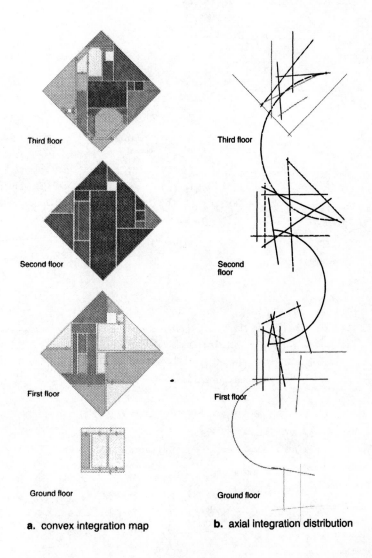

a. convex integration map   b. axial integration distribution

Isovists (see figure 9.14) illustrate how the transparency of the entry level contrasts with the opacity of the first floor. At the second floor, the living area seems to exercise a strong visual field, but closer inspection reveals that it is internal to its own function and the adjacent kitchen. The isovist from the kitchen is relatively impoverished, and that from the main bedroom is sparse. This last example also illustrates clearly the configurational effect of the glazed screens which have been inserted at the corners of rooms. A formal, compositional statement about tension

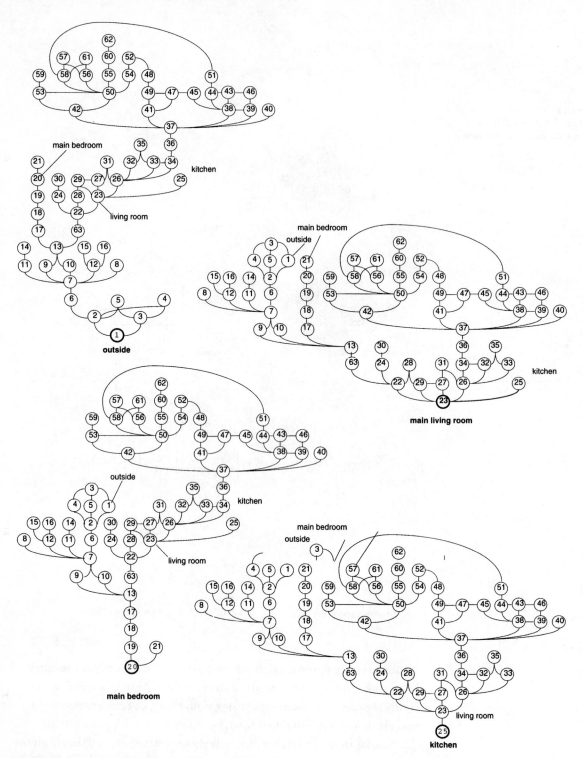

Figure 9.13
Justified permeability graphs from
the principal rooms of John Hejduk's
Diamond House A

Figure 9.14
Isovists from halls and rooms in John
Hejduk's Diamond House A

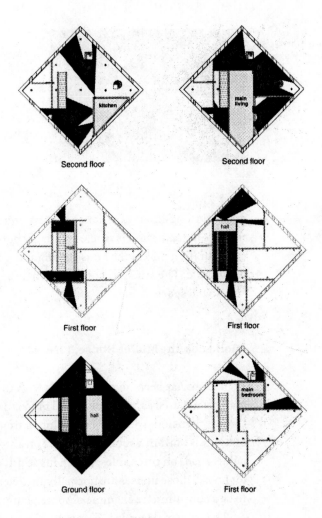

induced at the corner has created the potential for snooping. The three-
dimensional isovist of the visually most integrating space in the house
shown in figure 9.15 is almost entirely confined to the living area.

Critics have remarked that Hejduk's Diamond Houses appear rational,
precise exercises, but that they exhibit an emptiness and absence which is
not benign. Hejduk himself has suggested that they provide the structure
for a mental labyrinth but also that they talk about architectural banality.
The students cannot but agree. Like Botta's house, the tree-like overall
configuration of the Diamond House offers no possibility of fine-tuning to
take account of different social situations. It does not even constitute a

Figure 9.15
The visually most integrating three-dimensional isovist in John Hejduk's Diamond House A

dramatic 'one-liner' experience of entry and arrival. The extent to which the idea of separation is single-mindedly pursued in both composition and configuration makes the house configurationally banal and downright unsociable. The students concluded that the Diamond House epitomises 'antisocial space'.

Adolf Loos, the Muller House, 1929–30

Adolf Loos has become synonymous with the concept of '*raumplan*', normally translated as 'space plan' and taken to mean a maximally compact three-dimensional design, packed into a simple cubic shape.[4] The Muller house was built in a suburb of Prague on a steeply sloping site bounded by public roads on three sides, which made privacy difficult to achieve even for Loos, whose houses are normally introverted. It is generally thought to be a consummate example of space planning.

The principal facade is dominated by a central entrance recess. The house gives little of itself away to the street. The rear facade is terraced to follow the lie of the land. The full height first-floor windows illuminate the living room and give onto a terrace, whilst the central projecting bay above marks the position of the main bedroom. A large roof garden with panoramic views over the city is backed by a breakfast room. The east elevation overlooks an enclosed, private garden and is dominated by the dining room bay and bedroom terrace above. The west elevation is plain, with low-level entry to the garage.

The ground floor of the house is devoted to garaging and services (see figure 9.16a). The formal entry is elevated, and the visitor ascends formally to the reception rooms. The living room is entered theatrically, through an

Figure 9.16
Adolf Loos' Muller House, plans and convex break-up

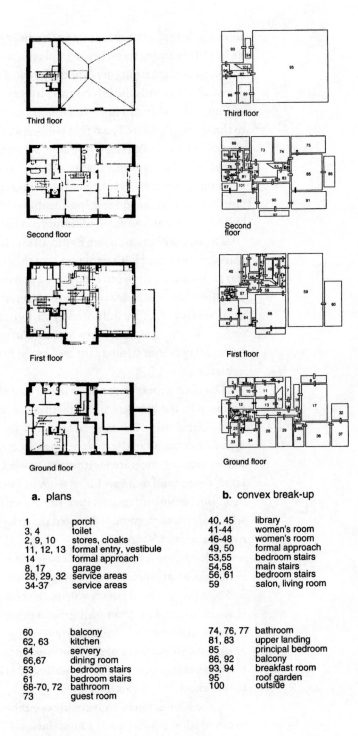

Third floor

Second floor

First floor

Ground floor

a. plans

Third floor

Second floor

First floor

Ground floor

b. convex break-up

1	porch	40, 45	library
3, 4	toilet	41-44	women's room
2, 9, 10	stores, cloaks	46-48	women's room
11, 12, 13	formal entry, vestibule	49, 50	formal approach
14	formal approach	53,55	bedroom stairs
8, 17	garage	54,58	main stairs
28, 29, 32	service areas	56, 61	bedroom stairs
34-37	service areas	59	salon, living room

60	balcony	74, 76, 77	bathroom
62, 63	kitchen	81, 83	upper landing
64	servery	85	principal bedroom
66,67	dining room	86, 92	balcony
53	bedroom stairs	93, 94	breakfast room
61	bedroom stairs	95	roof garden
68-70, 72	bathroom	100	outside
73	guest room		

arch. The circulation spirals up to the dining room, which is visually
linked to the living room below, and up again to a landing which controls
access to the remaining areas of the house. From this point, movement is
directed on towards the kitchen and library, round the central stair-well
and up to the bedroom floor, or laterally through a chicained side-passage
to the women's room. From this landing a direct high-level visual link is
also maintained with the living area, while the women's room is a
complex multi-level space which also overlooks the living room. The
bedroom floor and servants' quarters are conventional, save that the
family bedrooms are directly permeable to each other so that parents and
children can communicate without recourse to the corridor.

The convex break-up (see figure 9.16b), indicates something of the
complexity of the plan, particularly of the circulation areas which form a
fragmented zone between rooms. The convex integration map (see figure
9.17a), gives a much clearer picture of the structure of the plan. The segregated service areas are indicated by various shades of pale grey. The formal
route from the first floor entry to the main reception rooms and up to the
principal bedroom strongly integrates the house and appears highlighted
in black.

The dining room is the most integrated of the major functional spaces,
followed by the kitchen, the domain of servants and the only example on a
ring of circulation. Eating therefore draws the entire household together to
a greater extent than the main living space, the salon. The male-dominated
library is more integrated within the house than the more convexly-articulated, deeper and more secluded women's room. Upstairs, the main
bedroom is more integrated than the directly-linked children's rooms
which are, in turn, more integrated than the guest room which is located
over the women's room.

In this house, integration indexes status. The highest priority, and
hence the greatest measure of integration, is given to the formal reception
and entertainment of guests within the home. The configuration of space
is also dedicated to maintaining discrete separations between the various
household members. The axial map (see figure 9.17b), shows even more
clearly the importance of the relationship between formal and informal
circulation routes through the public and private domains of the house,
as it is experienced in movement.

In the Muller house movement assembles five large, independent rings
of circulation which pass through the levels to connect directly discrete

Figure 9.17
Adolf Loos' Muller House, convex and
axial integration maps

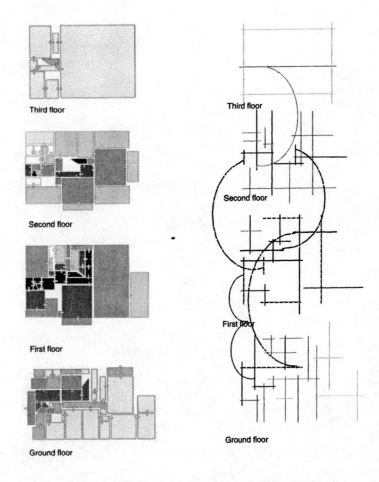

a. convex integration map   **b.** axial integration distribution

spatial domains within the house (see figure 9.18). The graph of space
unfolded from the outside shows the ring connecting the formal and
tradesmen's entry with the service functions and the gardens, and immediately above the ring constituted by the formal ascent to the reception
rooms and its return through the private stairs. Two small rings in the
centre of the graph are formed by the household's and servants' approaches
to the dining room, and by the withdrawing rooms for male and female residents. A final large ring links the formal and private approaches to the
bedroom floor. At this point, the locally-ringy family rooms contrast with
the deeper trees up to the servants' quarters and to the bathrooms.

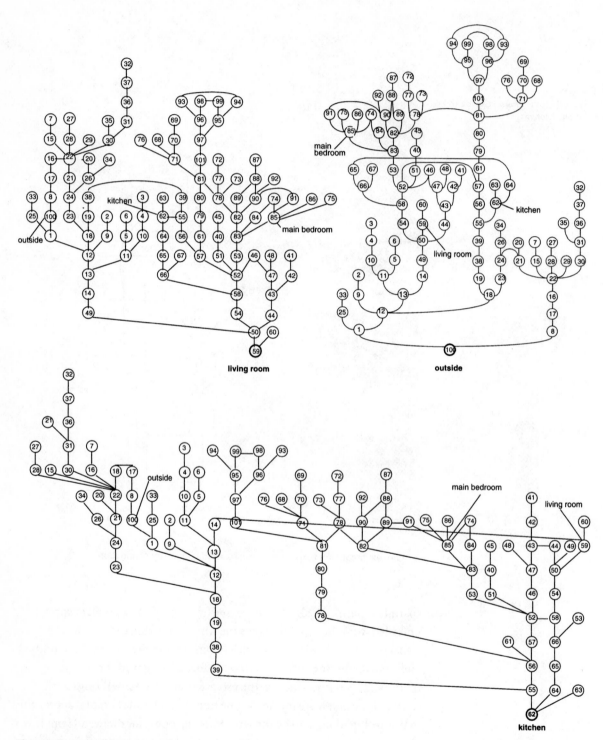

Figure 9.18
Justified permeability graphs from the
principal rooms of Adolf Loos' Muller
House

Figure 9.19
Isovists from halls and room in Adolf
Loos' Muller House

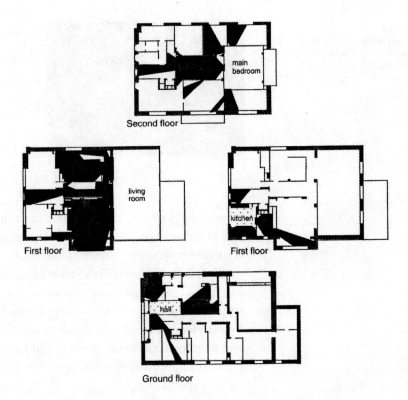

The graph from the kitchen clarifies the relationship of the reception
floor rings which allow for the ebb and flow of formal entertainment as the
household gathers to eat and disperses to smoke or gossip. The picture of
the configuration from the living room shows how the areas frequented by
the domestics are pushed maximally deep from those frequented by the
household. The main bedroom draws much of the internal life of the house
close to it, whilst preserving a strong separation from the trademen's entry
and those areas where servants work.

The isovists from major function spaces are generally expansive compared with those from circulation and service areas like the kitchen,
which are restricted thus denying any possibility for indiscreet surveillance from one part of the house to another (see figure 9.19). The isovist
stack from the formal entrance to the principal bedroom shows how the
guest is received with no small measure of 'pomp and circumstance' into
the Muller house, through a complex, dynamic and contrasting succession of visual fields. This formal ascent also takes in the most visually

Figure 9.20
The visually most integrating three-
dimensional isovist in Adolf Loos'
Muller House

integrating isovist, which is located in the hall at the principal intersection of routes in the heart of the house on the first floor landing and which
controls penetrating views in all directions (see figure 9.20).

The Muller house is dramatised by the way changes of level compose
heightened spatial contrasts and architectural effects. But this theatrical-
ity is only the most obvious manifestation of the fine-tuning of configuration to modulate the social dynamics of the house's many occupants: men
and women, parents and children, employers and domestics, hosts and
guests. The students' verdict on the Muller house was that it was
'refined space'.

Reformulating precedent

Despite the apparent stylistic and formal diversity of the four houses, the
students discovered that they permutated the fundamental configurational properties of space–depth (measured through integration) and rings
that were introduced at the beginning of the chapter. One example,
Botta's house at Pregassona, turned out to be shallow but tree-like.
Meier's Giovannitti House was shallow and ringy. Hejduk's Diamond
House emerged as deep and tree-like, and Loos' Muller house was deep
and ringy.

The integration order of functions turned out to be as revealing as the
average integration value of all spaces in each house. Each house used a
different function as the organising heart of the house (see figure 9.21). All
four architects agreed that sleeping should be accorded a relatively segregated position within the configuration of the house, but this was the only
point on which they were united. Unlike traditional and vernacular

Figure 9.21
Table of values for the four houses

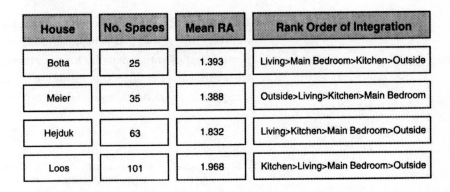

House	No. Spaces	Mean RA	Rank Order of Integration
Botta	25	1.393	Living>Main Bedroom>Kitchen>Outside
Meier	35	1.388	Outside>Living>Kitchen>Main Bedroom
Hejduk	63	1.832	Living>Kitchen>Main Bedroom>Outside
Loos	101	1.968	Kitchen>Living>Main Bedroom>Outside

houses, these homes were idiosyncratic in the way in which each constructed a living complex to support the radically different lifestyles.

Every home configures a way of life by constructing social interfaces between men and women, young and old, hosts and guests, owners and servants. Architects may choose not to consider this dimension of form-making but, because they configure built space as well as compose it for the eye, they cannot avoid its consequences. Architecture is able to enrich that experience by shaping a multifaceted, socially aware experience, or impoverish it by articulating one actor's point of view, or no one's.

Judged by these criteria, the students concluded that of the four 'stars' studied, two were real stars and two were not. Hejduk's Diamond House, whilst appearing the most daring of compositions, turned out to possess the most conventional of space configurations – deep, tree-like, segregated and functionally one-dimensional and banal. Botta's house drew on completely different compositional principles, but showed itself to be rather similarly configured and, perhaps, more fun to visit than to live in.

Although they seemed to be at opposite poles of the compositional spectrum – the former an airy, transparent, unitary and outward-looking volume and the latter a compact, opaque, sub-divided and introverted volume – the students found layers of spatial and formal subtlety in the houses of Meier and Loos which suggested great richness in the potential patterns of use and the experience of space for their occupants, although the lifestyles transmitted through the architecture could not be more different.

Careful analysis of precedent in basic design and in its architectural realisation showed the students a new perspective on the relation between architecture and life, but one which encouraged them to be more, rather than less, interested in the formal and spatial possibilities of architecture. However, they concluded that formal preoccupations are not enough, for truly innovative architecture resides in the marriage of configuration and composition to construct a social and not just a formal aesthetic.

Notes

1 Nigel Cross (ed.), *Developments in Design Methodology* (Chichester: John Wiley, 1984), pp. 245–64.

2 Joseph Rykwert, *Richard Meier Architect, 1964–1984* (New York: Rizzoli, 1984), p. 14.

3 K. Shkapich (ed.), *John Hejduk: Mask of Medusa: Works 1947–1983* (New York: Rizzoli, 1985), pp. 48–9.

4 M. Risselada (ed.),*Raumplan Versus Plan Libre: Adolf Loos and Le Corbusier 1919–1930* (New York: Rizzoli, 1988) p. 27.

Chapter ten

Decoding dwellings: the way ahead

Summary

Houses, it would seem, are more complex phenomena than accounts based on mode of construction or architectural style usually allow. Houses usually encode a wealth of social and symbolic information which is then taken for granted by their occupants, for whom they constitute a shared framework of spatial patterns and social practices that shape everyday life and which therefore seem as natural and familiar as breathing. Houses may even encode several perspectives on everyday life which sometimes co-exist without seeming to be aware of one another. However, social phenomena are durable in that they leave traces of the material form of their existence in the way in which the pattern of domestic space is arranged, in the kinds of objects which are found in different locations in the home and in the distribution of activities and behaviour which can be observed there over time. Space configuration, object arrays and people's routines can therefore be decoded so that the social and symbolic information are retrieved directly from the study of how houses are organised and used. These spatial descriptions are independent of people's experiences of and feelings about their homes. They speak directly to us about how the social universe is constructed and reproduced in everyday life without the need to invoke personal opinions and judgements about the meaning of home. A spatial account of domestic life may simply provide independent corroboration of people's perceptions about what their home means to them. More often than not, though, a spatial view enriches our knowledge about the relation between house form and culture by drawing attention to previously unremarked features of domestic life, or it may even expose deep-seated contradictions between people's beliefs about their home and their actual experience of dwelling there. This final chapter therefore stresses the centrality of clear, objective and quantitative spatial

From ideal types to genotypes

Previous studies that have addressed the social significance of domestic space have tended to capture the salient features of the home in an 'ideal type' which summarises what is invariant in the houses of a particular culture. Accounts such as Bourdieu's detailed specification of the structure and meaning which is inherent in the interior of the Berber house,[1] Cunningham's description of order in the Atoni house,[2] Humphrey's comparison of a traditional and a modern Mongolian yurt[3] or Tambiah's analysis of the social significance of the categories of space which are found in traditional houses in Thailand[4] have hitherto provided powerful insights into the social meaning of houses and homes in different parts of the world. These descriptions of domestic space help us to see how social rules and meanings are continuously constructed, constituted and renegotiated in time and space.

Yet however important these distillations of social knowledge may be, ordinary people's homes tend to be much more varied and idiosyncratic than the ideal type admits. Real houses are a complex expression of the social and individual worlds of their occupants, in which social structure and convention seems inextricably bound up with the idiosyncratic, whimsical, arbitrary or even chaotic circumstances of people's everyday lives. That this is so nearly always poses problems in understanding and interpreting the hidden order in houses and homes, for all to often what is different about a set of houses seems to be as important in expressing significant aspects of everyday life as what they have in common.

One way around this problem is to develop a more statistical account of both the structure and the variety which are exhibited in large databases containing dozens or even hundreds of examples of houses. The interface with the computer has become more user-friendly in recent years and technological advances already allow us to integrate quite different kinds of information about large samples of houses and to search systematically for correlations between candidate variables which might conceivably have influenced the layout in some way or another. Configurational analysis of even quite large and complex houses is just about instantaneous and the results of analysis can now be displayed in forms which are graphic and immediately accessible to intuition.

The growth and spread of the new information technologies allow us to ask more and more questions about domestic space arrangements, and to

Summary (cont.)

descriptions of large samples of layouts as the first step towards decoding the social logic of houses. At the same time it highlights the importance of building bridges to the broader range of research methods and investigative techniques which have been brought to bear on the study of houses and homes in order to enrich our interpretation and understanding of what is, after all, one of the basic building blocks of every human society.

ask more complex and open-ended questions at that. We are able to give clearer descriptions of the invariance that exists in large numbers of house plans, search for spatial 'genotypes' and dimension the extent of individual differences within the set. More important for architecture, we can if we so wish use these spatial decodings to generate new designs for houses which share the salient features of the existing collection, each an original, creative interpretation of the genuine article. However, none of this descriptive power resolves the underlying ethical issues, such as how the results of analysis should be interpreted or whether any lessons learned from the study of precedent should be reproduced without modification when building for the future.

It seems likely that in the future, studies of houses and homes will no longer be satisfied with identifying similarities in the spatial patterning of a set of houses in a particular region or cultural context. Increasingly, analysis will seek to pinpoint the typical ways in which different room functions and domestic activities are configured in people's homes, the importance of furniture and object arrays in providing the scenery and props for social encounter and interaction, how domestic space and its fixtures and fittings relate to explicit and tacit household practices, inter-personal behaviours, domestic habits and routines, the postures and gestures which people make in haptic space and even the language and concepts which people use when talking about what their homes mean to them. Increasingly, a configurational approach will reach out to related disciplines such as sociology, anthropology and psychology in addressing the social and personal interpretation of domestic space.

Representing domestic space

We have already seen that even the most simple of plans can be considered by breaking up the interior in several ways into its constituent elements and relations, be they fully bounded rooms, convex spaces, axial lines or visual fields. Each of these viewpoints may be equally valid and in almost all circumstances a comparison of the different points of view will yield insights into how domestic space is organised for social purposes. The latest generation of computer techniques permits these different spatial representations to be overlaid directly upon one another so as to recapture a multi-layered spatial experience of the interior, and then to explore how the house unfolds experientially to the moving observer in an animated 'walk-through' of the interior. It is now possible to model three-dimensional, convex and axial spatial volumes and to explore the changing sequences of three-dimensional visual fields which a spatial explorer encounters in moving about the house.

It seems likely that the next generation of theoretical advances will begin to unite the compositional and aesthetic preoccupations of architects and their critics with the configurational and functional approach which has hitherto been the distinguishing feature of space syntax. Experimental work is now being conducted on the integration analysis of shapes that permits the eye to retrieve useful descriptions of the shape and proportions of buildings. The relation between the new forms of modelling and a more conventional, proportional analysis of facades is suggestive but these 'non-discursive' techniques[5] are still in their infancy and the full potential of the new forms of computer modelling have yet to be fully understood.

We have seen that the configurational patterns which result from partitioning space are themselves lawful, and it is the lawfulness of space that is the raw material which can be exploited by different societies and sub-cultures to construct and constrain everyday domestic relations. Crudely, space is lawful because it is not possible for two entities to occupy the same space at the same time. Spaces can be assembled together into a larger continuous entity only by placing them next to one another or by putting them inside one another. Most of the time, people who use space do so 'with their feet on the ground' which means that its two-dimensional extent has a more immediate impact on human activity than does the experience of volumetric space.

More importantly, the spatial property of depth, whether from the outside or the generalised depth of each space in the house from all others, which is another way of conceptualising integration, is lawful in its operations. Depth from the outside and integration within the interior are the two dimensions of the layout of a house which usually turn out to have significant social connotations. The way these underlying dimensions are configured spatially constructs an interface among the house's inhabitants and relates them to visitors to the home.

All other things being equal, integration is strongest in the centre of a compact, regular plan or in the middle room in a chain of spaces which are connected together in a sequence, and partitioning rules can be derived to show precisely how integration is constructed in simple, functionless room arrangements. However, in the forms of domestic space arrangements that we normally encounter in different parts of the world integration and depth from the outside are usually manipulated, so that those spaces which draw the house together and are shallowest in relation to every other space in the house also contain activities which draw people together in activities which celebrate the group identity of the household, however this is socially constructed. Depth from the outside may be organised so as to open the heart of the house to outside influences or to curtail and control the penetration of visitors into the home. Likewise, the constituent space-types which make up the house locally usually exploit the logical potential of terminal spaces, bi-permeable spaces in sequence, bi-permeable spaces on a ring, or intersection spaces to act as the locus for occupation or movement about the domestic interior.

Tree-like layouts

More work needs to be done on the basic configurational characteristics of house plans. As evidence accumulates, it is becoming apparent that houses in many parts of the world exploit tree-like configurations to organise domestic space, though this is by no means universal. Tree-like homes share the property that movement about the interior and in relation to the exterior is highly controlled and predictable from the layout, a feature which is made use of in the way activities and functions are assigned to domestic space. Yet this does not mean that the social interpretation of domestic space is therefore easy and uncontentious for, as we saw in the small and simple tree-like houses of the Banbury region, the construction which can be put upon a spatial gesture like occupying the deepest terminal space in the home can be quite different depending on who the occupant is and what are the material circumstances which surround the act of 'being there'. Being locked as a prisoner in the deepest 'a' space with a guard occupying one of the 'b' spaces on the only route to the exterior is quite a different experience from, say, the householder's withdrawing voluntarily to an identically configured 'a' space to which intimate guests are admitted by way of a 'b' space anteroom. Both situations express inequalities in power and control but the former does so to the detriment of the occupant of the deepest space whilst the latter does it to his advantage. This simple illustration cautions against over-simplistic generalisations and points to the difference which exists between describing the objective properties of a house and the subjective interpretation of what those properties might mean either experientially or socially.

As with all forms of combinatorics, the task of enumerating exhaustively all possible tree-like justified graphs for a given number of cells can be shown to be futile even for small numbers of spaces and without taking any account of the complication that whilst two houses may have identical justified permeability graphs, this does not mean that they have identical floor plans. Adjacency is always the pre-condition for rooms to become permeable to one another, but two houses can have identical adjacencies, geometries and proportions and still have radically different patterns of connections between rooms. These issues make the social interpretation of house plans particularly difficult for archaeologists who have only the raw material of space as evidence of human habitation, since they cannot extrapolate with any degree of certainty from the precedent set by the layout of houses whose pattern of use is known to cases with identical configurational characteristics but where only the physical remains have survived. It is therefore fortunate that most archaeological remains contain evidence of material culture which permit an informed guess about what the different rooms in the house were used for.

Improbable trees

One notable exception where syntax has been put to work in recent years to try to shed light on a particularly intractable puzzle in the archaeological record, has been in the interpretation of the ruins of both the 'great houses' and the 'small houses' of the Native Americans of the American south-west, known as the Amasazi. The ruins of these people are well-preserved and have been studied for over a hundred years, but the relationship between the built environment and the social world of the Amasazi is still very much of a mystery. An important clue as to why there has been so little progress in interpreting the ruins may lie in the improbable, tree-like configuration of the room blocks which make up these monumental stone-built settlements (see figures 10.1 and 10.2). We have already seen that, as ordinary houses grow larger in terms of their syntactic size, it

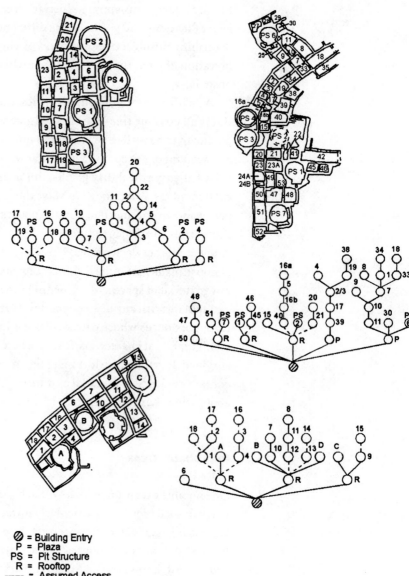

Figure 10.1
A selection of small houseblocks from
Pueblo Bonito, together with their access
graphs

⊘ = Building Entry
P = Plaza
PS = Pit Structure
R = Rooftop
——— = Assumed Access

becomes less and less likely that the additional cells will be added in a
sequence with the earlier cells but, for reasons of preserving accessibility
and daylighting, are more likely to be added in a shallow and branching
arrangement. The great houses of Chaco Canyon are a striking exception
to this spatial rule in that they have turned out to be some of the deepest

Figure 10.2
Plans and justified graphs of Kin Klesto great house

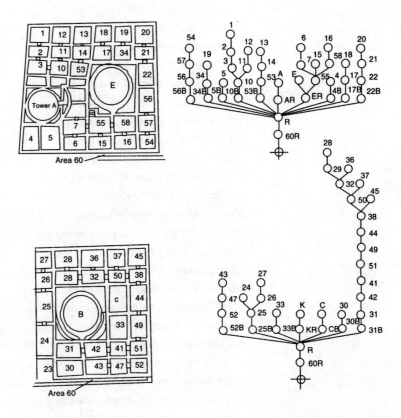

and most asymmetric complexes of rooms that have been recorded. Archaeologists have always been aware that the house blocks were deep and labyrinthine, but precisely how deep and tree-like the complexes of rooms are has only recently been revealed by three archaeologists who have worked independently using the analytic methods of space syntax to address the relation between configuration and function in Amasazi great houses.

Shapiro's work at Arroyo Hondo Pueblo,[6] which was occupied on two occasions from AD 1300–45 and AD 1370–1425, has detected that the configuration of the room blocks there changed over time from more integrated and accessible layouts in occupation phase one to room arrangements that were more segregated and inaccessible during occupation phase two. During phase one, there were more opportunities for internal spaces in the heart of the room blocks to exercise control over suites of adjacent and laterally connected rooms. Shapiro associated this form of spatial configuration with an extended family or clan-based social organisation which may have maintained control over limited portions of the pueblo without any over-arching centralised authority. During phase two, the individual house blocks became more asymmetric, less ringy and there were fewer strong local control points in each complex of rooms. It therefore became more difficult for non-residents to gain access to the deeper and more segregated parts of each room block and individual households were able to exercise more control over the social interactions between residents and visitors. The reason for these changes is not known, but Shapiro has suggested that they could have been produced by a change in the social organisation from extended to nuclear families, a change in the climate which precipitated a greater anxiety about and control over diminishing food supplies or a shift in the religious and ceremonial life of the people. At the same time, key plazas in the settlement became increasingly important integrating spaces within the pueblo as a whole, which may have been indicative of an increasing spatial differentiation between the private and public lives of the inhabitants.

Likewise, Cooper[7] and Bustard[8] have both used space syntax to extend their spatial knowledge about the archaeology of the great houses of Chaco Canyon, New Mexico which were built and occupied between the mid-AD 800s to the mid AD 1100s. These impressive ruins, which range from about fifty to eight hundred rooms in size, were first thought to have been large, densely populated villages but they are now believed to have been redistribution or ceremonial centres rather than centres of habitation. Cooper studied the justified access graphs of twenty-eight great houses. Bustard looked at eleven room blocks from three great houses and compared them with a sample of twenty small houses, also from Chaco Canyon.

Cooper found that the room arrangements in her sample of great houses were extremely variable in their layouts, which in itself supports the view that these were not apartment houses, as these might ordinarily be expected to resemble one another. The preponderance of extraordinarily deep, asymmetrical and tree-like plans which became deeper over time also suggests that these buildings were not used as houses. Some of the later room arrangements seemed particularly maze-like, with deep rings and unclear and restricted access from the rooms which fronted onto the plaza. As the rooms were unlit, orientation within these deep, meandering complexes must have been particularly difficult and the presence of corner doors between some rooms and occasional rings deep within the heart of the complex could only have exacerbated the problems of wayfinding. The plazas also became deeper, less accessible and more visually enclosed over time.

Cooper argued that the difficulty of gaining access to these buildings also casts doubt on the alternative hypothesis, that they functioned as storage buildings within a redistribution economy, since these would require easy, shallow access by large numbers of people from a large and relatively open public plaza, whereas 'the closed appearance of the Chaco Canyon houses and the increasingly asymmetrical and non-distributed plans would indicate that strong boundary control was more important than facilitating entry and social interaction'. Cooper therefore proposed that the great houses had more in common with monumental structures which might indicate that the occupants of Chaco Canyon were a more complex society dominated by some kind of managerial elite, a factor which could explain the inaccessibility of the room blocks though admittedly, in this case the question of use remains an open question where the possibilities have been extended rather than resolved by the use of syntax.

Bustard found that the small houses, which have ordinarily been interpreted as dwellings, also had a dominant tree-like layout which resulted from grouping rows of unlit, adjacent but unconnected back rooms in relation to a shallower front room which faced onto a plaza. She also suggested that this layout might have been preferred because it was easy to control and monitor. Bustard's findings for her smaller sample of great houses supported those of Cooper and Shapiro, particularly the trend towards increasing spatial depth and segregation over time.

However, Bustard also went on to compare the presence of archaeological floor-features such as fire pits, slab bins, mealing bins and other forms of built-in storage like shelves and platforms in her samples of small and great houses and to locate these in relation to three mutually exclusive architectural fixed features of the buildings, the building entry, plaza and kiva or pit structure rooftop. The large numbers of domestic floor features in small houses suggested that they were indeed dwellings, though there was some evidence from the numbers and arrangements of built-in features that not all small houses were equal and some functional specialisation may have been present in the society. The sample of small houses also revealed a consistent integration order for these activities and features,

which was as follows: plaza > rooftop > mealing room > fire pit > pit structure > no features > storage room. Mealing rooms seem to have been particularly important in that they acted as a transition between private, interior
space and public, exterior space. Bustard also detected a tendency for some
mealing rooms to be associated with more than one dwelling unit, which
suggested that a degree of co-operation in food processing may have
existed above the level of the individual household. Mealing rooms may
even have served as a means of economic and social integration by induc-
ing regular, face-to-face meetings among members of the local community.

Rooms with any domestic features were scarce in great houses, which
had the following genotype: plaza > rooftop > mealing room > kiva > fire pit
> storage > no features. Rooms with no floor features were distinctly more
segregated than the other spaces. Like Cooper and Shapiro, Bustard therefore rejected the hypothesis that the great houses were built as residences
either for an élite or for members of the population at large. She proposed
a mixed-use model for the great houses which may not have served exclusively either for storage, or for ritual or administrative purposes. All the
spatial changes which were identified by the authors had been overlooked
in the previous studies of the archaeology and architecture of the
American south-west, as these had concentrated on the shapes and
detailed measurements of the room blocks.

Ringy layouts

Tree-like domestic space arrangements produce strongly programmed
forms of domestic space arrangements. Compared with their tree-like
counterparts, plans with rings are more difficult to characterise as they
permit route choice by adding connections within the configuration over
and above the minimum necessary to ensure the continuity of the system.
Two important issues for interpretation in assessing the impact of rings are
first, who controls movement around the ring and second, how extensive
is the ring in linking together the parts of the complex? Trivial rings
which link only two or three immediately adjacent rooms can have only
localised effects within the layout. Large rings which link the physically
remote parts of the house together tend to have large-scale effects and the
act of blocking movement around the ring may be more obvious or less pre-

dictable depending on where the ring is cut. Spaces where rings intersect are usually powerful places occupied by key people or functions but this is not always the case, as the potential of a space to control movement among its neighbours depends also on how those neighbours are connected.

One of the most important distinctions in assessing rings is the difference between rings which are limited to the interior of the house and rings which intersect with the house plot so that access to the house is achieved by more than one entrance. Usually where a house has more than one entrance these are distinguished in some way in terms of function, or the people who may use each door, or the circumstances under which each is used.

Layouts that are ringy with respect to the exterior possess an important feature which is not characteristic of most tree-like plans: the house may be radically different in its configuration when it is considered in relation to its exterior than if just the interior spaces are taken into account. The reason that this is so derives ultimately from the laws of space rather than from social inclinations. In any tree-like room arrangement, whether the tree branches shallow or deep, the node that represents the exterior is at one pole of the justified access graph and the room or rooms which are deepest into the house are at the other extremity in a branching sequence which links together all the spaces in the house by way of the trunk of the tree. Eliminating the exterior, which will always be one of the more segregated nodes in the graph, has little effect on the overall configuration of the complex. However, where the exterior participates in a ring through the house, its elimination will have an overall segregating effect on those spaces that remain and the effect will be particularly pronounced where the ring is not just a trivial one that links together just the few spaces in the immediate vicinity of the entrance. It is therefore possible to speculate that whilst tree-like houses normally support strongly framed social situations where access to and movement about the house need to be controlled in the interests of an individual inhabitant or group of residents, ringy houses usually support social situations where the dominant interface in the dwelling is between an individual host and his guests or between some group of residents in the house and their visitors.

Many homes in different parts of the world are affected by seasonality, and a particularly clear illustration of a situation where external rings seem to play an important role in modulating people's way of living is to compare the pattern of space and behaviour in a ringy house during the summer when connections to the garden are taken into account, compared with how people use the same house in the winter when the rings with the garden are cut. As we have seen in the case of architects' houses in London and in the United States of America, ringy houses become more extroverted during the summer. They literally turn themselves inside-out and integrate with the garden. The same house can seem more introverted and closed in upon itself during the winter when the doors to the garden are kept firmly shut. Connecting or disregarding rings through the garden may affect the pattern of integration and also the balance of activities throughout the house, so that uses shift and migrate seasonally. The capacity of a house to absorb these seasonal fluctuations is normally considered to be a desirable quality and it is certainly a property that many architects intuitively seek after, though not always with success, perhaps because changing the connectivity of even one space may affect the whole house in ways which are difficult to intuit.

Most studies of houses which are concerned with the relation among the interior spaces do not differentiate the grounds in which the house is located into their constituent spaces but there may be circumstances when it is essential to do so. Several studies in recent years have paid particular attention to modelling the complexity of external space, looking at the relationship between the house and its plot, the interface between the house and the street and the visual and permeable spatial relations among the houses in a neighbourhood. It is quite common for the front-back orientation of the house to be associated with the public and private spheres of domestic life, express formal and informal social relations, provide appropriate settings for more ceremonial or more everyday, practical activities or be associated with the manifesting or hiding of objects in those rooms which front onto the street. As was found in the London terraced houses from chapter four, different sub-cultures within a society may differentiate themselves in gestures which turn out to be inversions of a set of common, underlying spatial principles.

Looking at a house with and without the exterior can also reveal interesting shifts in the perceptions of the householder and visitors. Often visitors are not given access to the whole house – an important exception being the guided tour of the home which may occur when a proud householder shows guests over the entire property – but it may even be normal for people's experiences of the domestic interior to be different and rather rare for everyone to have equal rights in the interior in the sense that some space is off-limits. A comparison of these partial readings of the domestic configuration as it appears to different groups of occupants is often illuminating. Sometimes the spaces used by different household members overlap but it is also possible that they intersect with one another minimally, or only through rings provided purely for circulation between the separate territories of the different groups of inhabitants. A final dramatic illustration of the construction of rings that are not found in normal, profane social space-time, is the different experience of people's houses mapped from the point of view of that most unwelcome of visitors, the burglar.

Residential institutions

There are, however, cases where the inclusion of rings can be particularly supportive or unsupportive of social interaction and encounter within the home, and a recent study by De Syllas[9] has highlighted the crucial role of rings in generating and controlling the behaviour of people in group residential homes for children, the elderly and people with learning difficulties. In one study of communal living, De Syllas compared three group homes for children who had been taken into the care of the local authority either because they seemed to lack parental care and control, or were the victims of a family crisis or domestic abuse, or had been discovered to have been committing acts of crime or vandalism, taking drugs or alcohol or engaging in under-age sex or because they represented a danger to themselves and others because of their aggressive or suicidal behaviour.

Despite having been designed by an eminent architectural practice, one of the homes had such a poor reputation among care workers that, at the time of De Syllas' visit, it was about to be closed down after having been in use for only two years. Staff running the home claimed that the building had 'a detrimental effect on the mental state of any child' and they argued that several children who had been admitted to the home had become more disturbed whilst they were living there. The architects had intended their building to achieve just the opposite effect, for it had 'been planned to give children as much freedom as possible in a homely environment' in the hope of encouraging improvements in the children's behaviour. The staff disputed this claim and they countered that, for the building to work at all, 'rooms have been locked and kept empty and access ways blocked' and that it was even necessary to keep the children locked in their rooms for most of the time to preserve a semblance of control over their disruptive behaviour. All parties seemed to agree that the crux of the problem lay in the relationship between the design of the building and the ways in which its occupants were using it. De Syllas compared the configuration of the 'rogue' home with two other children's homes that were of roughly the same size and date, which operated within the same management regime and which were known to work well, in order to highlight any spatial or organisational differences which might account for the apparent success of the two homes and the failure of the first.

Spatial analysis revealed an important difference in the design of the unworkable home which was that it had a series of internal rings which resulted from a pattern of dual circulation within the building. Not only did the home have a shared system of public corridors and staircases which provided access to the children's flats, staff accommodation, the communal living areas and service zones in the usual way, it also had a more private system of routes which passed through the interior of each of the flats that was occupied by a group of children and their resident care workers. A third set of rings allowed for a separate private access from the patio garden of each flat to a shared outdoor play area and to the world outside the home. All of these extra connections made it possible to circulate freely through the building without using the main, public circulation system.

De Syllas concluded that the building had been conceived of almost as a three-dimensional playground but its ringy circulation made it almost impossible for the staff to supervise, contain or control the distressed and disturbed children who were placed in their care. Instead of helping the children to recuperate from the experiences which had brought them into care, the staff found that the building required them to act the part of gaolers. The distinctive feature of the two other homes was that they had a clear spatial structure which, for the most part, took a tree-like form, the sole exception being the ring linking all the flats to the main entrance and shared dining area and to the service entrance by way of the kitchens.

De Syllas has carried out similar studies of group residential homes for people with learning difficulties and for the elderly. These have led to the conclusion that inappropriate rings in the plan can make the circulation more complicated and therefore more confusing than it need be, and that where this happens the building is experienced as larger and more institutional than is actually the case. On the other hand a simple, clear and generous pattern of routes within a group home can function as a social space in its own right, provide opportunities for residents, staff, guests and visitors to the building to meet one other informally and for staff to monitor the behaviour of residents in a discreet, unobtrusive manner.[10]

More recently, Peatross[11] has used space syntax to compare the spatial dimensions of control in three Alzheimer's units and three juvenile detention centres in the United States of America, and her research has drawn attention to how spatial rings in these institutions may construct a rich mix of static and moving people or separate stationary and moving people into two separate spatial groupings, with apparently deleterious effects. Some of Peatross' findings echo those of De Syllas. For example, she has suggested that the spatial form of the building may facilitate or restrict movement and co-presence among its residents and that under some circumstances it can even exclude residents altogether from the most integrated places in the layout. On the other hand, 'the integration core may sustain patterns of awareness, communication and encounter over and above those prescribed by the organisation'. Between these two extremes, the integration core normally acts simultaneously as a domain for probabilistic encounter and casual surveillance.

However, Peatross' detailed, first-hand observational studies of how the buildings were able to engineer patterns of mutual awareness or avoidance amongst its residents and between residents, staff and visitors have been able to shed new light on how space can work to make some buildings appear to be more institutional whilst others seem to be more informal and relaxed. In the more relaxed of her settings, Peatross found that the core of most integrated spaces usually supported the group activities of the residents. The way in which major routes cut through these spaces – day rooms, television lounges or multi-purpose rooms – meant that the residents' activity areas either lay directly on the ringy core of the building or were directly exposed to it visually. The result was that these spaces contained a unique and lively mixture of people sitting together in the foreground, whilst in the background the spaces were animated by a constant stream of people who could be seen moving around the building. Peatross described this phenomenon as the 'animated isovist' and suggested that visual fields which integrate static and moving people in a close association with the residents' shared spaces may be an acceptable way of normalising behaviour in what is, after all, an institutional residential environment. Peatross observed that the flow of passers-by in the background was the critical element in making the building appear relaxed and normal, not the size or composition of the static group of people who were present in the foreground. In the more successful group residential settings, people were observed to move about and to stop to talk to one another in places where they could be seen by other people, a factor which seemed to act as a multiplier effect in animating space and making it appear more relaxed and permissive. Thus, observed movement and social interaction in these environments were to a large measure configurationally driven.

In less successful environments which were judged to have a more institutional feel about them, the places which were provided for groups of residents to encounter one another were dead-end spaces, out of touch with the ringy routes which people took when moving around the building. This seemed to reduce the amount of global information that was available to residents. They were only aware of the factor of 'what is happening around here'. In more relaxed settings, the background spaces which residents were able to see whilst they were sitting together seemed to be able to offer them vital information and stimulus about 'what was going on out there'. This seemed particularly important in reducing and making palatable the more restrictive effects of confinement.

Peatross demonstrated that the degree of animation of the visual field of the group areas in residential care environments can be measured by observing the ratio of moving and static people who are co-present in a particular convex space and setting these figures against the numbers of static and moving people who can be seen when the occupants look out beyond the place where they are sitting (see figure 10.3). A further refinement measures the numbers of residents, staff and visitors in the foreground space and relates these to the numbers who are present in the background visual field. Issues such as 'are there more of us in here, or is out there livelier?' may make an important contribution to the social ambience of residential settings and may be particularly important in those cases where people are confined to an institution against their will.

Transitions and spaces

De Syllas' and Peatross' work on residential care environments has drawn attention to the differences between circulation routes and spaces designed for activities to take place. These distinctions also exist in ordi-

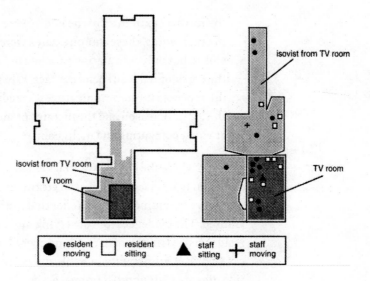

Figure 10.3
Snapshot of an 'animated isovist' from a typical residents' day room, showing observed activity within the room and outside it

isovist from TV room

isovist from TV room
TV room

TV room

● resident moving   □ resident sitting   ▲ staff sitting   ✛ staff moving

nary domestic space and the difference between rooms which are clearly intended to support activities and functions and those which are intended for circulation is, of course, itself a form of spatial labelling. There is a tendency to see transitions as mere circulation, intended to provide efficient access and egress or perhaps, more speculatively, to reduce unwelcome contact by insulating activities and functions from one another. This interpretation has been given to transitions on several occasions in this book, particularly where there seems to be an excess of lobbies and passage-ways over what is necessary to separate rooms, secure the boundary against trespassers, provide appropriate environmental conditions and so forth. Transitions have the effect of insulating spaces from one another as effectively as building walls and the 'social distance' which is built into transitions that engineer separations can be appreciated as 'felt space' just as much as where the separations are literally built into the bricks and mortar of the house. Strong arguments have been adduced that link the use of transitions in houses with the intent to assure that social separations within the home are strictly maintained.

No longer was it necessary to pass serially through the intractable occupied territory of rooms, with all the diversion, incidents and accidents that they might harbour. Instead, the door of any room would deliver you into a network of routes from which the room next door and the furthest extremity of the house were almost equally accessible. In other words, these thoroughfares were able to draw distant rooms closer, but only by a glaring paradox: in facilitating communication, the corridor reduced social contact. What this meant was that purposeful or necessary communication was reduced and contact, according to the lights of reason and the dictates of morality, was at best incidental, at worst corrupting and malignant.[12]

Even where the circumstantial evidence for a particular social interpretation to be placed on a spatial gesture is quite strong, counter-examples serve to remind the researcher that nothing should be taken for granted. The evidence from observing more complex organisations like residential settings which combine everyday living with close personal care, work environments, schools and hospitals shows that these circulation areas permit unprogrammed activity which does not directly support the organisation but function as highly permissive spaces where people are liberated from the statuses and roles that they occupy in the formal, organisational hierarchy. People interact more casually in corridors, they may even support forms of informal social encounter and negotiation which simply cannot occur in the more structured settings that are provided within rooms. Interpretations of how transitions feature in domestic space organisation should also allow for this possibility.

Space and labels

Once configured space is labelled to reflect the activities which are carried out in the different spaces, the functions they serve, the conventions governing which spaces are usually occupied by different members of the household and so on, this reintroduces the richness and variety of life into the more narrow morphological account and makes interpretation of people's domestic space arrangements somewhat easier, though rarely self-evident. The experience of a home is usually related to different viewpoints among household members and between inhabitants and visitors. Homes may reflect many differences between cultural categories, including gender divisions between men and women, power relations between hosts and guests, patrons and clients or householders and servants, generational differences between adults and children, differences in how people and household objects or domestic animals are accommodated in the home, lifestyle differences between the home as a locus for family life or as a place of work and so on. The strength with which these differences are encoded in the home may also vary from culture to culture, so that in some circumstances differences are weakly realised whereas in others they are pronounced.

Interpretation needs to bear in mind that the experience of the dominant group may be the most obvious and the most widely circulated interpretation of living at home, but it may not be the only view. For example, home is usually associated with benign feelings of security, safety and comfort but this may not always be so. For those where the home is the setting for domestic violence or abuse this is certainly not the case. Under these circumstances, spatial properties may be inverted so that features of the home that would normally be interpreted as supportive, such as having a clear physical boundary which protects the privacy of the occupants, become a burden rather than an asset.

Interpretations of domestic space also need to take account of time as an aspect of space as well as of different peoples readings of domestic life. An important piece of social information which may not be at all obvious from the layout of a house may be the difference between how it is occupied and used during normal social time and how the house is transformed to take account of the extraordinary or sacred times during which household rituals or family celebrations are enacted. People's homes are unlike the complex, non-residential buildings that can be directly but discreetly observed using conventional techniques for recording the presence of different kinds of building user, in that the introduction of a researcher into the domestic setting immediately violates the privacy of the home and so behaviour within the family is almost certain to alter to take account of their researcher-guest. In order to make a fuller interpretation of the house which includes social practices and invokes a temporal as well as a spatial dimension, it may be necessary to question residents closely about their everyday domestic routines and what happens on special occasions.

Spatial choreography

As research continues into the micro-use of space in the home, a new and promising line of inquiry is the relation between household activities and objects and the daily pattern of domestic routines in which people engage in the home. This has resulted in attempts to pin down the choreography of people's spatial experience through the study of kinaesthetics. The movements, gestures and postures are recorded which orientate and project the body in space. To give just one illustration, the task of food preparation and cooking in West Africa, where the floor is used as a working plane and free-standing portable equipment is used, inscribes a completely different sequence of balletic trajectories in space than is found in a conventional Western European kitchen, where cooking is dictated by the position of ergonomically designed, wall-mounted units with a level working plane set at a constant height of about nine hundred millimetres from the floor. Cooking in West Africa is a centripetal affair, where people co-operate in inward-facing groups to prepare a meal. In Europe it is usually an individual activity and even when the task of preparing for a meal is carried out in company, the positioning of the kitchen units usually ensures that the collaborators work side by side or even back to back, rather than facing one another. Many domestic routines and house-hold chores describe a series of arcs in three-dimensional space which encode behaviours that are so familiar that they are reproduced automatically. The extent to which these contribute towards a culturally specific 'space-sense' is still very much an open question.

An early application was in the study by Zhu[13] of the ritual practices of the imperial Chinese court in the Forbidden City palace complex, Beijing, that housed the emperor, his immediate family, his personal servants and a few important court officials. Zhu attempted to trace the dynamics of court life in relation to its built form and space configuration, enacted space inscribed in the unfolding of secular rituals such as those relating to the ascent to the throne, the grand audience, the celebration of the emperor's birthday, the declaration of a decree or the celebration of the winter solstice.

> In the hall of supreme Harmony, the emperor sat on the throne, facing south towards the greeting officials and nobles on the platform and in the courtyard square. Every action and every detail was governed by meticulous and subtle rules. The 'other side', the officials and nobles had to obey even more complex rules and to expend much more bodily effort, travelling long distances to reach the palace city and arrive at the position assigned to each in the courtyard square, where they stood in a symmetrical formation. The ceremony of greeting the emperor included

the most important and most impressive moment in the whole drama, the performance of the kow-tow: kneeling towards the monarch (that is towards the north) and touching the forehead to the ground nine times. This physically laborious act of showing reverence and respect expressed the asymmetrical relationship between the two parties. Indeed, physical bodily torture on both sides – albeit asymmetrically distributed – seems to have been a necessary part of the ceremony.[14]

Zhu argues that it is possible to reconstruct from these public displays of gesture and action, the elements and relations that constituted the ideological discourse of the Chinese imperial court.

Research is continuing into the relation between domestic space and the detail of how people move about in it, both purposefully and efficiently, in order to perform domestic tasks and chores and when drifting more aimlessly, perhaps just to inhabit and experience the different parts of the house almost as pure sensation. As Hillier has observed,

> any open space is a space in which possibilities have yet been eliminated, and every open space is continually structured and restructured by the human activity that takes place in it. If we do not conceptualise space in this way we have no way of reconciling human freedom and the human structuring of space. Human activity is never actually structured by space. In structuring space by physical objects we suggest possibilities by eliminating others. But the spaces in the interstices of the physical forms are still 'open'. Within these limits, the infinite structurability of space still prevails. In our cells we may dance.[15]

Thus, although the actions, movements, gestures and postures people take up in their homes are not spatially determined they may be spatially related, either because they are exploratory improvisations within a free, unconstrained environment or because they are the embodiment of conventional, even ritualised social practices or perhaps because they are involuntary behaviours that have been ingrained by habit.

Visibility and permeability

The relation between visibility and permeability is a vital component of how houses work spatially and are experienced by their occupants. Isovists or visual fields go some way to capturing the changing vistas that a moving subject experiences. As virtual reality becomes more sophisticated in simulating buildings and places so that it is possible to walk-through and explore, more of people's wayfinding strategies become accessible to research. Static descriptions of visual fields are increasingly being replaced by animations of promenades in which the transparency or opacity of materials, the play of light within the interior, and the changing sequence of visual fields can be simulated in order to study their effects on how people use and move about in buildings and places.

Some of this work is highly experimental but, like the study of movement and dynamism in architecture described above, it may turn out to have important practical applications. For example, in group residential homes for people with Alzheimer's disease or for those suffering from dementia, it is believed that some forms of wandering behaviours may be therapeutic in that they relieve the boredom and stress of living in a highly controlled, enclosed environment but other forms of confused wandering seem highly stressful and may even exacerbate people's symptoms. It is therefore important to know which kinds of space provide a positive stimulus to residents and which are deleterious.

Vernacular and historical studies

Studies of samples of traditional and vernacular houses have been continuing over the years and an extensive database has now accumulated on the morphology of houses world-wide. Several of these studies take as their starting point the approach that was pioneered in *Ideas are in things* of using a quantitative and statistical approach to search for regularities in a body of house plans that already exist in the historical record, in order to identify the way the houses are configured and to pinpoint the spatial characteristics of the locations of different household activities. This line of research is closely related to the studies of vernacular and regional house types which have been conducted over the years by Brunskill[16] and his colleagues at the University of Manchester, but it brings a new analytic dimension to their more conventional forms of historical scholarship. Recent research by Orhun into the typological variability of the traditional Turkish house[17] is typical of this genre.

Orhun's work, like much of the research which has been reported in this book, draws on a previously published first-hand survey and typological account of Turkish houses by the architectural historian, Eldem,[18] which was conducted in the 1980s. Despite the recent date of this field-work, many of the houses which he studied have since been demolished and so it is no longer possible to use direct observation of the interiors or interviews with the occupants to explore their everyday living arrangements. Traditional dwellings and ways of life everywhere are under great pressure to adopt a modern, largely western lifestyle and it is probably inevitable that the 'genetic pool' of domestic space-types will be seriously depleted by the start of the new millennium. It is therefore vital that those detailed field studies which are recording this vanishing heritage proceed in parallel with comparative and cross-cultural approaches which enhance our understanding of the richness and diversity of people's homes.

Orhun has subjected sixteen examples, selected to cover the range of typical Turkish plan-types, to a detailed configurational analysis. It has emerged that the relationship of the house to the exterior is an important spatial variable, which enables two configurationally distinct house-types to be identified: an 'introverted' type, with a deep integration core centred on the 'sofa', and a more 'extroverted' house, with a shallow core orientated towards the paved yard (see figure 10.4). These two types support different living patterns among inhabitants and distinct ways of receiving guests into the home. Even more important, the findings seem to relate to the relative insularity or openness of different sectors of Turkish society to outside influences, and to this extent, the house may be an important index of the progressive or conservative attitudes of its inhabitants. The contrast between deep and shallow integration cores and the proposition that these may express more introverted and extroverted houses may turn out to have a more general currency, particularly if these alternative spatial gestures reflect centripetal and centrifugal social forces which express the relative openness or closure of the home.

Configurational studies of this kind are unlikely ever to replace more conventional architectural accounts based on the material form of the dwelling, the mode of construction, the geometry and proportions of the plan, the use of materials and the detailed decoration of the facades. However, it is particularly difficult to escape from the architectural discourse once the buildings which originally gave rise to it no longer exist, and under these circumstances, the ability of spatial analysis to shed new light on existing bodies of data will undoubtedly continue to make an

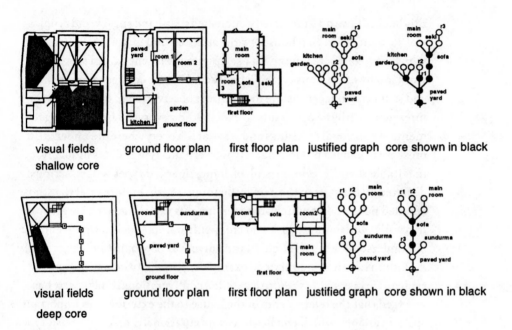

visual fields

shallow core

ground floor plan   first floor plan   justified graph   core shown in black

visual fields

deep core

ground floor plan   first floor plan   justified graph   core shown in black

Figure 10.4
Comparison of a typical shallow core and
deep core house

important contribution to our understanding of the evolution and typology of domestic space in different regions of the world. Where syntactic
analysis merely serves to confirm existing accounts, ideas or theories it
can appear to state the obvious, but in a more complex way. However,
where analysis points to a previously unobserved dimension of the data, as
it does in the case of Orhun's study, it is able to emancipate the researcher
from inherited frameworks and assumptions and propose a new way of
seeing the relation between house form and culture.

Existing scholarly accounts provide a very limited source for complete,
detailed samples of house plans, and as the importance of working on
large, statistically reliable samples has become clearer, researchers have
increasingly begun to assemble their own collections of plans culled from
local and national archives, building trade journals and architectural magazines, architects' drawings and brochures describing houses offered for
sale. Although this is still one step removed from first-hand survey work,
archival and documentary research paves the way for configurational
analysis to interface with issues which are normally located in the domain
of cultural studies, as we saw in chapter five which addressed – albeit
superficially – the social meaning of the home as a product of the specula-

tive housing market in late twentieth-century British, consumer-orien-
tated society.

Following this more semiological/linguistic approach, a much larger
study of the evolution of speculative houses in Britain between the
middle of the nineteenth century and the inter-war years has recently
been undertaken by Trigueiro,[19] who took as her sample five hundred
British house plans which she extracted from the leading building trade
journals of the day. All the houses were built for occupation by the middle
classes, a broad stratum which encompasses clerical workers and trades-
people at the bottom and members of the establishment, gentlemen and
polite society at the top. A cursory inspection of the plans revealed thirty-
five families of labels which were used to describe the three basic household activities of receiving, eating and cooking. This immediately
suggested to Trigueiro that a study of the semantics of room labelling
might prove fruitful. Powerful social messages seemed to have been conveyed by whether the main service room in the plan carried the label
'kitchen' or 'scullery', the reception spaces included a separate dining
room for eating, the space reserved for everyday living was designated a
'drawing room', 'sitting room', 'living room', 'lounge', 'family room' or
'parlour', and whether the layout included a more formal 'best' room for
the reception of guests.

In order to identify the relationship between status and dwelling type,
Trigueiro first established the total number of rooms in each house and
then the proportion of the available spaces which were devoted to three
key domestic activities; reception, service and sleeping. She found that
before 1894, the more reception rooms a house had the higher the social
status of its owner was likely to be. Houses for the upper middle classes
had four or more bedrooms and three or more reception rooms which must
include both a drawing room and a dining room, whereas middle-middle-
class layouts had only two reception rooms and three or more bedrooms.
For both these groups, the room in which food was prepared was invariably
described as a kitchen. Lower-middle-class homes had just one reception
room, which was never labelled as either a drawing room or a dining room,
and fewer than four bedrooms. Food preparation in this group might take
place in a kitchen but it could also be carried out in a room described as a
scullery, or in the living room. Out of the five hundred cases, 93% com-
plied with this description.

Between 1894 and 1914, high status was indicated by living in a house with both many reception rooms and many service rooms. Upper-middle-class homes had four or more bedrooms and a minimum of six living rooms, including at least two reception rooms and at least three service rooms. One of the reception rooms was invariably labelled either as a dining room or a drawing room. Middle-middle-class houses had at least three bedrooms and at most five living rooms, either two reception rooms and three service rooms or vice versa. Again, the largest and best-equipped of the service rooms was always referred to as the kitchen. Lower-middle-class plans had a maximum of four bedrooms and only three living rooms, none of which was ever labelled as a drawing room. Out of the five hundred cases, 98% followed this model.

After 1914, Trigueiro established that there was a reduction in the number of spaces allocated to both these functions, though after 1923 upper-middle-class layouts still had at least four bedrooms, and either a drawing room, dining room and kitchen layout, augmented by least one more minor service function, or a family room, dining room and kitchen plus two or more extra service rooms, together with a second, 'best' room in which to entertain more formally. Middle-middle-class houses had three or more bedrooms, one or two service rooms (invariably including a kitchen) and two or three reception rooms, one of these being either a dining room or a sitting room. Lower-middle-class houses had at most four bedrooms and three living rooms. Out of the five hundred cases, 98% fitted this description.

Trigueiro did not attempt a thoroughgoing sociological interpretation of these results. However, her findings clearly imply that the preoccupation of contemporary speculative builders with finding 'socially accept-able' ways of locating and describing the household activities of living, food preparation and food consumption in the layout in relation to the reception and entertainment of guests within the family home is not a new phenomenon since this is clearly the fundamental social dilemma which has generated the most common permutations of room labels in Trigueiro's house plans. Studies of the way in which people describe their houses, coupled to an analysis of how these descriptions relate both to the spatial attributes of individual rooms and to their overall position in the house, seem a promising line for future inquiry, particularly as terminology seems transient and driven by people's aspirations and pretensions as well as by their established values and achievements.

Trigueiro went on to make a syntactic study of the houses and their space-configurational features. The overall mean integration of the interiors of her middle-middle-class homes which were the most integrated subgroup in her sample at 1.475, is remarkably similar to the values for contemporary architects' houses (1.419) and modern speculative homes (1.423). If we consider the fact that the houses became more integrated over the eighty-seven-year study period, from 1.541 in the early 1800s to 1.433 by the 1930s then the similarity is even greater and suggests that middle-class homes in Britain are on a long-term pathway towards greater integration.

Trigueiro found that the tendency to greater integration was most marked in the upper-middle-class houses in her sample, from 1.568 to 1.424. If we consider these houses to be of a similar social standing to the modern architects' houses, this would tend to reinforce the suggestion of a downward tendency in the houses of gentlemen and professionals. The decline in values for the middle-middle-sector was 1.541 to 1.433, which could be compared with the average integration value of 'up-market' speculative modern houses, 1.349. The tendency to integration was least apparent in the houses of the lower middle classes, from 1.541 to 1.520. The comparable value for the 'down-market' sector of the Milton Keynes sample, considered separately, 1.497.

Trigueiro further noted that increased integration was accompanied by a greater syntactic differentiation among the constituent spaces of the dwelling and by a raising of the space:transition ratio from 1.3 in the 1840s, to 1.4 in the opening decades of the twentieth century and then up to 1.6 by the 1930s, suggesting that rooms in the houses were becoming spatially less insulated from one another. A low space:transition ratio (many transitions to fewer spaces) was a pronounced feature of the architects' London houses which were examined in chapter eight. Modern speculative houses have a space:transition ratio (1.5) more like their early modern counterparts. Again, the process took place differently in the dwellings of different status groups within the middle classes.

Finally, Trigueiro returned to the social meaning of the different functional labels in the home, focusing on the receiving / eating / cooking triad which was discussed earlier. Here she argued that the space used for cooking was likely to have been used only by members of the household and so it could be located at the opposite social pole from the 'best' space where visitors were usually received. The room where meals were eaten, whether informally as a family or whilst hosting a dinner party, was the setting which brought the conceptually separate domains of cooking and entertaining into direct association with one another.

By plotting the proportions of most integrated function spaces in the sample which were devoted to each activity over time, Trigueiro has detected a shift in the focus of integration over time from the public – reception / dining centred – to the private – dining / cooking centred – sphere. In upper-middle-class homes the integration focus moved from an adjacent and directly-linked pair of rooms, the drawing room and the dining room, into the dining room. The transfer seems to have taken place around the turn of the century. In middle-middle-class houses the double reception room remained popular until about the time of the First World War, and then after the war the integration focus moved not to the dining room but to the kitchen.

Lower-middle-class houses did not possess a drawing room or a separate dining room. Some of these houses amalgamated eating and cooking in a well-integrated room, leaving a separate, more segregated 'best' space for the reception of guests. This eventually became the 'traditional working-class' way of living that was noted in chapter four. Others put the activities of eating and reception together in the most integrated space and separated out food preparation and cooking. After the war, if cooking took place in a separate space, this tended to be more integrated than the eating and reception space. This eventually became the 'new middle-class' way of entertaining described in chapter four.

Middle-class homes in Britain therefore evolved during the nineteenth and early years of the twentieth centuries, from a relatively segregated spatial system that was centred on the interface between the family, servants and visitors to a more integrated layout which was family-centred. Trigueiro's findings suggest that the scenery was already being put into place for the development of the modern, nuclear family during the Victorian period. If this is so, the continuities with Victorian homes which were observed in the speculative houses of Milton Keynes would seem not to be superficial. However, large-scale longitudinal syntactic studies of this kind are exceedingly rare and clearly much more work needs to be done that relates developments in space configuration to the sociology of the family.

Research in this field is required as a matter of some urgency, as the number of houses built in Britain is set to rise by some 4.5 million new homes over the next decade. Because of the way housing finance in Britain is structured, most speculative house builders still cater for a model of the family based on a stable partnership between two young adults and their joint offspring, but the formation of new households is already known to be greatest amongst people living alone, and what is more, post-modern families seem to be much more diverse and loosely structured in their make-up and to show a greater tendency over time to oscillate between periods of lone-parenting and serial monogamy than was the case in previous generations. The relation between these broad demographic and social changes and ordinary people's varied lifestyles and images of home needs to be better understood, if the supply of houses is even crudely to match the demand for a decent and acceptable 'home of one's own', let alone to encourage a degree of self-expression or to enrich people's lives. These problems are by no means unique to Britain, but the solutions which emerge in different social and economic conditions are likely to be different. So also are the spatial characteristics of the houses needed to support people's lives in different parts of the world.

The morphology of domestic experience

An important limitation on studying the labelling of house plans which was a feature of Trigueiro's lower-middle-class homes and which is endemic wherever resources are constrained, is that a single space may have to adapt to accommodate several, often incompatible, functions over the course of a working day. A recent study by Monteiro[20] has attempted to study this process in more detail through a close examination of how daily family activities are distributed in the houses of low and middle income households in Recife, Brazil. The study sample comprised 101 houses from three neighbourhoods in Recife; a favela (shanty town), a public housing estate and a middle class residential neighbourhood which contained a mixture of flats and houses (see figure 10.5, 10.6 and 10.7). However, instead of analysing the spatial configuration of the houses, which in the favelas might consist of just a single room, Monteiro directly analysed the spatial pattern of activity in the home following the model set out in the introduction to this book which analysed the spatial configuration of people inside a Mongolian yurt.

Monteiro's research aim was to capture the morphology of domestic experience, including which activities were perceived as compatible and

Figure 10.5
Typical favela houses in Recife, Brazil.

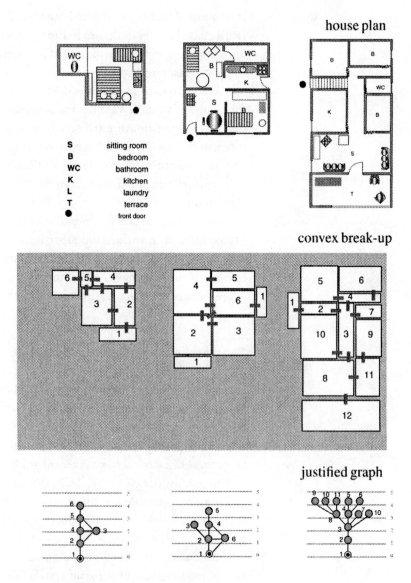

S	sitting room
B	bedroom
WC	bathroom
K	kitchen
L	laundry
T	terrace
●	front door

house plan

convex break-up

justified graph

which incompatible where different activities usually took place, how the pattern of domestic activities was distributed within the dwelling and what were the spatial attributes of the different spatial settings. To that end, two main methods were used for data collection. In order to obtain data on people's patterns of daily activities, Monteiro used a 'multiple sorting procedure' to elicit information about people's subjective percep-

Figure 10.6
Typical public sector houses in Recife, Brazil

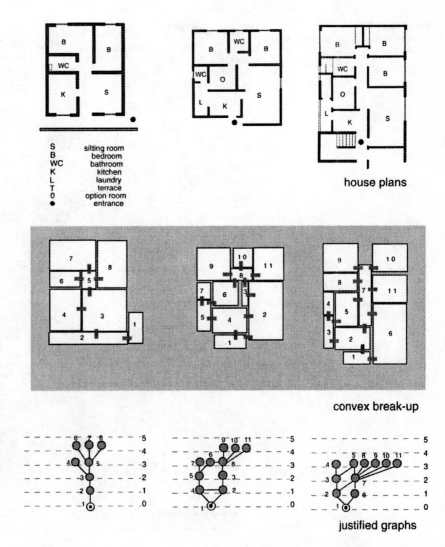

S sitting room
B bedroom
WC bathroom
K kitchen
L laundry
T terrace
O option room
● entrance

house plans

convex break-up

justified graphs

tions of which domestic activities could go together and which should be kept apart. After a lengthy familiarisation process, respondents were invited to select from a set of eight labels those room names by which they called all the places in their home, to choose all the activities which they normally performed there from a list of twenty-five, and then to match activities to places. Respondents were also asked to draw a plan of their house or to permit the researcher to visit their home to draw it. All the respondents were interviewed in their own homes, which also permitted

Figure 10.7
Typical middle-class houses and flats in
Recife, Brazil

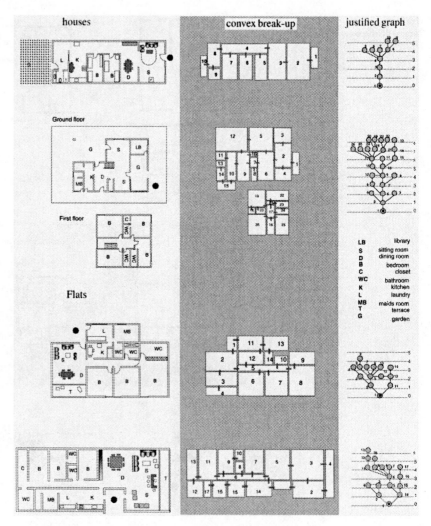

Figure 10.7
Typical middle-class houses and flats in
Recife, Brazil

the interviewer to observe directly the use of space in each house. Care
was taken to record all objects and furniture which might hold clues as to
where domestic activities were taking place and to register any transient
evidence of activities which might have occurred in each space, such as
cups and plates containing leftover food, books on the table or toys on
the floor.

The results of the interviews were first mapped onto the plans of the
houses and then the overall pattern of domestic activity was analysed
configurationally. Five activities were dropped from the original list at this

stage, mainly because they took place outside the house. Two syntactic variables were associated with each activity; depth from the exterior of the dwelling and degree of integration within the home. The activities were further grouped into five analytic categories; domestic chores (ironing, cooking, washing-up or washing clothes), interactive leisure (watching television, playing with the children, chatting, meeting friends), passive leisure (reading, listening to music, studying and dating), communal needs (drinking coffee, eating lunch, dining) and private needs (having a wash, taking a bath, sleeping, resting or making love).

Monteiro found that activities tended to group in different integration bands. The first, most integrated band, contained communal needs, followed by interactive leisure pastimes. Domestic chores were grouped in the second band, as were passive leisure activities. The third band of activities involved satisfying personal needs, and these tended to adopt a more segregated setting. However, the detailed rank order of integration of all the activities was found to vary markedly by house type (see figure 10.8) so as to produce quite distinctive groupings of activities in each of the different spatial settings.

Activity patterns in the favela houses were strikingly integrated, which might be expected where these are likely to be taking place in different parts of the same room or in the same room at different times of day. What was unexpected was the extent to which the houses were integrated by household chores, particularly cooking. Monteiro concluded that these houses in particular reflected a woman-centred world view. The extreme integration of most of the activities in the home was bought at the expense of decreased segregation and privacy when carrying out personal, private activities. Here, Monteiro observed, privacy seemed to have been more a matter of timing than of space, particularly as the more integrated activities normally occurred quite deep within the house. The shallow spaces nearest to the door were usually used for passive leisure activities.

Activities in the public sector flats revealed a completely different spatial experience of dwelling. The integration pattern strongly reflected the general tendency for interactive leisure activities to be the most integrated, domestic chores to band together in the middle range of values and personal activities to be the most segregated. However, the association of activities to places which were either shallow or deep from the entrance was much stronger than in the favelas, and here the greatest distinction was between interactive leisure activities which were the most shallow

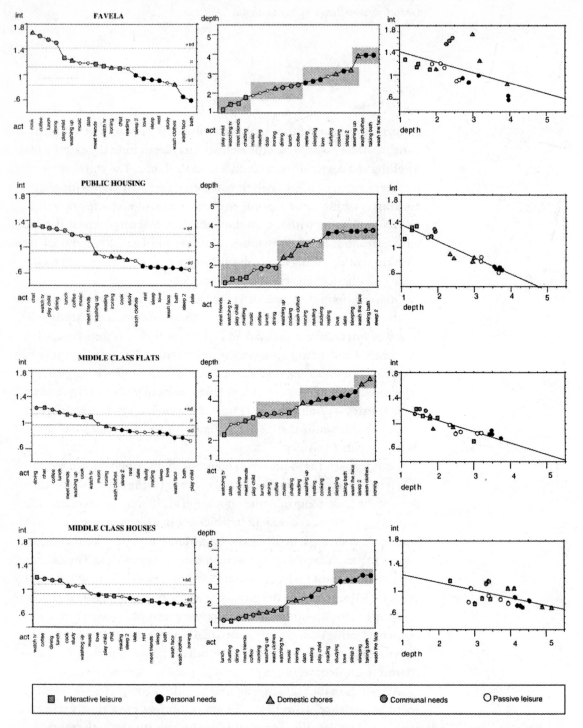

Mean integration values for the twenty domestic activities

Depths from the exterior of the twenty domestic activities

Correlation of integration and depth for the twenty domestic activities

Figure 10.8
The relationship between activities and syntactic measures in favela houses, public sector houses and middle-class flats and houses.

and passive leisure and personal needs which were very deep in the home and also quite fragmented from one another. Monteiro concluded that the public sector flat plans were particularly inflexible in this respect, with all the interactive activities being concentrated into one shallow sitting room which became the only social place in the house.

Middle-class flats showed a more variable distribution of activities to places. The first band of well-integrated activities comprised a mixture of communal needs, interactive leisure and household chores. The middle band also contained an even more heterogeneous mixture which included all types of activity except communal needs. The third, segregated band contained only personal needs. Monteiro observed that the main entrance to these flats led directly into the dining room which then acted as a main distributor to the remaining rooms in the house. As the space was both well-integrated and shallow, it naturally became the principal locus for social activity among family members whilst at the same time, 'this kind of flat invited free and easy hospitality, since the visitor's first view is of the family at the dining table'.

Finally, although middle-class houses showed many similarities to middle-class flats in the ranked distribution of activities according to their integration into the overall pattern of household activities, the houses were more segregated than the flats, and the interactive activities were spread more widely across all integration bands and the domestic chores associated with laundering clothes appeared at the extreme of segregation. Further inquiry elicited that the laundry is normally done by a maid in these homes. The middle-class houses also differed from the flats in how activities were distributed shallow to deep in the home. Here the shallowest activities take place at least two steps into the dwelling, and the shallowest activities are drawn mainly from the category of interactive and passive leisure. However, in marked contrast to the previous cases, some private needs also occur quite shallow in the home, a factor which was explained by the existence of a separate library, office, or 'best' room at the front of the house which combine the properties of being manifested to the exterior and quite shallow in the house with being relatively segregated. Monteiro concluded that 'the pattern of domestic activity in this case shows a more flexible use of space and a more heterogeneous and rich disposition of space functions'.

Monteiro's findings pointed in the direction of the extent to which activities are rooted in the their spaces, that is, they occur within defined boundaries and require special furniture and equipment to support them and so have very little spatial flexibility, with more loose activities which can be performed in any convenient location, as they do not need many props.

A second factor seems to relate to the importance of time as an aspect of space. Particularly in the favela houses where many activities are compressed into a single room, but also in the more spacious public sector flats and even in the generous middle-class flats, incompatible activities struggle to take place in the setting which has what are perceived to be important and supportive spatial characteristics, such as being both shallow and well-integrated.

Architects tend either to associate particular rooms or spaces in the home with specific activities and functions or to note that in some houses a spatial setting appears to accommodate more than one use, in which case it is perceived as a flexible, multi-purpose space. However, recent comparisons between more 'westernised' and more 'traditional' homes in the West African city of Ilo-Ife have revealed that people's lifestyles differ markedly in how activities and objects are organised within the family home, the extent to which one or two key functions appear to dominate a space to the exclusion of others or that several potentially conflicting activities are assigned to the same space but are separated in time, the degree to which household objects and equipment are rooted in a particular place or whether they migrate from place to place as people retrieve and make use of them, the compatibility or incompatibility of the array of objects and types of activities that share a particular space and the extent to which specific activities or objects are excluded from particular rooms in the house. It would seem that at least in some cultural contexts, a more complex picture is required in order to understand precisely how household activities and objects are classified, distributed and assembled in the homes of different sub-groups within society.

Many studies of the relation between house form and culture in a specific socio-cultural context, like those that have just been reported above, have shown that the differences between class, occupational or ethnic groupings within a single society are at least as marked as the differences between one society and another. It is fairly safe to assume that different sub-groups within society are likely to be a source for typological variety. However, this is not always so, as one recent large-scale study of one hundred and sixty traditional Hausa houses from the historic core of the ancient city of Kano in northern Nigeria, by Muhammad-Oumar[21] has revealed. This work set out explicitly to explore the influences of ethnicity and occupation upon domestic space organisation by comparing the houses of smiths, traders, craft workers, government officials and religious leaders among the ethnic Hausa, Fulani and Kanuri, and also those of Berber and Tuareg migrants from North Africa.

In spite of this diversity in the ethnic origin, occupation and income of the households studied, Muhammad-Oumar has identified a clear and consistent genotype for the traditional Kano house which is strongly related to gender divisions within the home. A typical Kano house has a deep, tree-like morphology with an integrating courtyard located three or four steps into the home from the exterior, one or more shallow, male-orientated entrance spaces and a set of rooms which may be either shallow or deep from the outside but which are always segregated, terminal spaces. The courtyard is a female-orientated space. Syntactically it is the largest, most accessible, best-connected, most integrated and strongest controlling functional space in the house, but access to it by visitors is strictly limited by powerful social conventions and even the male members of the household are discouraged from loitering there. The rooms, locally known as *daki*, are at the opposite pole configurationally and socially. Shallow rooms are normally allocated to male members of the household whereas the deeper rooms are usually occupied by women and their young children, but rooms are never shared by adults of the opposite gender. They are the most intimate and personal of spaces, where their occupants sleep and where they receive intimate friends and close relatives. Interposed between the courtyard and the exterior is a third type of space, shallow and male-orientated. There is always an entrance hall to the house which may lead directly to one or more adjacent, shallow reception rooms and there may also be an open, outer yard which may also be connected to one or more reception rooms as well as controlling the pathway to the main, inner courtyard. Whilst the entrance hall is strongly male-orientated, the outer yard may be appropriated for co-operative women's work during the day. In a small minority of larger houses, these male-dominated spaces may contest with the woman-centred courtyard as the focus of integration in the home.

Each Kano house is unique in the sense that its construction and detailing, overall shape and layout, number and size of rooms and household composition and family circumstances are all different. At the same time, over 95% of the houses surveyed were found to be variations on these two underlying genotypes. Relations between men and women appear to override all other factors in determining how traditional Kano houses are planned and the ways in which they evolve physically, through a process of expansion and contraction, as family circumstances alter. What is not described in space is inscribed in rules governing the behaviour and conduct of household members. The small number of houses which do not conform to either of the genotypes are 'big houses' which, as their local name implies, are much larger than the norm in terms of metric area and the number of rooms and are shared by between five and eight related, usually quite wealthy families.

Muhammad-Oumar's work is one example of a new generation of syntactic studies which couples a first-hand, field survey of a large sample of houses to directly questioning the householders about their use of space, the kinds of activities which go on in different places in the home, the occupation of domestic space by men, women and children, where objects are kept and how people perceive and relate to their homes. The descriptive methods which syntax offers the researcher are now well-established and so the task is increasingly one of interpreting what the observed regularities in the space patterning of people's houses mean to them, personally and socially. This usually involves obtaining access to people's houses to record the positions of architectural features, fixtures and fittings and items of furniture, the location of decorative and utilitarian objects, and the quality and condition of the interior finishes and decor. Householders may need to be questioned about how they make use of space and it may be necessary to inquire separately of the men, women and children of the house to obtain a complete picture of daily life. Finally, it may be informative to ask people, as Muhammad-Oumar did, about how they feel about their houses, whether they are satisfied with their homes and what further improvements they would like to make to the interior if they were able to do so. Sometimes, it proves useful to ask the residents to draw their houses and to compare their subjective mappings with the more objective picture of space obtained by the researcher.

It is occasionally observed that an 'insider's view' of their home must necessarily be more authentic and valid than that of an 'outsider', whether this is applied narrowly to mean the difference between a resident's account of his own home and that of the observer of or researcher into the morphology and social meaning of the house, or more broadly in suggesting that someone studying a culture anthropologically, from the outside, cannot understand it as well as someone who is of the culture, that is, born into it and raised according to the world view which obtains there. In fact both views are likely to be flawed, and so each can in principle inform the other. An insider is rarely attentive to the things he takes for granted as he assumes that this is how things are done the world over. It takes an outsider to point out the strangeness and arbitrariness of what seem to an insider to be quite normal social practices. Conversely, an outsider may not appreciate the nuances which lie behind observed socio-spatial phenomena, or even worse, he may misunderstand them altogether by interpreting them according to his own preconceived assumptions. Perhaps the most fruitful situation is where the two views can work together in partnership to share and test ideas, but there is probably no reason to suppose that one stance is ethically superior to the other.

Precedent in design

It is fortunate that this is so, for architects are rather rarely 'of the culture' for which they design. This is as true of architects designing popular housing within their own cultural context as it is of architects who are commissioned to design and build houses abroad, for the professional education of most practising architects guarantees that they will have embraced the attitudes and values of the intelligentsia, perhaps even of the *avant garde*. Even where architects are prepared to live for a while amongst the people for whom they are designing, this does not necessarily ensure that they are able to grasp the essential features of their way of life.

Amorim[22] has investigated the extent to which a house can be viewed as the unique expression of an architect's personal style or, alternatively, is the product of shared assumptions about how the modern home should accommodate basic human needs or functional, programmatic requirements, using Brazil as the context for his inquiry. Amorim first set out the basic, functional specification for a house which was taught in schools of architecture in Brazil during the 1950s, 1960s and 1970s, as part of a 'design methods' approach to education which aimed to help students identify fundamental design requirements at the briefing stage. The method involved specifying each activity in the home as a node or bubble and representing all functional relationships between activities by lines

Figure 10.9
The transformation from 'bubble
diagram' to plan.

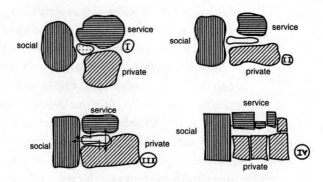

Figure 10.9
The transformation from 'bubble diagram' to plan.

linking nodes, in order to arrive at a topological, shape-free 'bubble
diagram'.

Amorim described the essentials of the design method as follows: 'first,
classification of living activities according to a particular set of requirements; second, grouping of similar activities generating sectors; third, providing duplicate facilities to attend similar activities which may overlap
others; fourth, definition of barriers to guarantee the necessary independence of the sectors'. The sectors which were assumed to be basic to
the design of a house were a social sector to accommodate group activities
among inhabitants, a private sector which ensured the requisite degree of
privacy for each individual member of the family and a service sector
which contained the support functions that maintained the dwelling's life.
These were connected together by means of a fourth, mediator sector and
linked to a fifth sector, the public realm beyond the home.

As the student refined his or her design ideas, the diagram gradually
acquired the properties of shape, adjacency, connectivity and proportions
until it became a 'functional house' that could be translated easily into a
proposal for a real building (see figure 10.9). Amorim conceived of this
'functional house' as a 'topological gene' which carried information about
how the modern Brazilian home should organise activities, support individuals and groups and generate and control social relationships. The
method acquired the status of a science in schools of architecture and it
also became popular amongst practising architects as a way of reducing the
apparent complexity of the design process.

Amorim analysed the configurational characteristics of the 'functional
house' and compared it with those of a sample of one hundred and forty
modern houses built between 1950 and 1970 by Brazilian architects who

were working in the city of Recife. As well as marking the period during
which design methods became a popular educational tool in schools of
architecture, this also coincided with the popularisation of modern architecture in Brazil. The sample of houses was heterogeneous and included
examples from the middle, upper-middle and upper-class socio-economic
groups, terraced, semi-detached and detached houses, one, two and three
storey dwellings and cases of homes which were designed by architects,
engineers and draftsmen. It also included several seminal works of architecture which became synonymous with the new approach to design, a
number of houses which were published in local or national periodicals
and substantial numbers of anonymous suburban buildings.

A conventional convex break-up was made of each house which was
represented as a justified permeability graph in the normal way. The
spaces in each house were then classified according to their named uses
and to whether they belonged to the social, private, service or mediator
sectors. Where spaces in a sector were located together in a separate
spatial sub-complex they were consolidated into one node in the graph. In
this way, the original sample of one hundred and forty plans was distilled
down to just twenty-four graphs, which were then analysed for their properties of depth from the exterior, integration value and space-type and
compared with the graph of the functional house (see figure 10.10).

Amorim discovered that despite the vast array of house layouts which
could arise in theory out of the potential array of labels and spaces, only
twenty-four non-equivalent graphs with either four, five, six or seven elements were found in the houses of Recife. In terms of the combinatorial
possibilities, there are thirty-eight non-equivalent ways of combining a
four-element graph, and four hundred and twenty ways of permutating a
five-element graph. Yet just sixteen cases, 10.7% of the sample, used a
four-sector system (including the exterior as a sector), 60% of the houses
used the basic five-sector system, but among these only seven types of
graph were found, corresponding to just 1.66% of the repertoire. Amorim
did not go on to calculate the combinatorial possibilities for the six and
seven-element graphs which had a duplicate sector, because of the combinatorial explosion of cases, but it is self-evident that he found only a frac-
tion of the possible combinations.

The designers of these houses did not seem to be completely sub-
ordinate to the stereotype encapsulated in the graph of the functional
house. At the same time, the houses bore a strong family likeness to one

Figure 10.10
Sector typology of modern Brazilian houses.

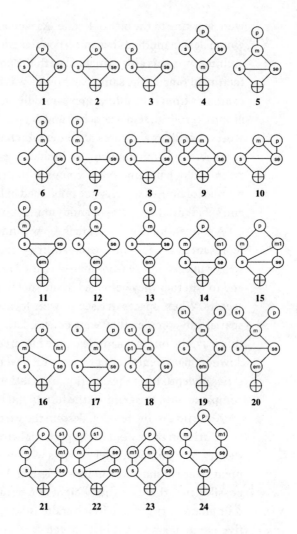

another. The topological size of the graph was strongly related to socio-economic class in that the higher the social stratum, the more complex the specification for the house and the greater the number of nodes in the functional graph. Each of the sectors was associated with a particular space-type and location in the graph. The private sector activities of the houses tended to take place in either 'c' or 'a' type spaces which were located in deep and segregated positions in the graph. The service and social sectors assumed shallow locations in the graph and were located in ringy 'c' or 'd' type spaces. This was generated by the need for the family's social spaces to be close to the main entrance to the house but away from the service zones. These were usually occupied by servants, who had a separate service entrance which brought this sector into a shallow relationship with the house. The public sector was predominantly 'c' type space, but it invariably reverted to 'a' type if an external mediator was included as a buffer zone between the house and its public exterior. The mediator was more varied in its local morphology, an attribute which Amorim termed the 'joker effect' because of its unpredictability. The rank order of integration of these functions was either social = service < private, 57.86% of the sample, or social < service < private, 34.29% of the sample. The remaining 7.85% were atypical cases.

Amorim was therefore able to show that the houses had a common underlying design specification which was based on the ideal of the functional house and which governed the relationship between the major activities in the home. He suggested that this amounted to a paradigm for the design of houses which restricted the vast number of possible housing layouts to just a few, relatively standardised plans. It emerged that these houses were far more than just the expression of an architect's individual style. It now seems possible that modern houses in some parts of the world may come to exhibit the invariance which is more usually associated with traditional and vernacular homes. However, it seems also to be the case that social rules may have combined with functional ones in arriving at the genotype of the modern Recife house. Even though they are undoubtedly influenced by an educational system which can be accused of pandering to fashionable intellectual trends, it seems that many practising architects are still in touch with their cultural roots.

Intervening

People seek to understand the role of domestic space in shaping and constraining culture for a variety of reasons. For some the quest is purely intellectual whilst others study the relation between house form and culture in order to glean information about how society and its institutions are evolving over time. Recently, attention has focused on the production and consumption of houses as commodities, particularly amongst architectural historians and cultural theorists. It is now widely acknowledged within the social sciences such as archaeology, sociology, anthropology and cultural geography that architecture is a powerful instrument for representing, moulding and classifying the world. It is particularly important to acknowledge the social nature of space and its symbolism and meaning in relation to the study of houses and homes.

However, architects and designers can also claim to have a more practical and immediate interest in the way people live, in that they study houses and homes in order to intervene in the housing process, either by modifying existing dwellings or by the design of new ones. This places a particular responsibility on architects to understand the social nature and significance of the phenomena they create, especially as the profession has undoubtedly misconceived the relation between people and buildings in the recent past, most notably in the design of social housing. This book is a small step on the road to creating a more complete understanding of the social content of houses and homes.

The built environment is the most mundane, enveloping, the largest and the most socially significant artefact that humans create and, within the built environment, the most basic, widespread and necessary of buildings is undoubtedly the house. Yet still the house constantly presents problems, challenges and puzzles which only serve to remind us that we do not fully understand the artefacts we make. We may aspire to participate in a society where a comfortable, acceptable and affordable house can be obtained by everyone who requires one, but this goal seems as distant today as it ever was. Much of the choice which is held out to people in the design of houses turns out to be spurious and whole sectors of society are excluded altogether from the housing market.

These are undoubtedly large and complex social problems which reach far beyond the modest investigations which have been presented in this book. At the same time, the theories and methods which lie behind the case studies that have been presented here are rooted in a concern for a more democratic and social vision for architecture. The techniques which have been used here to decode people's dwellings can also form the basis of a more intelligent approach to architectural design. As the approach which has been sketched out here becomes more widely accessible and better established, it has the potential to form a shared language amongst those who study, design, build, manage, evaluate and dwell in houses. The shared, comparative study of houses from all over the world can only enrich our collective understanding of the material culture of people's everyday lives. It may even begin to turn that vision into reality.

Notes

1 Pierre Bourdieu, *Echanges et communications: mélanges offerts à Claude Lévi-Strauss à
l'occasion de son 60e anniversaire* (Paris:
Mouton, 1971), pp. 151–69.
2 Clark E. Cunningham, 'Order in the Atoni
House' in Rodney Needham (ed.), *Right and
Left: Essays on Dual Symbolic Classification*
(University of Chicago Press, 1973), pp. 204–38.
3 Caroline Humphrey, 'Inside a Mongolian
Tent', *New Society* (31 October 1974), 273–5.
4 S. J. Tambiah, 'Animals are Good to Think
with and Good to Prohibit', *Ethnology* 8 (1969),
424–59.
5 Bill Hillier, *Space is the Machine: a
Configurational Theory of Architecture*
(Cambridge University Press, 1997), pp. 88–145.
6 Jason Shapiro, 'Fingerprints on the
Landscape', *Proceedings of the First
International Space Syntax Conference* 2
(1997), 21.1–21.20.
7 Laurel Cooper, 'Comparative Analysis of
Chacoan Great Houses', *Proceedings of the
First International Space Syntax Conference* 2
(1997), 22.1–22.12.
8 Wendy Bustard, 'Space, Evolution and
Function in the Houses of Chaco Canyon',
*Proceedings of the First International Space
Syntax Conference* 2 (1997), 23.1–23.22.
9 Justin De Syllas, 'Aesthetic Order and Spatial
Disorder in a Children's Home', M.Sc. thesis,
University of London (1989).
10 Justin De Syllas, 'Living in the Community:
a Study of the Domestic Life of People with
Learning Difficulties Living in Local Authority
Hostels', NHS Estates (1994).
11 Freida Peatross, 'The Spatial Dimension of
Control in Restrictive Settings,' *Proceedings of
the First International Space Syntax
Conference* 2 (1997), 14.1–14.16.

12 Robin Evans, *Translations from Drawing to
Building and Other Essays* (London:
Architectural Association Press, 1997), p. 79.
13 Jian Fei Zhu, 'A Celestial Battlefield: the
Forbidden City and Beijing in Late Imperial
China', *AA Files, Annals of the Architectural
Association School of Architecture* 28 (1994),
pp. 48–60.
14 Ibid., p. 56.
15 Hillier, *Space is the Machine*, p. 345.
16 R. W. Brunskill, 'A Systematic Procedure for
Recording English Vernacular Architecture',
*Transactions of the Ancient Monuments
Society* 13 (1965–6), pp. 43–126.
17 Deniz Orhun, Bill Hillier and Julienne
Hanson, 'Spatial Types in Traditional Turkish
Houses', *Environment and Planning B:
Planning and Design* 22 (1995), pp. 475–98, and
Deniz Orhun, Bill Hillier and Julienne Hanson,
'Socialising Spatial Types in Traditional
Turkish Houses', *Environment and Planning B:
Planning and Design* 23 (1996), pp. 329–51.
18 S. H. Eldem, *Türk Evi* (Istanbul: TAÇ Vakfı
Güzel Sanatlar Matbaasi, 1994).
19 Edja Trigueiro, 'The Dinner Procession Goes
to the Kitchen', *Proceedings of the First
International Space Syntax Conference* 2
(1997), 19.1–19.16.
20 Circe Monteiro, 'Activity Analysis in
Houses of Recife, Brazil', *Proceedings of the
First International Space Syntax Conference* 2
(1997), 20.1–20.13.
21 Abdulrazzaq Muhammad-Oumar, 'Gidaje:
the Socio-Cultural Morphology of Hausa Living
Spaces', Ph.D. thesis, University of London
(1997).
22 Louis Amorim, 'The Sector Paradigm',
*Proceedings of the First International Space
Syntax Conference* 2 (1997),18.1–18.14.

Index

Printed in the United Kingdom
by Lightning Source UK Ltd.
99065UKS00001B/17-20